The *Alternative* Kitchen Garden

an A-Z

Emma Cooper

Permanent Publications

Published by

THE QUEEN'S AWARDS
FOR ENTERPRISE:
SUSTAINABLE DEVELOPMENT
2008

Permanent Publications
Hyden House Ltd
The Sustainability Centre
East Meon
Hampshire GU32 1HR
England
Tel: 01730 823 311
Fax: 01730 823 322
Overseas: (international code +44 - 1730)
Email: enquiries@permaculture.co.uk
Web: www.permaculture.co.uk

Published in association with

Permaculture Association (Britain), BCM Permaculture Association, London WC1N 3XX
Tel: 0845 458 1805 Email: office@permaculture.org.uk Web: www.permaculture.org.uk

First edition © 2009 Emma Cooper
The right of Emma Cooper to be identified as the author of this work has been asserted by
her in accordance with the Copyrights, Designs and Patents Act 1998

Designed and typeset by John Adams

FSC
Mixed Sources
Product group from well-managed
forests and other controlled sources
Cert no. TT-COC-2200
www.fsc.org
© 1996 Forest Stewardship Council

Printed in the UK by Cambrian Printers, Aberystwyth

Paper from FSC certified mixed sources

The Forest Stewardship Council (FSC) is a non-profit international
organisation established to promote the responsible management of
the world's forests. Products carrying the FSC label are independently
certified to assure consumers that they come from forests that are
managed to meet the social, economic and ecological needs of present
and future generations.

British Library Cataloguing-in-Publication Data

A catalogue record for this book is available from the British Library

ISBN 978 1 85623 046 9

Contents

Contents

Foreword
by
Mark Diacono

If you're new to growing food, relax and enjoy this book: It brings together the many spokes of growing edibles into one hub, drawing together techniques, processes and concepts, pleasures and possibilities, experiences and insights without sparing the failures. This is gardening as a whole and as it should be. If you are already converted, rest assured that this stream of thoughts and experiences, exciting ideas and fascinating facts make *The Alternative Kitchen Garden* a book to grow with, in all senses.

There's a lot of talk at the moment that this, now, is the time to grow your own, but what we are seeing is a more enduring reconnection and fascination with what we eat. Since the 1950s, we have seen the wider population who used to grow at least a little of what they ate fall by the wayside (though allotmenteers and kitchen gardeners have never gone away). Undoubtedly our obsession with 'saving time' and the availability of cheap food has played a key part in this, but the tendency of some garden writers to cloak the pleasure of growing in endless jargon, to dress up complex techniques as critical and create an expert/novice divide has done little to encourage and inspire. Happily Emma is helping to put this to rights.

It is one thing to 'do', quite another, as Emma does, to multiply the value of doing by enthusing, inspiring, encouraging and enabling.

Through her website, blogging, podcasts and now this book, Emma beautifully conveys the simultaneous inconsequentiality and enormity of growing: Planting a tree, while a matter of hole-digging and backfilling, engages us with our cultural heritage and becomes an opportunity for creativity and expression, as well as offering a gift to the future. And as you'd expect if you're familiar with Emma's work, it's a generous book, linking people, organisations and the reader throughout, joining the dots as it goes.

Many books present the reader with what feels like a mountain to climb. Emma's gift is in breaking down barriers, inviting us into the resulting space and presenting numerous ingenious opportunities to fill it. What and how we do this is up to each individual.

Now I'm off to sow some quinoa.

Mark Diacono is head gardener at River Cottage and runs Otter Farm, the UK's only Climate Change Farm, home to experimental orchards of 'foreign' foods including almonds, pecans, persimmons and apricots – as well as the olive grove. The aim of the farm is to take advantage of global warming to grow these crops and sustainably add them to the British larder without the food miles and subsequent heavy carbon load normally associated with them – a beautifully virtuous circle of working with climate change in a way that helps arrest its acceleration.

Mark is author of Veg Patch – River Cottage Handbook No.4, *recently published as part of the River Cottage Handbook series.*

www.rivercottage.net
www.otterfarmblog.co.uk

The Author

Emma Cooper lived a very uneventful life until she met her husband, Pete. She went to The University of Birmingham, earned a degree (a BSc (Hons) in Physics and Astrophysics), and then started a string of office jobs of an increasingly computery nature.

At one of those jobs she bumped into Pete, and together they have embarked on a journey towards a greener lifestyle. It started off relatively simply, making good use of the local recycling collections and moving towards organic food.

In 2001 they bought a house, and Emma wandered out into the garden and planted a few herbs and vegetables in pots on the patio – merely to cut down on the family Food Miles. She soon developed a towering obsession with edible plants and is on a quest to grow them all, from the humble spud to the exotic achocha and beyond.

Over the past 8 years, Emma's garden has developed from an unloved urban back yard into an edible paradise, albeit a rather untidy one. Because this is a place where wildlife is welcome and nothing grows in straight lines.

Pete is normally quite happy to leave the gardening to his wife, although he has made a few contributions of his own – most notably building the Grow Dome, installing several large water butts and insisting on chickens. Princess Layer and Hen Solo arrived in 2006 and happily munch their way through more than their fair share of the home grown veggies, plus the occasional slug when Emma insists.

In the autumn of 2006, Pete left the world of air-conditioned offices and vending machine coffee to work from home. He seemed to be having so much fun doing it that Emma joined him early in 2007. Since then she has had far more time to spend in the garden, although it's a shame that it has coincided with two of the worst possible growing seasons of recent years! And although there's not as much spare cash to spend on gardening goodies, it doesn't matter – making the garden more self-sufficient has been huge amounts of fun and very rewarding.

When she's not in the garden, Emma can be found huddled over a gardening book from her over-stuffed bookshelf, or in front of the computer. Emma writes about environmentally friendly gardening, keeps a regular online diary (blog) about her gardening exploits and green issues and records a (fairly) regular online radio show called The Alternative Kitchen Garden, which draws its audience from all over the world.

For Pete

**without whom none of this
would have been possible**

The *Alternative* Kitchen Garden

Introduction

The Alternative Kitchen Garden is a philosophy, an evolving idea of what a kitchen garden could and should be in the 21st century. In the last few decades of the 20th century the Western world became more and more industrialised. Kitchen gardens, once an important part of most homes, became all but extinct as highly mechanised agriculture and cheap food imports made them seem unnecessary. But at the start of the 21st century, numerous food scares and increasing awareness of environmental and health issues are bringing home food production back into the public eye.

Many people have not had a chance to learn the practical skills that growing edible plants requires, but the Alternative Kitchen Garden is a friendly place where all are welcome. The emphasis is on trying things out, finding what works for you and what grows well in your garden. There are only two real rules – be kind to the environment and have some fun in your garden!

The Alternative Kitchen Garden is also a very real place. It has incarnations across the globe, wherever people are trying to tread lightly on the Earth and raise some plants. But the original Alternative Kitchen Garden, my garden, is in urban Oxfordshire. It came into being in 2001, when my husband Pete and I bought our first home. It was born out of a concern for the environment, but has thrived because I have developed a profound respect and fascination for the plants themselves. Their beauty and generosity astounds me, and there is always something new to see.

Initially, the Alternative Kitchen Garden was simply a few pots on the patio. My first plants – herbs and leaf beet – grew and some of them even gave us a harvest. I was hooked, and they were soon joined by anything which might grow in a container – garlic and potatoes, then strawberries and then a patio orchard of dwarf fruit trees.

The garden itself had long been neglected and was mainly ropey old lawn with the added bonus of hidden treasure – ankle-breaking pot holes, buried lumps of concrete and the rusty remains of largely unidentifiable items. We had neither the time nor the inclination to dig, and so we covered it in black plastic sheeting weighed down with bricks. It wasn't pretty, but it was an improvement – there was now a clear path right down the garden to the enormous bramble patch at the bottom. If I had been Sleeping Beauty I would have been waiting for my Prince to hack his way through it.

On the day that Pete trod on a hedgehog that had made its way under the black plastic (a dark, damp environment being a haven for both slugs and snails and the things that eat them!), we decided that the plastic had served its purpose and needed to go. Don't worry about the hedgehog – their prickles act as shock absorbers and the hedgehog lived to see another day. By the time we removed it, the plastic had been down for a couple of years, and the grass was history. But the bindweed lived on. We replaced the plastic with woven weed-control fabric and a mulch (covering) of bark chips. Aesthetically this was much more pleasing, and gradually we reclaimed the garden. With some help from my parents we beat the brambles back but this left the garden open to an alley at the bottom. The time had come for the first major garden project – a new fence. We decided to paint it forest green, a job which took us several months as it was sandwiched into our meagre free time. In the meantime, the brambles were making a come back and when we were finally ready to put the fence up it was once again a battle against the blackberries. But once the fence was up the garden started to look and feel like a garden, and far fewer of the fat neighbourhood cats could muster the energy to scale a six foot fence in search of their usual toilet sites.

By 2005 the fence was in place and the first raised beds had appeared – built from large concrete blocks that give the place rather an industrial feel until they're softened by the planting. My gardening blog (internet diary) was in full swing and plant mania was starting to take hold. I became a seed hoarder, collecting plants that I wanted to grow as and when I had the time, energy and space. I saw and lusted after a Grow Dome – an enormous greenhouse with a geodesic dome. Having visited a working one, I ordered my own and it arrived in July 2005. At that time we were cash rich and time poor, a situation that many people find themselves in. It would be two more years before my flat pack Grow Dome became a proper greenhouse.

2006 was the year that Pete discovered he has an obsession with large butts – water butts, that is. And although it was a long, hot summer, for most of it we had plenty of rain water saved up with which to water the plants. For me, 2006 was the year that I grew my first really unusual plant – achocha – and from then on I was hooked. 2006 was also the year that the chickens arrived. Hen Solo and Princess Layer were delivered along with their five-star chicken accommodation, the eglu. They have added another dimension entirely to the garden, and despite the fact that they occasionally escape and munch things they shouldn't we wouldn't be without them.

In 2007 things changed abruptly. Pete and I both became self-employed, time rich and cash poor. We finally finished putting up the Grow Dome, and despite the atrocious English weather that summer the Alternative Kitchen Garden produced a crop of sweetcorn that both we and the chickens enjoyed. I started saving my own seeds, and growing things from pips.

And at the beginning of 2007 I started the Alternative Kitchen Garden podcast – an internet radio show, free to download, and covering a different gardening topic in every show. The first ever episode was on one of my favourite plants, Jerusalem artichokes, because they're so easy to grow and provide a good harvest even from containers. In its first year the Alternative Kitchen Garden show covered many topics, from compost and slugs through to chickpeas and tiger nuts.

Although it's snowing as I write this (in mid March), I have high hopes for the Alternative Kitchen Garden this year. The Grow Dome is ready for action, I've started a Goji Garden based on forest garden principles, and a new raised bed is waiting to be planted with potatoes. There's almost no budget for the garden, but it doesn't matter. From tiny seeds an enormous glut of courgettes will grow!

The *Alternative* Kitchen Garden

A is for...

A is for...

Achocha

Achocha is an unusual thing to find growing in an English kitchen garden. It's one of the Lost Crops of the Incas, an ancient food crop from the Andes. But if you think about, so is the potato, and very few people could imagine life without the humble spud.

Achocha is a climbing plant, with light-green divided leaves. It does grow flowers, but you'll have to look closely to see them because they're small and very pale. You might find it easier to look for the hoverflies that swarm around them. Hoverflies tend to look like small wasps, but they fly in completely different ways and are very shy – approach one and it will flit away. They don't buzz, either, and have no sting. Hoverflies are very useful to have in the garden because their larvae eat greenfly.

Once the flowers have been pollinated, tiny fruits will start to grow. They're easier to see, being a deeper green than the leaves. They'll grow into an interesting tear drop shape, a bit like a garden gnome's hat. If you pick them when they're small then you can eat the fruits raw in salads. They have a very 'green' taste, sometimes described as being like green pepper. As the fruits grow larger they develop hard, black seeds that look like tiny stealth bombers. At this stage you'll have to split the fruits open to remove the seeds before you can eat them, and they're better cooked – on pizza, or in stir fries and curries. Achocha is a very versatile vegetable, which is good because it's also one of the most prolifically fruiting plants you'll grow. They're practically unstoppable until they're cut down by frost.

Achocha is a tender plant. You can sow your seeds indoors a couple of weeks before the last frost date for your area, or outside where you want them to grow once the risk of frost has passed. Treat them like runner or climbing French beans, and make sure you have something for them to grow up – as soon as the seedlings start to grow their climbing tendrils you need to split them up and plant them out, or they'll start to climb each other and become hopelessly entangled.

Achocha vines aren't too fussy about soil type, but they like a warm (not hot) environment – perfect for the average English summer. Your seedlings might be attacked by slugs and snails, but otherwise achocha is pretty much trouble-free. It can grow upwards of six feet tall though, so either use a tall support or pinch out the growing tips when they reach the top. I grew mine up a trellis, and then they tried to take over the washing line as well. If you've got an eyesore in your garden that you want to cover for the summer, a pergola that looks a bit bare or a gap you want to fill for privacy, then achocha is your plant!

Achocha is in the Cucurbitaceae plant family, along with courgettes, pumpkins, cucumbers and melons. You'd be wise not to grow it in the same place each year, but it won't cross with other plants in your garden, and so it's easy to save seeds from.

A is for...

Allotments

Allotments are pieces of land that are leased out to people who want to grow food crops. They're a very Victorian concept – popularised because it was believed that having an allotment would kill two birds with one stone, giving working men something to do of an evening other than go down to the local pub and providing them with an additional source of food to stretch their rather meagre budgets.

However, it was during the Second World War and the Dig For Victory campaign that allotments really came into their own. With a blockade seriously cutting into Britain's imported food supply, the British people were encouraged and exhorted to grow as many of their own vegetables as possible. They did, motivated by a sincere desire to help with the war effort, but also by their rumbling tummies.

After the war, allotments became less popular and went into a serious decline. Although each local council is obliged by law to provide allotments if a number of local residents request them, allotment sites are under siege by developers who see their land value rather than their community and environmental value. Many high profile battles have been waged – some won, and some lost. One of the fiercest battle grounds of recent years was Manor Gardens Allotments, a site a century old that found itself (literally) in the path of London's 2012 Olympics. Despite their lengthy campaign, the allotment holders have been moved to a new site and the Manor Gardens allotments have been bulldozed.

However, allotments all over the country are undergoing a resurgence. There's a new wave of interest in self-sufficiency and healthy eating after a number of really scary food stories in the media. People are also trying to incorporate exercise into their increasingly sedentary lifestyles, to get ever more obese children to eat vegetables, and to save the planet by cutting down on chemical use and Food Miles.

Some allotments are still run in a traditional way, generally by male gardeners with many years of experience and set ways. But some are more forward-thinking. The new wave of kitchen gardeners is younger, greener and - in many cases – female. The emphasis here is on sustainability, community and fun. Some allotment sites have plots for wildlife gardens, communal orchards, schools programmes and a great deal of help available for newcomers. Others still have large tracts of overgrown land and offer little help other than routinely spraying 'failing' plots with weedkiller.

For the committed kitchen gardener, an allotment brings a new world of opportunities simply because of the space available. You need a lot of ground to grow all of your own potatoes, for example, and pumpkins are generally enormously sprawling plants. A field of wheat might raise the eyebrows of your allotment neighbours, but it's a definite possibility. On a swampy site you could even consider growing rice. Getting an allotment can add a great deal to your life, not least the vast gluts of courgettes that you'll be handing out to friends and foes alike in the height of the summer. But it is also a big commitment, needing regular attention and (at least to begin with) some hard work. Your local allotment site may have plenty of spare plots, or a waiting list longer than your arm. But if you're thinking about getting an allotment, or waiting for your turn to come, there's no reason why you can't start growing straight away. Even if you only have containers on the patio, a window box, or pots of herbs on the kitchen windowsill, there's plenty of things you can grow.

A is for...

Apples

The apple is one of the quintessential British fruits. It grows well in our soils and climates, and over time local varieties have been bred to take advantage of the conditions available. Where would Britain be without cider, scrumping and apple pie?

But these days most of the apples in the supermarket are imported, often by air, and frequently pretty but tasteless. Orchards have been grubbed up to make way for more profitable crops, and apple biodiversity, culture and history are all being lost.

If you want really tasty apples, you have to look for them. Common Ground, a charitable organisation that aims to celebrate and conserve uniquely British traditions, holds yearly Apple Day events across the country. At an Apple Day event you can taste local varieties, drink cider and apple juice made from a single type of apple rather than blends and take part in all kinds of apple-related antics. You might also be able to bring home your very own local apple tree to grow in your garden.

Ask most people to think about an apple tree and their mind will fill with the image we were familiar with as kids – a large tree, with a rounded crown and glossy red apples. But not everyone has the space to grow such a delight in their garden. There is an apple tree to fit in most spaces though – with varieties available on dwarf rootstocks, training methods to keep trees small and growing along fences, or even step-over apples that can be used as edging for beds. I've coveted a step-over apple tree ever since I first saw one (in the kitchen garden at Chatsworth, I think), but they don't really fit into my garden and they'd be pecked to death by the chickens, who eat any tree foliage within reach.

I have one apple tree, 'Saturn', grown as a minarette, which is basically an upright cordon. The tree is on a very dwarfing rootstock, so will never grow too tall, and is kept pruned so that it doesn't have any long branches but grows a lot of small fruiting spurs. I chose the variety for its disease resistance – a good start in an organic garden. To begin with I grew it in a container, but it was never very happy because I'm not good at regular watering. A couple of years ago I planted it out into the garden and it hasn't looked back. We ate our first fruits last autumn, and although I think I picked them too soon, they were still lovely – and a nice glossy red.

My apple is part of a mini orchard – four minarette trees, with a plum, a cherry and a pear making up the quartet – in the chicken run. Although the chickens do a certain amount of damage to the lower foliage, they do keep pests down and fertilise the trees for me.

In many places, local fruit varieties are making a comeback. Farmers are finding that they can make a living if they sell the fruit directly to the public via farmer's markets or box schemes. And local ciders and single-variety juices go down a treat, too. If you really can't squeeze an apple tree into your garden, then see if you can find a local community orchard where you can help out with the upkeep in return for a portion of the apple harvest. You might even find someone at work with an old apple tree who can't make use of all the fruit and would be grateful for your help with the harvest.

And just in case you think that the apple is being unfairly lauded, the day before Apple Day each year is All Fruits Eve – a chance to celebrate all the fruity wonders this country has to offer.

A is for...

Annual

An annual plant is one that completes its entire lifecycle in one season – or sometimes less. Many weeds are annuals – growing from seed, flowering and setting seed before you've even managed to get your gardening gloves out of the tool shed. Most of the common vegetables are grown as annuals, too, but they're not quite as precocious.

Some of the vegetables that we grow as annuals are, botanically speaking, something else entirely. Runner beans and peppers are perennial plants in their native habitats, living for several years. Here in the UK they are killed off by frost in the winter, but by digging up runner bean roots and storing them in sand in a frost-free place over winter, or bringing your pepper plants indoors to a sunny windowsill, you can sometimes get a head start on the growing season.

There are also biennials – plants that take two years to complete their lifecycle. They grow from seed during the first year, overwinter and then flower and set seed in their second year. There's quite a few common plants in this category, including parsley, chard and leaf beet, carrots and beetroot. Usually the part we want to eat becomes worthless as soon as the plant has flowered, and so the plants are grown as annuals. If you want to save seed from your biennial plants, you'll have to leave some in the soil until they flower.

One of the major problems that a kitchen gardener faces is annual and biennial vegetables that want to 'bolt' – complete their lifecycle at an unseemly pace. There's lots of reasons why a plant may bolt, but they mostly come down to stress. If a plant is stressed, by water shortages, a lack of vital nutrients, unhelpful weather or pest attacks, then it goes into survival mode with just one aim – reproducing before it dies.

With some bolting vegetables, like onions and garlic, the harvest can be saved by cutting off the flower stalk. With others, like coriander, there's very little you can do. Try growing Oriental brassicas instead – they're still edible once they've bolted! Or choose 'bolt resistant' varieties of plants, and then try to keep them happy.

There are some edible plants that have significant ornamental value when they've bolted. If you've sown too many lettuces and you have a glut, then leave some of them to bolt. The humble, dowdy lettuce will change before your eyes into an ornamental glory of the border – growing into a pyramid of leaves topping out at about three feet tall! If you leave it to set seed you can save some for next year, but don't collect seed from plants that have bolted prematurely – that's a genetic characteristic you don't want to encourage.

The advantage and disadvantage of annual plants is the same – you have to sow new seeds every year. Growing plants from seed is immense amounts of fun, and very rewarding, but it's also time consuming and fraught with pitfalls.

If you want a lower maintenance kitchen garden, then choose perennial plants – most fruit is perennial, and some vegetables are too. Consider designing and planting a forest garden, copying the way that nature does it. Or you could grow annual plants and let them self-seed and grow where they want to grow. This laid-back approach is completely alien to many gardeners, but is not without its beauty. All you need to do is set the ball rolling and then keep an eye on anything that's getting out of hand. There's always something to see and something to harvest in these types of garden, especially if you learn to see the positive qualities of weeds.

A is for...

Aubergine

Aubergines are in the same plant family as potatoes, tomatoes and peppers. They're not as commonly grown here in the UK, though, at least partly because they're sun-loving vegetables. You might get away with growing one in a pot on a sunny patio, but for a really good crop you'll need a greenhouse or a polytunnel.

If I followed my own advice, I wouldn't grow any aubergines because I don't like them. Generally speaking, kitchen gardeners should only grow things they're going to eat – there's nothing more demoralising then spending time and effort nurturing an edible plant and to then not get anything in return. But occasionally I make an exception, for educational purposes!

And the truth is that, like peppers, aubergines are very ornamental plants. The variety I grew, Calliope F1, had greyish green and furry leaves. It was described as spineless (aubergines being quite prickly plants), but that wasn't entirely true. I grew mine in a container in the Grow Dome (which wasn't finished at the time, but the outside structure was complete). My plants grew the most amazing pinkish purple flowers, which then developed into the cutest tiny fruits you'll ever see. Where they join to the stem of the plant they look like they're wearing little green pixie hats.

If you don't fancy stripy aubergines then there are many others to choose from. The familiar ones are enormous black and glossy fruits, but you can get white ones, pink one and even green ones. Fruits range from tiny and round to enormous and long. They're certainly a plant that gives you plenty of visual interest while you wait for the fruit to ripen.

Aubergines need a long season, so sow your seeds indoors in late winter when you're sowing your tomatoes and peppers. You'll have to keep them frost free, so you can't plant them outside until late spring – in the meantime they'll need as much light as possible to avoid lanky growth, and you may need to keep potting them on into larger pots and feeding them.

Once they've been planted out into their final position they'll need a regular supply of water, particularly when they're flowering and fruiting. A fertiliser that is high in potash (potassium, the K in NPK) should be applied once a fortnight once the flowers have appeared. A tomato feed or home-made comfrey fertiliser is ideal. In WWII, when potash was just another thing that was hard to get hold of, wood ash was used to supply it to fruiting vegetables. Don't apply a general fertiliser instead – too much nitrogen at this stage will encourage leafy growth rather than flowers and fruit.

Harvest your aubergines when they're fully mature – when they've reached the size stated on the seed packet and taken on their final colouring. Pick them while they're glossy – once the skins start to go wrinkly the fruits will be more bitter. Harvest time is likely to be in August.

Aubergines don't suffer from too many problems. In the greenhouse they might be attacked by red spider mite and whitefly; outside they can fall prey to aphids. They grow 60-90 cm tall, depending on the variety, and the taller ones (and larger fruited varieties) will appreciate the support of a cane. If you have a sunny windowsill, you can even grow them indoors. The main point to bear in mind is that you need to choose a variety that is suited to your climate – you're much more likely to get a bountiful harvest from an early variety in the UK.

The *Alternative* Kitchen Garden

B is for...

B is for...

Basil

For some people, summer isn't summer unless they've got fresh basil to enjoy with their home grown tomatoes. I have to admit it's not one of my favourite herbs, but if it is one of yours then you'll be relieved to hear that it's easy enough to grow — if you remember that it's not like other herbs.

For a start, basil is a tender annual. You have to grow fresh plants each year, and they do not — under any circumstances — like the cold. Try sowing your basil seeds or planting out your basil plants when you plant out your tomatoes. It is possible to grow basil entirely indoors; I have a friend who kept several plants alive and healthy on a self-watering tray on his desk at work.

Secondly, although it brings to mind hot, summer days, basil isn't part of the group we call Mediterranean herbs. It doesn't cope well with heat waves and droughts, it likes a plentiful supply of water.

The basil family has many members, all with their own unique flavour. The most popular one for culinary purposes is sweet basil, commonly 'Genovese'. It has lush green leaves of a decent size, and is easy enough to grow. You can also get purple basil, essentially the same plant in a different colour, that's not quite as productive. Bush (or Greek) basil has tiny leaves; lettuce-leaved basil is well named.

A walk on the exotic side will bring you to Thai basil or even Holy basil (a ceremonial herb in India, but also used for teas) or a host of other beauties. If you like basil then by all means give them a go – but bear in mind that these more unusual plants are likely to be harder to grow then their plainer cousins, and also that there probably isn't a self-help group for people who develop a basil obsession.

B is for...

Beans

Beans are a mainstay of the kitchen garden – providing fresh green pods, shelled haricot verts and dried beans for winter storage. Runner beans have a special place in English hearts, but French beans are more versatile. And since they are easy to save seed from, there's a wealth of heritage varieties; some people even collect them.

When faced with the bean catalogue, the first choice is whether you want climbing or dwarf French beans (known as pole and bush beans in the US). Climbing French beans will wind their way up canes or a trellis, and crop over a long period. Plants that make use of vertical space are always helpful, especially in small gardens. Dwarf French beans are easy to grow, bushy and largely self-supporting.

French beans are tender plants, sown indoors a couple of weeks before the last frost date, or outside only after the risk of frost has passed. They transplant happily, and grow well in containers. Early and late crops do well under cover, because French beans don't need to be visited by pollinating insects to produce pods. If you have the right microbes in your soil (they will arrive by themselves, over time, or you can buy them) then they will even take nitrogen from the air and 'fix' it into the soil, making their own fertiliser. If you leave the roots in the soil when the harvest has finished, they'll pass any excess onto the next crop.

Regularly harvesting the pods encourages the plants to grow more, but if you want to dry the beans, then don't pick fresh pods from those plants – it will delay the drying process. Even so, you may need to uproot the plants at the end of the season and hang them upside down indoors to finish drying.

Runner beans are sown at the same time, but have to be planted out in the garden because they need the attentions of bees to bear fruit. They are technically perennial and if you dig up the roots, store them in damp sand in a frost-free place over winter, and then replant them in spring then it's possible to get them to grow again – and possibly to crop earlier than their spring-sown siblings. But since growing from seed is easy and convenient, attempting to over-winter your beans may not be worth the effort. Runner beans climb and need support (although there is a dwarf variety, Hestia).

Broad beans are hardy and sown in the autumn, or early in the new year, to provide a protein-rich harvest in late spring and early summer. Here, again, there are choices to be made – white beans or green beans, long pods or shorter and fatter ones. The average plant height is 75cm, but there are taller ones that need support and dwarf varieties that shouldn't.

Broad beans are unusual in the plant world because they have square stems, not round. The flowers are very pretty, white with black centres, and are scented. They appear early in the year, making them an ideal food source for bees and other beneficial insects. If you're lucky you'll find seeds of the famous 'crimson flowered' broad bean – a beautiful addition to any kitchen garden.

There are many more types of bean (including yard-long beans, lab lab beans, soy beans and chickpeas), most of which are fairly marginal in the British climate. Some have low yields that mean they're not worth the space they take up in a small garden – if a large harvest is your only goal. If you enjoy experimenting then they make interesting test subjects.

B is for...

Bees

Bees are having a hard time these days. No one is entirely sure why, with theories ranging from disease to pollution to interference from mobile phone masts. What we do know is that we'll miss them when they're gone – bees are one of our main pollinating insects, and as such of enormous economic benefit. Many people are afraid of these stinging insects (including me – I was stung by a bee and it hurt like hell), but the countryside would look very different without them.

There are lots of different types of bees. They're usually thought of as living in colonies or swarms, but in fact most bees are solitary. Some build nests in the ground whilst others seal their eggs in with sections of leaf they've chewed off. They range in size from tiny to huge, and are commonly seen at different times of the year. But identifying what sort of bees you have is difficult, because they're all busy and none of them sit still long enough for you to get a good look.

The main thing we can do to help our bees is to give them something to eat. Bees like pollen and nectar, and if we can provide them with flowering plants right through the season then they'll have an all you-can-eat buffet to choose from. It may sound as though that's much easier to do in an ornamental garden, but the truth is that lots of the showy blooms that gardeners love are useless to bees. They're either bred to have no pollen (allergy free!) or they're just too darned frilly for the bees to make it past the petals. What bees love are the simple, open flowers that are easy to incorporate into a kitchen garden. Herbs are great – lavender, thyme, mint, pot marigolds, borage. Broad beans flower early in the year and are great for bees. They also love the flowers on soft fruit and if you've got a comfrey patch then let a couple of plants flower and watch the bees go wild. And in my garden one of the raised beds is out of bounds to humans for several weeks in late spring as the Welsh onions around the edge flower and attract every bee within flying distance. In fact, I'm in the process of moving the Welsh onions to other parts of the garden because although not wanting to disturb the bees is a great excuse for avoiding the weeding, I would like to be able to plant out the sweetcorn in peace.

These days you can even buy specially made nests for solitary bees – although Ken Thompson's research at the University of Sheffield (entertainingly written up in his book 'No More Nettles') suggests that it's very hard to encourage bees to use them. A collection of dry stems, or lengths of bamboo cane, is good for many insects including some bees, or you can try drilling different sizes of hole into a log. Sometimes bees nest in compost heaps, which can be somewhat disconcerting, but if you try not to disturb them they will be gone before you know it. Otherwise a general approach to improving the wildlife value of your garden works wonders – the more different habitats you create then the more chance there is that a particular species will decide to call your garden home. But more about that later.

B is for...

Birds

I'm very lucky that, even though I live in an urban area, I am surrounded by birds. Their song wakes me up in the morning – and in the long days of summer it's often the last sound I hear at night. To be truthful it is often less than idyllic, as they can be very loud, but I wouldn't have it any other way.

We have a flock of sparrows living in the eaves, starlings who are probably nesting in the attic, and a pair of blackbirds who think nothing of stealing all my blueberries every summer. The bird table is the domain of some immensely fat pigeons, there's usually a robin on hand when I'm digging, and a few weeks ago I saw a heron on a roof down the street.

Encouraging birds into the garden is relatively easy – hang up a bird feeder or two and they will come. The more different types of food you make available, in different ways, then the more birds that will come. Some are insect eaters, some only eat seeds, some will chow down on whatever's going. Some have no bird table manners and prefer to eat off the floor.

If you want to make them feel welcome in the long term, then stop using chemicals in the garden. Build your wildlife from the ground up, by encouraging soil micro organisms and creepy crawlies – the bottom of the food chains which have birds and mammals at the top. Give them some shelter – birds love trees and bushes, anywhere they can see the prowling neighbourhood cats without becoming their lunch. A source of clean water is also invaluable, especially in very dry or cold weather when natural sources are few and far between.

Once you've encouraged all of these birds into your garden then you may well start to regret it. Although they will help you deal with your pest problems, they can also be pests themselves. They'll dig up your seedlings, peck at buds and steal any soft fruit you haven't netted. In winter pigeons become the main pest, helping themselves to those sprouts you've grown for Christmas dinner. Or so I'm told - I've never grown sprouts (and probably never will!) and the pigeons in my garden have never shown an interest in the purple sprouting broccoli, almost certainly because they've become accustomed to a diet of white breadcrumbs and bird seed.

There are many ways to discourage birds from becoming pests in the garden. You can string up old CDs or plastic bags, anything that either makes an unpredictable noise or flashes of light. You can build a scarecrow or buy a plastic owl or sleeping cat – but you'll need to move them around because the birds quickly work it out when things are static. With soft fruit you have two options – either net it, or get used to the fact that the birds will take their share before you do. But that's quite a small price to pay for a garden full of life.

B is for...

Bokashi

Bokashi is the first real innovation in home composting for years, although if you want to be picky then Bokashi isn't composting at all.

A Bokashi system involves an airtight container or some kind (usually a bucket with a tight fitting lid and a tap) and a regular supply of Bokashi bran. Armed with both of these things then householders can process waste which would otherwise go straight to landfill – items such as cooked food, meat and cheese, fish and dairy that have no place on a regular compost heap. With a Bokashi bin you can store this unpleasant waste in the kitchen for a few weeks, and then safely put it onto the compost heap – thereby saving the planet into the bargain.

The engine that powers the Bokashi phenomenon is EM – Effective Micro-organisms, a collection of microbes that effectively pickle organic waste. Anything that you put into a Bokashi bucket will come out looking much the same, but smelling strongly of vinegar. This makes it unattractive to vermin, and when added to a compost heap the waste quickly breaks down. According to the literature, Effective Microorganisms save us from ourselves – cleaning up our water supply, our soil and even our bodies.

Impressed by the rhetoric, I bought a Bokashi system a few years ago. Ideally you need to have two Bokashi buckets. When one is full you need to let it sit for a fortnight before you can empty the waste onto the compost heap; in the meantime you'll be filling the second bucket, adding a handful of Bokashi bran each time you add some food waste. There is therefore an initial cost to starting Bokashi composting – although there's no real reason why you can't just buy your own suitable containers and a supply of Bokashi bran. The bran itself isn't that expensive, but don't buy it in bulk because the microbes don't live for ever.

The system does exactly what it is designed to do. Any food waste that you put into the bucket will pickle, meaning that it doesn't rot down. Most people will consider the vinegary smell to be better than that of rotting food, but that's a matter for personal opinion. The waste looks pretty much the same coming out of the bucket as it did going in – which isn't entirely pleasant. And it tends to be rather wet, so unless you mix it well with dry materials when you add it to the compost it has a tendency to form a stodgy, intractable layer that will not compost down and will stink to high heaven when you empty the compost bin.

Using the Bokashi system does have an unexpected benefit – you get up close and personal with the food waste that you make, rather than simply sending it off to landfill and forgetting about it. When you come face to face with the fact that you're throwing away half of that take away curry every Friday night, or that despite your best efforts no one in the house really likes that tuna casserole, then you may start to re-think your shopping and eating habits.

After about two years of using my Bokashi system, I gave it up. I was fed up of tipping icky food waste onto the compost heap – and sick of seeing it again when it failed to rot down. We'd also cleaned up our wasteful act, and it was taking a long time to fill the bins. The Bokashi bins themselves have been given a new lease of life. With their tight fitting lids and good taps, they're the perfect container for making comfrey liquid feeds.

B is for...

Borage

I can't now remember why I decided to grow borage in the garden. Although borage is edible, it has hairy leaves that make it fairly unpalatable, and it is reported to taste like cucumber – not one of my favourite flavours. It's the star-shaped flowers that are more often used, added to salads to liven things up, or frozen into ice cubes to add a decorative touch to long, cool summer drinks.

For my first attempt to grow borage, I sowed the seeds in a window box.

They germinated and grew quite happily, but borage is a tall plant (growing up to 60 cm) and it wasn't entirely comfortable in a lofty position.

That year I was also taking part in a Garden Organic member's experiment to test plants that attract beneficial insects to the garden. They'd included marigolds, phacelia, coriander and fennel in the experiment. I grew them all except the fennel, which is a very tall plant and too big for the space I had available. In the end the phacelia took over and crowded everything else out – a worthy trait in a plant that is more often grown as a green manure.

Phacelia has abundant purple flowers that bees love, so if you're growing it as a green manure it's worthwhile allowing some to flower – especially as it flowers over a long period.

Over the course of the summer I recorded all of the insect activity on my experiment plants – which wasn't a long job as there really was hardly any. I was looking for ladybirds, lacewings, hoverflies and spiders. All I got was bees (not something to complain about).

But one day I found out where all of the ladybirds, at least, had gone. The borage plants in my window boxes had developed a minor aphid infestation, and I was keeping an eye on it to see whether I would need to take any action. In the end I didn't have to – all of the plants were home to ladybird larvae, in various stages of development. Despite the hairy stems they were happily tucking into the aphids, growing big and strong and becoming the next generation of predators in my garden.

I dutifully noted this result on my experiment sheet and it got an (anonymous) mention in the final report from Garden Organic.

Last year's borage (grown from the same packet of seeds) had another surprise up its sleeve. When the flowers first emerged, they were pink. I hadn't heard of pink borage before, and thought it might be a separate variety – but it isn't. Some plants grow pink flowers that turn blue as they mature; most have flowers that are blue from start to finish.

When you sow your borage seed (which you can do right through from March to July), take a good look at the seedlings. Borage is very good at self-seeding, and you'll need to recognise its offspring so that you can either weed them out (if they're in the wrong place) or avoid weeding them out if you want more plants.

B is for...

Broccoli

A few years ago, Pete and I signed up for an organic veg box delivery, to decrease our ecological footprint whilst increasing our intake of fruit and vegetables. It served up some unknown delicacies, including Jerusalem artichokes and sprouting broccoli. Whilst Pete has a difficult relationship with all members of the cabbage family, after my first mouthful of buttery purple sprouting I was hooked.

Sprouting broccoli is not the easiest plant to grow. You sow the seeds in spring, usually in pots or in a nursery bed, and transplant the seedlings into their final growing position in midsummer. They stay in place until the following spring, when you finally get your harvest. In the meantime, you have to protect the plants from all of the beasties and diseases that plague brassicas. The plants are tall, and take up a lot of space; they need to be planted at least 60cm apart.

But sprouting broccoli is harvested in early spring, during the 'hungry gap' when not much else is cropping. And the plants are generous. Keep cutting the florets before they flower and the plant will keep growing more, until either it's exhausted or you're sick to death of sprouting broccoli. In the midst of a glut it's hard to motivate yourself to sow seeds for next year, but you'll regret it if you don't!

Although sprouting broccoli is becoming more common as we return to more seasonal patterns of eating, it can be hard to track down and is often expensive. If you develop a taste for it then you'd be well advised to find a space to grow your own. If you grow other members of the cabbage family you should keep them all together and move them around the garden each season, to prevent the build up of pests and diseases. Don't over water or over feed your broccoli – too much lush green growth jeopardises the plant's ability to survive harsh winter weather. The best defence against cabbage white caterpillars is to net the plants and prevent the butterflies from laying their yellow eggs on the underside of the leaves. Alternatively, constant vigilance and hand removal of the eggs and any caterpillars saves the plants from being decimated.

Until recently, your choice of purple sprouting broccoli variety was limited to 'early' or 'late' – plants that either crop in March or April. It's now possible to get some named varieties, and if you have the space, growing more than one extends your harvesting period.

White sprouting broccoli is said to have the best flavour. Perennial nine star sprouting broccoli stays in the ground for several years, providing a low-maintenance harvest of florets that are a cross between broccoli and cauliflower. However, its flavour is said to be inferior, and you'll have the usual problems with pests and disease.

For 'wok broccs' (summer sprouting broccoli), seeds are sown in spring to provide a summer harvest. This is ideal if you can't face waiting a year for sprouting broccoli, but less so if you're too squeamish to wash caterpillars (rampant in the summer months) out of your dinner.

Sprouting broccoli is one of those plants that just doesn't grow well in containers. It's too big, and takes up space for too long. However, there are some alternatives you can try - look for broccoli raab (or rapini) and kailaan (also known as Chinese broccoli). Other Oriental vegetables have edible flowering shoots, too.

The *Alternative* Kitchen Garden

C is for...

C is for...

Calendula

Calendula is the Pot Marigold, *Calendula officinalis*. It has been bred into some outrageous colours and fluffy blooms, but in its original form it is orange and daisy-like – and totally stunning.

It makes a good addition to a kitchen garden for two reasons. The first is that it is edible – you can liven up your salads with a few Pot Marigold petals, or use them to add a saffron colour (at a fraction of the saffron price) to cooked dishes.

The second is that they're a great companion plant. They'll attract all kinds of beneficial insects to your garden, because of their large and open flowers. Bees and hoverflies, in particular, will be most grateful.

The plants also have uses in herbal medicine, and are said to actively repel some garden pests. They're easy enough to grow, happy in most soils and a sunny position. If you're not eating the flowers you'll have to remove them as they fade, to promote further blooms and also to prevent them self-seeding throughout the garden. Apart from being vulnerable to slug attack when they're young, Pot Marigolds are generally problem free.

Don't confuse Pot Marigolds (*Calendula*) with the other sorts – French and African marigolds are Tagetes.

C is for...

Carrots

Home grown carrots are lovely – fresh, crunchy and ultra-carroty. And if you grow your own you get a lot more choice than you would in the supermarket. You can grow long and straight carrots, or go for the gourmet Chantenay roots (which look more like a conical cartoon carrot). You can also get carrots with round roots, and in pretty much all the colours of the rainbow – from white right through to deep purple.

   If you don't have much space then you'll want to stick to baby carrots –

early varieties, or the ones with short roots. They'll be ready more quickly and you'll have a more productive garden as a result. The stumpy ones are good in containers. If you want to grow impressively long and straight specimens then be prepared for some hard work – they need very well-worked soil, or they hit obstacles and fork. They'll also fork if the soil is too rich, so never feed carrots that are growing in the ground. With a selection of varieties and successional sowing you can have carrots pretty much all year round, with early varieties growing under protection in February through to maincrops that are harvested in October and can be stored through the winter.

Of course, that's an ideal scenario. I haven't cracked it yet. I'm great at growing baby carrots, but haven't managed to grow any larger ones. And even if you get the growing conditions just right, you'll have to contend with the dreaded Carrot Root Fly.

The carrot root fly is an interesting beastie. It lays it eggs in carrot patches, and the eggs hatch into maggots that eat their way through your carrots. Affected plants are stunted and eventually die, and the carrot root fly can attack parsnips and parsley as well (because they're in the same plant family). There are generally two attacks every year, in April / May and July / August.

Carrot root fly find carrots by their smell. So if you're disturbing the foliage (by weeding or thinning) then you're effectively banging a carrot root fly dinner gong – do it as little as possible, and remove any thinnings to the kitchen or the compost heap. You can attempt to disguise the carrot smell by planting other things alongside your carrots. Onions are usually recommended, but you can also plant your carrots with flowers, or surround them with scented herbs.

Carrot root flies fly quite low, so planting your carrots in pots, raised beds or behind low barriers can help to keep the fly out. But the only sure way of avoiding carrot fly problems is to cover your carrot crops with fleece. Only remove it to weed and thin your carrots, and put it straight back when you've finished.

At the end of the season, dig up all the remaining carrots – you can store them in boxes of damp sand for the winter, if you want to. Dispose of any infested ones and then dig over the surface of the carrot bed. The birds will then find and eat any over wintering carrot fly pupae. Encouraging the birds to check over the soil after you've cleared a crop is generally a good idea – they're much better at spotting insect pests than we are, and get a good meal in return for their help.

Carrots are one of the best candidates for one of the greats joys of growing your own – oddly shaped vegetables. Because they fork at the drop of a hat, they grow into some weird and wonderful shapes – frequently suggestive. It makes them harder to peel, but who would pass up the chance of a good laugh with Sunday lunch?

C is for...

Cats

Love them or hate them, cats can be a real pain in the garden. They dig up newly planted beds, use bare soil as a litter box, flatten plants and kill garden birds. If you don't have a cat of your own and find your garden the recipient of unwanted attentions from neighbour's cats then it can be extremely irritating.

Local cats are always leaving me 'presents' in the garden, the disposal of which is not a fun job. Coffee grounds and other smelly things (like citrus) can move them on for a time, but if you want to be largely cat-free you'll have to take stronger action. When we erected the six foot fence around the garden, our cat problems dropped significantly. There are very few ways in and out now, if you're not agile enough to scale the fence – and most pampered house cats aren't. We also have a PIR (Passive Infra Red) sonic deterrent. It senses movement and produces an ultrasonic noise that's irritating to cats (and dogs) but not humans or birds. Even so, in the past I have resorted to throwing water at cats who won't take the hint.

If you want to cat-proof your garden, cover bare earth. If you've sown seeds or don't want to cover soil then try putting down barriers to prevent cats from squatting on it. Stones, sticks, thorny twigs, string, meshes and temporary wobbly fences should all do the trick. Once plants are growing strongly you can generally remove these defences.

Things you may have around the house that are said to repel cats include coffee grounds and citrus (as previously mentioned), chilli pepper and lavender. Cats return to established toilet spots, finding them by smell, so if you do have to clean up a mess make sure you mask the smell as well – or you'll be doing the same thing again tomorrow morning. You can also buy proprietary repellents, including Silent Roar (made from big cat dung) and sprinklers that spray animals when they're triggered.

Of course, cats aren't all bad. They might help with rodent problems, make much-loved companions and are territorial – so if you have a cat of your own then other people's aren't likely to be a problem. You may even want to set aside a part of your garden for kitty.

C is for...

Climate Change

People talk about Climate Change a lot, and it finally seems as though almost everyone agrees that it is occurring – but that's as far as it goes. There are still plenty of people who don't believe that we are responsible for Climate Change, and more still that do believe but aren't prepared to do anything about it.

The theory behind Climate Change is that ever since we began digging up and burning fossil fuels in large quantities during the Industrial Revolution, we have been releasing more carbon dioxide into the atmosphere than it can cope with. This excess carbon dioxide is trapping heat in the atmosphere and causing the whole planet to warm up – which is why it's also called Global Warming. A temperature rise of a few degrees may not sound much, and some people (especially during the 'height' of an English summer) may feel that it would be a good thing – but the effects of Climate Change are nowhere near that simple. In fact, it's hard to think of a more complicated subject than how the climate works. We're nowhere near figuring it all out, which makes it even more silly to be messing around with it.

There are obvious signs of climate change all over the planet – the most publicised being the loss of ice in the Arctic and Antarctic – but what it means for Britain is less clear cut. It may get warmer. Or the change in ocean flows might cut off the Gulf Stream that keeps us warm and hence it may get colder. It's generally agreed that the weather here will get less predictable – with more 'extreme' weather events likes floods, droughts and gales.

There's plenty you can do to help reduce your impact on the environment (and I'll cover that later in Footprints), but there's also a lot you can do to help your garden deal with a changing climate.

Discover the secrets of water-wise gardening, so that your garden will cope as well as possible during long dry spells; make as much compost as possible and add it to your soil, for all of the benefits that organic matter bring; get to know your garden – learn about your soil and the various microclimates you have; reduce the amount of impermeable hard landscaping you have, so that excess rain has a chance to drain into the soil rather than run off; if you live in an area prone to flooding, build raised beds; choose the right plants – sun-loving perennials are very drought tolerant, but there are edible plants that like damp and/ or shady conditions too; investigate varieties with in-bred resistance to drought, pests or disease; save your own seeds so that your vegetables adapt to your local conditions; make your garden wildlife friendly so that you have a robust garden ecosystem that has the best chance of adapting to changing conditions.

C is for...

Coffee

There are lots of people who would struggle to live without coffee. Unfortunately, growing your own supply isn't really a viable option – coffee is a tropical plant that needs a heated environment to survive in Britain. You can buy seeds and try growing a coffee plant indoors, but even if you do get it bear fruit you'll need to process the beans yourself too. It sounds like an interesting project, and one I might try at some point, but for most people the closest they will ever come to a coffee plant is in a botanical garden.

Since we're shipping in our coffee from tropical climes, we should make the most of it. Waste coffee grounds make an excellent addition to the garden. They're nitrogen-rich, so they are a compost 'green' that needs mixing with 'browns' to make good compost. You can also use them directly on the garden as a mulch. You'll have a garden that smells of coffee for a few days, but the mulch will deter slugs (they're said not to like caffeine) and stop cats from using your beds as a toilet. It may even confuse carrot flies and keep your carrots safe – as long as you keep topping it up. And organic matter and nitrogen will be added to the soil and feed your plants, whilst a thick mulch will suppress weeds and conserve moisture in your soil. You can even add coffee grounds to water to make a nitrogen-rich liquid feed for hungry plants.

Because coffee grounds are damp, they go mouldy very quickly if they're stored without air – so try and use them quickly, although mouldy grounds can safely be added to the compost heap. They are slightly acidic, so they make a great mulch for acid-loving plants. If you're adding a lot of them directly to your soil then keep an eye on your soil pH to make sure it stays in a suitable range for your plants.

Coffee grounds are great for worm composting too, but again you'll have to be careful not to make you're the environment too acidic for your worms – you can balance coffee grounds (and other acidic materials, like onions and citrus fruits) by adding garden lime or crushed egg shells to the wormery.

So next time you make a pot of coffee, don't throw the coffee grounds away. You can add them to the compost heap (filter paper and all) or sprinkle them onto the garden. If you have a coffee machine at work then consider collecting the grounds and bringing them home (I did that for a number of years and yes, my colleagues did think I was bonkers) – you'll be saving the company money on their waste disposal as well as saving the planet. And if you frequent a coffee shop or pass one on the way home then ask them for their coffee grounds too. Some are only too happy to help, and Starbucks even has a special 'Grounds For Your Garden' scheme. Not all branches participate, but those that do put out baskets of coffee grounds (repackaged into their original bags) for customers to take home and compost.

C is for...

Comfrey

My garden is largely fuelled by cardboard and comfrey. Cardboard makes an excellent addition to the compost heap, but comfrey is even more of a godsend. It's known as the permaculture plant because it has so many uses.

You may recognise wild comfrey – it grows vigorously along the edges of rivers and has a tendency to self-seed. The variety called Bocking 14 is sterile and much more well-behaved; it's the one to choose if you're looking for comfrey plants for your garden. Comfrey is easy to grow, happy in most soils and pest and disease resistant. You can cut several pounds of leaves from each plant, several times a season, so even a few plants make a big difference.

You can use fresh comfrey leaves as a mulch, or dig them into planting holes. Because they contain very little fibre, the leaves decompose rapidly, making nutrients available to other plants. You can also use comfrey as a compost activator, to speed up the composting process.

Comfrey leaves rot down into a sludgy liquid, which means that they can be used to make liquid feeds. The usual way of making a liquid feed works for lots of plants, and can be used for comfrey feeds, nettle feeds, seaweed feeds and even turning your weeds into a liquid feed. It's very simple – you fill a bucket with leaves, top it up with water, cover it and leave it alone for a couple of months. The leaves decompose in the water and make a very nutritious liquid feed – that stinks to high heaven. I tried it once, and it took me several days to work out that the rotting sewage smell wasn't caused by a fault at the local sewage farm, but was coming from my comfrey bucket at the bottom of the garden. So although this works very well, it's not going to make you popular in urban areas.

But the unique composition of comfrey leaves means they rot down without water. So if you fill a bucket with comfrey leaves, weigh them down with a brick, put a lid on it and leave it for a couple of months then they rot down into a dark, treacly liquid that hardly smells at all. When you want to use it, you simply dilute it 10:1 with water.

Comfrey liquid feed is rich in potassium and perfect for fruiting vegetables like tomatoes and peppers. You can water it on, or spray it onto the leaves for a foliar feed. It's good for crops in containers, and once you've paid for the plants it's completely free, always available and has no carbon footprint.

You can even use comfrey to make your own potting compost, by layering chopped comfrey leaves with well-rotted leaf mould. And as if this weren't enough, comfrey is edible, although it's hairy leaves aren't appetizing to humans. Animals are less fussy and comfrey leaves make a nutritious addition to their diet. Our chickens will even eat it, sometimes.

Bocking 14 has pretty purple flowers that bees love. I delay cutting the comfrey so that the bees can have their share. My comfrey plants are at the back of a raised beds, where they grow too large and overshadow the crops, and where the attentions of the bees make weeding hazardous. Every summer I make a mental note to move them somewhere else when they're dormant over the winter, but I haven't done it yet.

C is for...

Compost

Compost is one of nature's miracles, turning waste organic matter back into its component parts so that they can feed more plants and animals. It happens everywhere, but in the garden we prefer to keep this process under control in a compost heap.

When things rot they're eaten by a host of bacteria, fungi and animals, collectively called decomposers (or detritivores). These organisms need nitrogen and carbon.

Nitrogen is present in 'green' materials – fresh leaves and stems from garden plants, tea bags, coffee grounds, vegetable peelings and mouldy fruit. Carbon is found in 'browns' – dry materials like fallen leaves, twigs, paper and cardboard.

To make compost successfully, you need a mixture of 'browns' and 'greens'. It's not an exact science, but try to add roughly the same amount of both. If you have a lot of grass clippings, balance them out with some scrunched up cardboard or newspaper or the straw your guinea pig has been using as bedding. When you add kitchen waste, try wrapping it in newspaper. Not only does it help turn the waste into a balanced compost 'meal', but it cuts down on the number of flies in the compost bin.

Compost needs to be wet, but not sodden. If your compost is dry then you can add water (or urine – it's a good source of nitrogen); if it's wet then simply add more dry materials.

You need air in there too. The easiest way to add air is to add a good mix of materials. A few twiggy bits or cardboard tubes every so often work wonders, and if you add them as you go along then you won't have any problems.

That pretty much sums up the easiest form of composting – cold composting. With a cold compost heap you add materials whenever you have them. You don't have to turn it and you don't have to worry about building it in layers. A cold compost heap takes several months to make useable compost (longer in cold weather). Having two means you can fill one whilst the other is rotting down.

A cold compost heap doesn't kill off weed seeds, perennial weeds or diseased plant material – so don't add them. Don't add cooked food, dairy products, meat or poo from animals that eat meat. They might attract rats, and they will certainly smell.

Your compost heap will deal with vegetable peelings, grass cuttings, tea bags and coffee grounds, poo from vegetarian animals, cardboard, paper, straw, and garden plants. If you're not sure whether you can compost something, look it up – almost all gardening books have a section on composting, and there's a lot of information on the internet. Think of all the 'rubbish' you can turn into compost.

Don't be in too much of a rush to use the finished compost – the longer you leave it, the better it is. Compost has so many uses that you can never make enough. Dig it in to your vegetable patch, or use it as a mulch. Sieve it and use it in homemade potting compost or rake it into your lawn. The thrill of using your compost makes the effort you put into making it worthwhile.

Compost is the perfect way to add organic matter to your soil, and feeds an immense number of soil organisms that are at the bottom of the food chain. If you want healthy plants and wildlife in your garden, start by building a compost heap.

The *Alternative* Kitchen Garden

D is for...

D is for...

Daisies

I don't have daisies in my garden. That's mainly due, I think, to not having a lawn – one of their favourite places to grow. If I did have a lawn then I certainly wouldn't be weeding the daisies out, as I think they're pretty. I do have daisies thriving in the driveway. I weed out all the grasses and the dandelions and leave the daisies alone, and they're gradually growing into spectacular clumps.

As children many of us become familiar with daisy flowers – their snowy white petals and yellow centres, and the fact that some of them have pink tips on the back of their petals whilst others don't. Their habit of closing up for the night, only to open up again in the morning, is interesting, and of course they're prefect for making daisy chains.

Because daisies are simple flowers, and bloom for much of the year, they also have a considerable value to wildlife. Bees appreciate them, as do hoverflies. And in actual fact, daisies (*Bellis perennis*) are edible. Their leaves are best eaten when young, and can be added to salads or cooked. The flowers and petals are edible, too, but possibly more decorative than tasty. According to Ken Fern (in his excellent book *Plants for a Future*), they can even be used to make an insect-repellent infusion.

I haven't tried eating my daisies, turning them into herbal preparations or spraying them on to repel bugs. I just like them – every time I go out into the driveway and see them blooming, it makes me smile.

D is for...

Dandelions

One summer's day, when I had been battling the weeds in the garden (hand-to-hand combat) for months, I sat back and decided that all of the dandelions in the garden were one plant – connected together at the roots. And when I thought about it I decided that all of the dandelions in the world were one plant, connected together at the roots. It isn't true, of course. Dandelion flowers turn into dandelion clocks and spread their seeds on the wind, making new and separate plants elsewhere. It was just a delusion brought on by the futility of weeding.

Dandelions are the arch nemesis of many a gardener, because of their long tap roots that seem to go on for ever and have a tendency to snap when pulled. And each section that breaks off can, if left in the soil, grow into a new dandelion plant. But a dedicated weeding campaign will get them under control – there are now no dandelions left in my garden.

But even if there were, it wouldn't be the end of the world. When you stop seeing them as villains, many weeds can be considered as useful plants and certainly have been in the past. Dandelions produce fresh, green leaves nearly all year round. They make a nice addition to a salad, although most people find them too bitter to eat in any quantity. If you want a gourmet treat, blanch them by covering them with a light-excluding bucket or plant pot, and they will have a much more subtle flavour.

Dandelion roots are edible too, and have been used in the past as a coffee substitute. If you can find some nice fat burdock roots to go with them, you could even make your own old-fashioned dandelion and burdock drink.

And have you heard that trick of using a banana to ripen other fruits (like those pesky tomatoes that resolutely remain green at the end of the summer)? The ripening effect comes from the ethylene gas that the bananas produce. Dandelions produce the same gas, so if you have something you need to ripen and you don't have a banana handy then you could see whether a dandelion or two does the trick instead.

Now that wild food is trendy, if you've eradicated all of the dandelions from your garden then you may be feeling a little envious of those who have not. If you really want to, you can buy dandelion seeds and treat them as a crop. A quick flick through this year's Organic Gardening Catalogue offers the cultivated variety of the common dandelion (*Taraxacum officianale*) and also the Italian dandelion, with pretty red leaf ribs. Dandelions are also included in one of their edible wild flower mixes.

Whilst cultivating these plants in the garden does take some of the excitement out of foraging in the countryside, it does also take out the risk. You won't have to worry about trespassing on private property, harvesting contaminated plants, identifying plants correctly or depleting wild stocks. But if you go on holiday and leave a neighbour in charge of watering, you may find that they've helpfully weeded out your entire salad crop by the time you get back.

D is for...

Dead-heading

There are lots of regular jobs in the garden that could be classed as 'enjoyable pottering' or 'chores', depending on your point of view. Some people hate watering; others find it a peaceful way of starting or ending the day. Likewise there are people who find weeding a wonderful way to get up close and personal with their plants, and others who find it drives them to distraction (I suspect it depends on the nature and volume of the weeds!).

Ornamental gardening, to me, seems to involve far too much dead-heading – the removal of faded flowers to promote the growth of more. I understand the reasoning behind it. If a plant is allowed to flower and set seed then it has done its 'job' for the year and will either die (if it's an annual) or lapse into contented leafiness (perennials). But although it certainly gives you an opportunity to see and smell the flowers up close, I find dead-heading dull.

And that's why I currently have violas self-seeding in the containers on my patio and Welsh onion seedlings popping up all over the garden. But it's also the reason that I was able to save a considerable amount of dwarf marigold seeds last year, and didn't have to buy new ones this year (and won't need to for years to come).

One of the nice things about kitchen gardens is that the need for dead-heading is reduced. Many of the most beautiful flowers belong to fruiting plants – think of apple and cherry blossom, tomatoes and beans – and allowing them to set seed is the whole point. Other flowers are edible – nasturtiums, pot marigolds and chamomile – or otherwise useful, like lavender, and hence are removed from the plant before they fade.

Many edible plants are encouraged not to flower at all, and are removed to the compost heap when they do (including salad crops and herbs). And allowing others to complete their lifecycle gives you an ample supply of seed for years to come and to share with other gardeners. So even if you find a Zen-like calm whilst dead-heading, stop snipping sometimes and see what happens.

D is for...

Decomposers

Most people have heard the term 'food chain' – the idea that every plant and animal is food for another, until you get to the animals at the top. It's a useful concept, but very simplistic. In fact, each and every plant and animal in nature is food for many others and the whole thing is much more of a 'food web'. If you tried to draw a realistic diagram the paper would be black with connecting lines very rapidly.

But there's still a hierarchy of organisms – some which are predominantly food for others, with a small number of large predators at the top. It's the animals at the top of the food web that we know and recognise, but the engine driving the whole process are the organisms right at the bottom – the decomposers.

Decomposers eat the remains of plants and animals, or their waste products. They're also sometimes called detritivores, because they live on detritus. Their brand of waste disposal might not be glamorous, but it's key to the functioning of the whole system. If they didn't munch their way through all of the dead animals, dying plant material and (let's face it) poo then we wouldn't be knee deep in the stuff because we wouldn't be here – there would be nothing left for us to eat.

You may think that in a nice, neat English garden that this kind of thing only happens out of sight, in the compost heap. And to a certain extent you would be right, but given something to feed on there will be decomposers everywhere, and the garden will be the better for it.

There's a whole army of decomposers in the garden, some of which will be familiar but many of which are practically invisible and nameless. Earthworms are much loved for their contribution to soil health. Wood lice aren't as popular, as they tend to be found on damaged fruit and vegetables – but although they look guilty the actual damage may well have been done by slugs who then slimed away and hid. Slugs and snails also play a role in decomposing plant material, as do millipedes. Springtails are tiny, white creatures with a tendency to bounce around. If you've closely examined the contents of your compost bin then you will have seen them; otherwise you won't. But there are also legions of bacteria and fungi that do a lot of the hard work.

Not only are these guys invaluable at breaking down organic matter into new plant nutrients, but they themselves become food for other creatures – mainly spiders, centipedes, beetles and mites. And they become food for more obvious animals like hedgehogs, birds and frogs. So if you want visible wildlife in your garden then it pays to make a nice home for the decomposers at the bottom of the pile.

Since decomposers feed on decaying organic matter, it doesn't cost much to feed them. You won't have to keep popping out to the garden centre to pick up a bag of Rot-A-Lot Decomposer Food. Just don't be as tidy in the garden. When you're clearing away plant material, consider whether you could leave it in place for longer – perhaps over the winter. That might not be a good idea in the vegetable patch (where plant remains can encourage pest and disease problems) but there will be other areas in the garden where it's possible. Or you can collect all of your decaying organic matter in one place – the compost heap, a five-star resort for decomposers. And then when you use the finished compost, the decomposers will treat your garden like an up-scale new development, and move in pronto.

D is for...

Digging

Gardening is thought of as a sedate, well-mannered pastime, but it's really a hot bed of seething passions. If you want to see them in action, then simply find another gardener and criticise their compost. Or try and convince a pesticide junkie that organics is the way to go. Or just turn up at the local allotment open day wearing a t-shirt bearing the slogan "I Dig No-Dig".

It seems there's very little room for compromise on this issue – you're either a digger, or a No Digger, and never the twain shall meet. Conventional horticultural wisdom is that digging improves soil structure, by removing compaction and leaving an open, free-draining soil that plant roots can easily penetrate. It gives you a chance to dig soil improvers into the soil, and if you do it in autumn then winter frosts will help to break down heavy soils into a fine tilth ready for spring sowing.

On the other hand, digging is very hard work and a common cause of injury in unwary gardeners. If it's done wrongly you can damage your soil structure as much as your back and actively encourage weeds to grow. And by adding a lot of air into the soil you're increasing the rate at which organic matter breaks down.

No Dig gardening allows people who can't dig to have a garden. It preserves and enhances the natural soil structure, encourages soil organisms to flourish and reduces the loss of both organic matter and water. Because you're not bringing new weed seeds to the surface, you won't have to do as much weeding either. Mulches are used to add organic matter – letting earthworms and other soil organisms incorporate it for you. And a No Dig system is almost always a bed system – where there are distinct planting areas and paths, and compaction is prevented by never stepping on the soil in the beds.

The disadvantages of the No Dig system is that it can be slow to bring about soil improvement, and soil borne pests are not exposed to birds by digging. It also has a problem dealing with perennial weeds – some of which can only really be removed by digging them out.

My philosophy is that if you're happy digger, then dig. If the thought of all that digging is putting you off having a vegetable patch, then be reassured that it's not necessary. You may have to dig out some perennial weeds before you start (although if you're not in a hurry you can use a long term sheet mulch) and if your chosen spot has been walked on then you may need to relieve soil compaction before you start. Or you can just build a raised bed, add top soil or compost on top the ground and let nature take its (gradual) route to improving your soil structure. As long as you don't tread on your beds, your spade is likely to spend almost all of its time in the shed.

D is for...

Diseases

Reference books on plant pests and diseases make uncomfortable reading, with endless lists of things that can go wrong. Personally I prefer a holistic approach, concentrating on plant wellbeing.

Plant health has strong parallels with human health. Plant diseases are caused by bacteria, viruses and fungi. A healthy plant is less likely to be affected by disease (and pests) and can fight off infection. A diseased plant looks unhealthy, either because it is wilting or because it has discoloured or deformed leaves.

To promote good plant health in your garden, don't cram in too many plants; a lack of air flow around the leaves promotes fungal diseases. Mix and match your planting so that there aren't big blocks of similar plants together. Diseases (and pests) find it harder to take hold if their favourite plants aren't all next door to each other. And some plants actively improve the health of their companions – chamomile is known as the 'doctor plant' and is said to improve the health of plants nearby.

In the vegetable patch, separate crops by time as well as space using a crop rotation. If you plant the same crops in the same place every year then diseases build up in the soil and have no trouble attacking your plants.

Keep plants stress-free by making sure that they have enough water – neither too much (waterlogging encourages fungal rots) or too little. The right amount of feed is also important – too much nitrogen encourages soft growth that is vulnerable to attack. Weeds cause stress (by depriving crops of water, nutrients and light), affect air-flow and spacing, and can be vectors for disease.

Hygiene is important. Keep tools clean to avoid transporting diseases around your garden, and wash pots before you reuse them. Beware of importing disease problems from elsewhere. Club root is a serious disease for plants in the brassica family (cabbages, cauliflower, broccoli, sprouts, etc.) that causes damage to the root system and stunts growth. It is caused by a fungus (a slime mould) that can live in the soil for 20 years, even if suitable host plants are no longer grown. Because it is soil borne, club root can be transferred in soil – by exchanging plants with someone with infected soil, or even on muddy boots. There is no cure, so be careful what you bring home.

It's not all doom and gloom. Plants and seeds sold by reputable companies should be disease free, and many varieties of fruit and vegetables have in-bred resistance to certain diseases. With companion planting and crop rotation you can prevent a build up of disease, and keeping plants happy and stress-free is much easier in an organic garden than for plants fed a chemical diet.

Some problems are inevitable, especially when plants are tired. Courgettes, for example, generally succumb to powdery mildew – but there's usually no need to take action as it does not affect the remaining fruit.

The best way to ensure that your garden remains healthy is to spend a lot of time in it. Keeping an eye on your plants gives you early warning of potential problems. Any suspect plants or foliage can be removed before disease spreads, and ailing plants can be fed a pick-me-up (a seaweed-based foliar feed is full of trace elements and a good booster) or moved to a better position. But there's no reason to become a garden hypochondriac – a happy plant is much tougher than it looks.

The *Alternative* Kitchen Garden

E is for...

E is for...

Earth

Almost all soils are made from tiny particles of rock, formed over thousands of years. The depth of soil varies considerably, but is divided up into two layers – topsoil and subsoil. The topsoil is the soil in which your plants grow. This is where they send out their roots to find food, water and air. The subsoil, underneath, isn't a nice environment for roots. Some plants send down deep tap roots, but mostly there's not enough air there for anything to grow.

The soil you have depends on local geology, and it's not something you can change. Its type is determined by the size of the rock particles it's made from. Sand particles have a diameter of between 0.06mm and 2.0mm, and feel gritty. How much water a sandy soil holds depends largely on the size of the sand particles; coarse particles mean a very free-draining soil, while smaller ones hold more water in place for plants.

Silt particles are smaller, down to 0.002mm, but to a large extent they behave like sand particles - with better water-holding properties. A wet, silty soil feels quite silky.

Clay particles are less than 0.002mm in diameter and have almost magical qualities. They have an electrical charge, usually negative, and attract positively-charged plant nutrients. This might sound complicated, but in essence clay particles in your soil grab hold of passing plant nutrients – giving plants time to take them up - rather than letting them wash out of the soil. The electrical charges on very small clay particles also play a large part in building soil structure, which means that clay soils can be easier to work with. They hold water better, too. Wet, clay-rich soil can be moulded into shapes.

Investigate what type of soil you have, and learn to live with it – because changing it is a large-scale process, expensive and unsustainable. The ideal soil for gardening – loam, a mixture of all three sorts of particle – is hard to find. Sandy soils, although they dry out rapidly in summer, warm up quickly in spring and allow earlier planting. Clay soils are fertile and hold water, but are slow to warm up. And when they dry out they develop large cracks.

There's a second component to soil, organic matter, and this we do have some control over. Organic matter, formed from dead plant material and animal remains, adds plant nutrients and improves soil structure to the point where it holds water and makes it available to plants but also allows excess water to drain away.

Adding organic matter to your soil (e.g. compost, well-rotted animal manure, green manures, surface mulches) is of benefit, whatever your soil type. Adding organic matter to a free-draining sandy soil helps it to hold water and nutrients. Organic matter in a clay-rich soil makes it lighter and easier to work, and helps to stop big cracks and clumps forming. The improvement in soil structure makes more air available to plant roots, and the organic matter itself is home to many organisms that play a part in improving soil quality for you.

Organic gardening is all about caring for your soil, so that it takes care of your plants. People who mindlessly concrete over it, pollute it with toxic chemicals and spray it with pesticides, herbicides and fertilisers should be paying their soil more attention.

E is for...

Earwigs

Earwigs get a lot of bad press because they can be a pest in an ornamental garden. They like munching their way through petals and young leaves, especially on showy and prized plants like dahlias and chrysanthemums. They come out to feed at night, which no doubt adds to their reputation. They're easily recognisable, with those large pincers at the rear.

   An easy way to deal with earwigs is to build an earwig trap. Stuff a flower pot with straw or hay, turn it upside down and balance it on top of a cane. Earwigs will find it as they're seeking out a cosy place to while away the daylight hours – and you can check the trap daily and dispose of any earwigs that you find.

In the kitchen garden, earwigs are much less likely to be a pest. I don't remember ever seeing one in the garden, although I'm sure I have, so they haven't done anything to warrant my paying attention to them. In fact they can be allies, since they eat aphids and the eggs of moths (including codling moth, the apple pest) and the evil vine weevil.

Earwigs hibernate in tufts of rough grass, piles of dead leaves and hollow stems (as do many other beneficial insects), so if you want to encourage them it pays not to be in too much of a hurry to tidy up the garden in autumn. Earwigs lay eggs in the soil in late winter that hatch in early spring. In a good year there may even be a second generation.

E is for...

Eden Project

At the turn of the millennium, an ambitious project aimed to turn a disused clay pit in Cornwall into a sustainable visitor attraction and education project. The scale of the task was almost unimaginable – manufacturing thousands of tonnes of soil out of mineral wastes and composted bark, creating a substantial drainage system to reuse rainwater, planting over a million plants (some of them in locations so precipitous that the gardeners have to abseil to reach them) and designing and building the largest dome greenhouses in the world. The result, the Eden Project, has to be one of the horticultural wonders of the world.

I've been lucky enough to visit Eden several times. If I lived closer I would have a season ticket. If I lived in Cornwall I would work there. I would sweep the floors, if that's all they needed – I love the place that much.

It is constantly evolving, but currently consists of three biomes (a biome is a community of plants from a specific climate). The largest of the domes holds the Rainforest (AKA Humid Tropics) biome. It's hot, and humid, with water constantly misted into the atmosphere. There's a long, winding path right to the top, so you can get a view of the rainforest canopy. It's not for the faint-hearted, but there's a chill out room and an escape route for those who find they can't take the heat.

Here you can see all of the useful plants that come from the tropics, including bananas, rice, coffee and chocolate. Most gardeners will never have the opportunity to grow any of these plants, and it's wonderful to see them reach their full potential.

My most memorable trip to the Rainforest biome was for an evening Eden Session – when we listened to the Dhol Foundation drumming from the very top. The Eden Project isn't just about plants, it's also about art, music and culture.

The smaller dome houses the Mediterranean (Warm Temperate) biome. Here you can see the Mediterranean classics, grape vines and olives, along with plant communities from similar climates. Among the displays there's usually plenty of edibles to see – often tomatoes, peppers and aubergines and herbs.

Outside, in the base of the clay pit and growing right into its walls, is the Cool Temperate biome. Although Cornwall has a mild climate, all the plants are growing outdoors and could grow equally well in your garden. On my last visit I saw achira, yacon, and oca as well as more familiar vegetables. In front of the restaurants there was a vegetable garden planted up as a huge rainbow, with squashes and peppers and marigolds interspersed with leafy greens.

The Eden Project is all about education, regeneration and sustainability. It was here that I first heard the phrase 'Waste Neutral'. With recycling bins throughout and an enviable composting programme, Eden is actively reducing its waste. And they're closing the waste loop. By buying as many recycled products as possible they're aiming to offset the waste that they do produce, and become waste neutral.

A visit to Eden is not complete without a walk through their shop. Even the most ardent environmentalist can just go nuts here, guilt free. There's local food and gifts to take home, green books and DVDs and ranges of organic clothing. There are even plants for sale, and seeds, so that you can attempt to recreate Eden in your own back garden. Even if you take away nothing but photographs and ideas, it's still a wonderful place to visit.

E is for...

Edible

I started growing edible plants because I was concerned about Food Miles. That concern wouldn't have got me much farther than a couple of pots on the patio. What has brought me the rest of the way is an increasing fascination with plants.

We are dependent on plants and animals to provide for almost all our needs. Food, clothes, building materials and medicines all come from plants. We satisfy our vices with plants – tea, coffee, tobacco, alcohol and many illicit drugs are plant-based. The fossil fuels we use to power our lifestyle were once plants or animals.

Plants do, effortlessly, things we struggle with. They create microclimates, filter toxins, run entirely on solar power, silently pump water hundreds of feet and manufacture their own food.

We should be in awe of plants, but all of this wonder takes place on a daily basis, right under our noses, and we take it for granted. We're only just starting to realise that a daily dose of plant life can brighten our moods, and that digging around in the dirt can lift our spirits. We have forgotten that the plants that feed us, clothe us and house us can also heal our souls. And, given half a chance, will save us from ourselves and heal the planet too. Tree planting schemes improve air quality; algae are being considered as carbon dioxide scrubbers to combat climate change and plants can even clean up toxic spills for us.

A lot of people worry that an edible garden won't be attractive. If I had the chance I'd send them all to RISC's incredible roof garden, to see how wrong they are. Edible plants are beautiful, and fascinating. Useful plants can add far more to a garden than purely ornamental ones.

There's nothing quite like fruit tree blossom to herald the spring. In summer, lavender and sweet peas will scent a room far more pleasantly than a synthetic air freshener. If you like big, brash flowers then you can't go wrong with the yellow trumpets that squash plants grow, or the bright colours of nasturtiums. Chillies and rainbow chard are both vaunted for their ornamental value, but if you want something really impressive then try growing a passionflower. The fruits on the hardiest species (*Passiflora caerulea*) are edible, but not supposed to be very tasty. The plants are herbaceous, cut down by frost in the winter. If you can give the roots some protection then you increase the chance of the plant returning the following year. *P. edulis* is said to have much nicer fruits, but it is more tender. Perhaps it will grow well in a container and survive the winter by being taken into an unheated greenhouse....

Growing edible plants (or useful ones – perhaps you'd rather grow your own plant supports, twine, medicinal herbs or dye plants) does wonders for your well-being, enhancing both physical and mental health. It puts you in touch with the seasons and the wonder of the natural world.

Edible plants come with their own in-built reward system. Once you've dug your first potatoes, shelled your first peas or popped the first raspberry into your mouth then you'll probably be hooked. And whatever you decide to grow - whether it's vegetable staples, gourmet treats or unusual edibles – at the end of the day you can pick it, serve it, eat it and have the satisfaction of saying "I grew that". Priceless.

E is for...

Environment

It's said that the environmental movement began when we saw the first photos of Earth from space. Before that, I suppose, it was easy to believe that whatever waste we threw out into the environment just went away. Now we know that there is no 'away'.

Since the Industrial Revolution, we've stumbled from one environmental catastrophe to the next. When we worked out that the smoke pouring from factory chimneys was causing local air pollution, we built larger chimneys. The result was cleaner air around the factories, and acid rain in neighbouring countries.

We frequently develop new products, only to run into problems downstream – quite literally in the case of numerous chemicals that have a detrimental effect on the water quality in rivers.

It was the hole we made in the ozone layer (which allows more UV radiation to filter down to the planet surface and cause skin cancer in humans and other nasty environmental effects) that brought home the realization that pollution can be invisible, a concept we're still struggling with now that we know our carbon dioxide emissions are contributing to a change in the climate.

Industrialization and globalization have meant that we can now affect the environment on a global level – things you do at home have knock-on effects on people all over the world. Unfortunately our political systems haven't really caught up yet, and dealing with global environmental problems is a painful and slow process.

And so it's vitally important that we 'think global, act local' – keeping global environmental issues in mind, but concentrating on the things that we have some control over, the things we do on a daily basis.

By now we all know the basics of what we should be doing – recycling, driving less, cutting down on our energy use and searching for environmentally friendly products and services. But beyond that, solving environmental issues is complicated and the best solutions are frequently unclear. There's lots of corporate 'green wash' clouding the water, and concerns that the economy will collapse if people stop buying all those unnecessary products. And environmental issues are often emotive – nothing makes suburban blood boil faster than the suggestion of fortnightly rubbish collections, for example.

We're all on a journey to living a more sustainable life. Some of us are taking the first, small steps; others are way ahead. Still more have yet to make a start. Wherever you are on the path, a garden is a great thing to have. Gardens remind us of what we're working towards, help us make a positive contribution to sustainability and - when times get tough – give us a tranquil space (however tiny) in which to reflect on our progress. As long as you don't go nuts and buy endless amounts of stuff for your garden, it's hard to go wrong.

E is for...

Experiments

The unique combination of soil, climate and much more means that gardening in your garden is different to gardening elsewhere. You can read up on horticultural best practice and learn all about soil and plants and wildlife, but in the end there's no substitute for getting your hands dirty and learning by experience what works in yours.

Permaculture recommends that when you start a new garden, you do nothing for the first year except watch closely. You'll learn where the sun reaches throughout the year, and which parts of the garden are always shady. You'll be able to point out the frost pockets and damp patches. After that year you'll be in a position to put everything from ponds and compost heaps to different plants in the best possible place. You'll know exactly what sort of soil you have, and where it needs improving.

In practice, most people don't want to wait, but gardens are dynamic things and develop as you go along anyway. If a plant is in the wrong place, you can usually move it. But the underlying idea is valid – you'll get more out of your garden if you learn how it works.

If you want to, you can add to the body of gardening knowledge by participating in organised trials. Garden Organic members do so every year, with experiments across the whole range of organic topics. As I write this, I have yellow tomatoes growing in the Grow Dome, part of a Garden Organic experiment to determine whether a new variety or an old variety is better. Hundreds of people across the country will be doing the same thing, and Garden Organic will collate our responses.

Gardening magazines and seed companies often run similar trials, offering free seeds to gardeners who will send in their results and opinions.

And there's no reason not to try out new things on your own. Perhaps there's a new seed variety that catches your eye, or something in a gardening magazine that sparks an idea. Ideas come to me in the depths of winter, when there's no real gardening to be done and my green fingers are itchy. One year it occurred to me that my Bokashi buckets would be ideal for making liquid feeds, and that adding Bokashi bran to the mix might cut down on the whiff. At the time I was still using the buckets for Bokashi composting, but now I can confirm that they are perfect for liquid feeds. As to whether Bokashi bran does cut down on the pong… I haven't tried that one yet.

Once I'd eaten my first Jerusalem artichoke, which arrived in an organic vegetable box delivery, I thought it would be nice to grow them. Since I didn't have much space, I wondered whether they would grow in containers. I saved the next batch of tubers, planted them in pots on the patio and… well, you can read about how well that one worked out later on!

My experimental crops for this year include kiwano or Jelly Melon. There's also goldenberries, tomatillos, oca and mouse melons! Last year the chickpeas were a dismal failure, the tiger nuts were disappointing and the peanuts got eaten by slugs – but the garlic harvest was enormous, I ate my first home-grown apple, and grew my first aubergine. There's really no such thing as a failed experiment – even if the outcome isn't what you expected, you'll have learned something and be ready to try again.

The *Alternative* Kitchen Garden

F is for...

F is for...

F1

A lot of modern varieties of vegetable seeds are F1 hybrids. They're expensive – generally you only get a handful of seeds in a packet that costs a couple of pounds or more. The reason that they're expensive is that producing F1 seeds is an intensive process.

F1 stands for First Filial, and it is the first generation of seeds or plants resulting from a cross between two very different parents. The result is a new variety with desirable characteristics and 'hybrid vigour', which means that the new plants grow quickly. The problem lies in keeping the parent plant varieties pure and stable, so that the F1 generation is always the same.

The lack of genetic diversity in F1 plants makes them ideal for mass production. They grow uniformly, fruit uniformly and crop all at the same time. Perfect for farmers, perfect for supermarkets. But these qualities make them less ideal for kitchen gardeners. Although many people wouldn't particularly object to having very uniform crops, the fact that they all ripen at the same time could be a problem – a feast and famine situation is generally something to be avoided in a vegetable plot. And although many F1 hybrids have inbuilt pest or disease resistance, they are often bred with qualities other than flavour in mind, and so do not deliver the best that home grown produce can offer.

Plant breeding is a slow process. Desirable traits have to be carefully encouraged in several generations of plants, with undesirable traits removed – by selecting which plants to continue breeding from and which to discard. Being the first generation from different parents, F1 hybrids are genetically unstable. The upshot of this is that if you grow F1 hybrid plants, allow them to flower and set seed, collect the seed and sow it again next year you will most likely get an odd collection of plants that bear little resemblance to their F1 parents. This is the F2 generation and you may get something good, or you may not.

This means that F1 hybrids are a problem if you want to save your own seeds and grow similar plants from one year to the next, or conduct your own plant breeding experiments. In that case you should opt for open-pollinated seeds, which are more likely to 'come true' and have offspring like the parents but with enough genetic diversity to adapt to the different conditions that occur in gardens.

F1 hybrids are one of the flash points among kitchen gardeners. Some gardeners have no desire to save their own seeds, and value the reliability of F1 hybrids. Others resent the strangle-hold that seed companies have on the seed market and the fact that many modern varieties are bred with farmers in mind. They prefer to save their own seeds and only sow open-pollinated varieties.

If you want to avoid F1 hybrids, you have to do your homework. Although seed packets will generally say if the contents are F1 hybrids, seed catalogues often don't. F1 hybrids will be mixed in with open-pollinated (and even, these days, old 'heritage' varieties) and you may not be able to tell which is which. If you want to be sure then fire off an email or ring the supplier up and ask – and if they can't tell you, order from someone else. Or just place your order with a company that doesn't sell F1 hybrids at all – like Real Seeds.

F is for...

Fertilisers

Fertilisers replace plant nutrients that have been used up. This is particularly relevant in kitchen gardens, because we remove so much plant material... and eat it. So it seems like a sensible idea to replace lost nutrients – but there are issues with fertiliser use.

Most fertilisers only replace the three macronutrients (nitrogen, phosphorus and potassium) that plants need in the largest quantities. Feeding plants a steady diet of these three nutrients is like giving kids nothing but fast food – it's not nutritionally balanced and it's doesn't do them any good in the long term.

Fertilisers, particularly chemical fertilisers, change the soil chemistry. They make life difficult for many of the organisms that live in the soil, and using nothing but fertiliser can make your soil a barren place. That's not good for plants either.

And when you're buying fertiliser you're bringing materials into the garden, no doubt transported from far away, and adding to pollution and climate change. The soluble nature of many fertilisers mean that they can wash away in heavy rain, causing problems elsewhere.

The organic approach to feeding plants is to concentrate on improving and feeding your soil. If you have good soil, your plants are better able to extract the nutrients and water they need, and grow better as a result.

The best thing you can do for your soil is to make as much compost as possible. Compost recycles the plant nutrients in garden waste, kitchen waste and paper/cardboard and turns them into the perfect soil improver. Applying compost adds nutrients to the soil, promotes a healthy soil environment and improves the soil structure.

Having said that, sometimes a fertiliser is necessary. Container-grown plants need feeding - a small volume of soil cannot provide them with all of the nutrients they need. And there are hungry plants that need extra food to provide bumper crops – like tomatoes, courgettes and some fruit bushes.

The important thing to remember when choosing a fertiliser is to pick the right one for the job. Even if you limit yourself to organic fertilisers, there's a lot of choice; the one thing they have in common is that they all smell funky.

Seaweed features heavily in organic fertilisers, because it's a good source of the trace elements (micronutrients) that plants need in small quantities – a bit like we need vitamins and minerals. Seaweed extract is a liquid that can be applied at any time, and is great for giving a boost to struggling plants.

Liquid feeds are very fast acting when you water them onto the soil. But even faster still is using them as a foliar feed – applying them directly to leaves. When applying foliar feeds you have to make sure that they're not too strong – so read the instructions carefully. Seaweed extract makes a great foliar feed. Not only does it give plants a very quick boost, but the fishy tang it adds deters some sap-sucking insects.

Whenever you're using a fertiliser, remember to follow the instructions. Using too much is a waste of money and won't do your plants any good. And if your plants just don't seem to grow well, try and solve the underlying problem rather than just reaching for a fertiliser. You may have problems with your soil structure, or the nutrient balance in your soil may be wrong – having your soil tested will show whether this is the case.

F is for...

Fixation

Gardening books and magazines often say that beans and other plants are 'nitrogen-fixing' – they can take nitrogen from the air and turn it into a useful plant nutrient, so they don't need fertiliser. And if you leave the plant roots in the soil when you clear the top growth away, any surplus nitrogen will be left behind to feed the next crop. A lot of green manures are nitrogen-fixing, and are designed to feed the crop that comes after them.

Whilst this is all true, it's only half the story. You might remember the other half from biology classes at school – symbiosis. Nitrogen-fixing plants form a partnership with rhizobia bacteria in the soil, and it's these bacteria that do the nitrogen fixing. If the bacteria aren't present, then fixation won't take place.

When you're growing nitrogen-fixing plants in ground that has been used for vegetable growing for a long time, then this usually isn't an issue. The bacteria build up in the soil and can persist for many years, even if the ground isn't currently being used for growing nitrogen-fixing plants. There are different strains of bacteria that partner up with different crops though, so if you try something unusual (like chickpeas) then you might not have the right bacteria present.

And if you're growing on new ground, or in potting compost, then you may well not have any rhizobia present. The good news is that, after a few years, they will magically appear. In the meantime, though, your crops will be poor as the plants struggle to feed themselves.

If you want a quick fix, it's now possible to buy various strains of rhizobia (often called inoculants, or bean boosters) that you add to the soil before sowing your beans. If you're not having problems with your peas and beans then it's not necessary, but if your plants are disappointing then it might be worth a try. Remember to get the right strain for the beans or peas that you're going to plant. The bacteria have to be in place for germination, or shortly afterwards, for the partnership to take place.

If you do have the right bacteria, than any pea/ bean plants that you pull up at the end of the season will have nitrogen nodules on their roots – pale little bobbles, the same colour as the roots themselves. Once the rhizobia have arrived in one area of the garden, they can be spread around to new areas by transferring a shovelful of soil.

Because I grew most of my plants in containers and sterile potting compost, I never had rhizobia in the garden – and my beans were usually disappointing as a result. This year, however, when I pulled up the dwarf French beans that were growing in the Grow Dome they had nitrogen nodules on the roots. They were growing in home made compost, so the right rhizobia for French beans have obviously arrived and will be spreading around the garden as I use the compost. Had I known they were there I would have left the bean roots in the soil, but I didn't.

When I pulled up the broad beans, growing outside, they didn't have nodules. I may try out an inoculant for them next year.

F is for...

Footprints

The Ecological Footprint is a way of collecting together the various impacts we have on the planet to give one number that tells us how sustainable our lifestyles are. It counts up how much land we need to grow our food and how much land we've built upon. It takes into account the land from which we get our natural resources – timber, water and mined products – and also includes fudge factors for things like energy production that don't have a land value.

When you calculate your Ecological Footprint (calculators are available online) you get a number – the area of land required to support your lifestyle. If you use several different calculators then you'll come up with different answers, because they ask slightly different questions and involve different fudge factors.

Your Ecological Footprint will be compared to your fair share of the planet's resources. This is a simpler calculation, adding up all the productive land and then dividing it by the number of people on Earth. The end result is always the same – if you live in an industrialised country then your Ecological Footprint is much larger than your fair share.

You'll probably be told how many Earths we would need if everyone lived the same lifestyle we do. We only have one planet, but it's a useful representation of how unsustainable our current lifestyles are. We're expecting more from the planet than it can supply, and environmental damage is the inevitable result.

You can also calculate how much carbon dioxide your lifestyle emits – how much you personally (or businesses, or countries) contribute to climate change.

Measures of general environmental impact, like Footprints, are always going to be estimates. The science is complicated and there are lots of things we don't know about environmental issues – science is an unfolding story of finding more questions than answers. The value of Footprints lies in their ability to bring home to us just how unsustainable our lifestyles are. Because once you know there is a problem, you can take steps to solve it.

Gardening may seem like a low-risk activity in terms of environmental impact. Doubly so if you grow your own food, because you're cutting down on all of those pesky food miles. But your garden has its own Footprint, and the choices you make about how you garden have an effect on it.

Easy ways to ramp up your Garden Footprint include heating your greenhouse, buying in plants and tools and indiscriminate use of power tools. And the person who invented patio heaters clearly didn't have the environment in mind – the energy used when you're trying to warm up the outdoors is immense.

But there are easy ways to minimise your Garden Footprint too. Collect as much rainwater as possible (there's energy involved in collecting, purifying and pumping mains water). Make compost, to cut down on the need for soil improvers and fertilisers. Be careful what you buy. Many garden products are transported long distances and contain a lot of 'embodied energy' (the energy required to make something). Keep the use of power tools to a minimum and avoid heating the greenhouse. If you have plants that can't be brought inside and die in cold weather then section off a small area of the greenhouse and heat that.

Reduce, Re-use, Recycle and Rot and your Garden Footprint will be low.

F is for...

Forest Gardens

Over thousands of years, plants have evolved in different ways to take advantage of the light that is available to them. Trees grow tall so that they can spread their leaves above other plants and get to the light first. Spring bulbs live out their entire lifecycle – growing leaves, flowering and reproducing – before the trees above them grow their thick covering of leaves. Plants have different heights, leaf shapes and lifecycles to exploit particular sets of conditions, called ecological niches.

Plants aren't happy outside of their niche. A sun-loving plant won't thrive in the shade. A shade-loving plant quickly fries in too much sun. Bog plants don't like drying out, and desert plants don't like being wet.

A forest garden is designed so that every plant is growing in its ideal niche, and that all the niches are filled – so that the garden is as productive as it possibly can be. The idea is to have plants with as many uses as possible. There would be medicinal herbs, and you might also find yourself with the raw materials for basket weaving, soap, dyes or plant feeds. Forest garden plants are usually perennials, or annuals and biennials that self-seed and reproduce without human intervention. They're categorised into 'layers' – the height at which they grow.

The first layer is the canopy, large trees that provide shade and fruit and a valuable wildlife habitat. Small forest gardens may only have one tree in the canopy layer – or they might 'borrow' trees from the surrounding landscape. There's also a layer of smaller trees, and then one of shrubs. Soft fruit is in this layer, and there are lots of fruiting plants that will be happy in a forest garden – including familiar berries such as raspberries and currants.

Small herbaceous plants make up the next layer – things like herbs and leafy greens. The soil surface in the forest garden is yet another layer, covered in low growing plants. Underneath them is the root layer. You wouldn't grow annual crops like carrots and beetroot in a forest garden, but there are some more unusual root crops that would thrive here and provide a harvest.

The final layer is a vertical one. In a natural environment, climbing plants make their home growing up trees and taller plants. A forest garden makes use of vertical spaces such as walls and fences; there's a surprising number of climbing plants with edible fruit or other uses.

If it's done right then a forest garden is very low maintenance. All you do is pick your harvests and intervene occasionally to restore the balance if a plant tries to take over. I'm experimenting with a miniature forest garden – I have three goji berry bushes, and I've planted them out in their own bed with an under-planting of strawberry seedlings that will hopefully grow into a healthy ground cover. My Good King Henry is there too (it's much happier in the ground than it was in a container), and I have plans to add more plants later on.

Although forest gardening is not a new concept, it's more common in tropical climates. Temperate forest gardens are still new and experimental, but forest garden projects are springing up around the UK. One of most established is the RISC roof garden in Reading (Berkshire) - if you're impatient, skip ahead to R and read all about it.

F is for...

Freecycle

Even though we live in a consumer culture addicted to buying new things, there are still plenty of people who haven't given up on second-hand goods and hand-me-downs. Car boot and jumble sales, charity shops and eBay are popular for a variety of reasons. Some people just don't have the financial resources to shop elsewhere, others are bargain hunters and still more are trying to live a more sustainable lifestyle.

The latest weapon against waste and over-the-top consumerism is Freecycle and other similar schemes. The idea is simple – if you have something that you don't want anymore, you post an advert to an email group to see if someone in your local area would like it. They then come and pick it up, and no money changes hands. You can pass on almost anything, from a couple of paving slabs or some rubble to baby clothes and televisions. As long as it's legal and suitable for a family audience, anything goes. You can't swap or sell things though – if you want to do that then visit eBay or use a classified ad.

People can also place Wanted adverts on Freecycle – if they're in desperate need of something that someone else may have kicking around in the garage or the attic. People moving into new homes regularly ask for pieces of furniture; new mums-to-be are grateful for anything for baby.

Freecycling can be engrossing if you live in an area which a high traffic group. Your inbox can rapidly fill up, and you have to be quick off the mark if you want to be in with a chance of getting some of the popular items. The person who posts the advert decides who gets the item. There are no set criteria for the decision, so some will simply go for the first person to apply, while others will give it to the most deserving cause. Sometimes collection has to take place on a particular day.

Although Freecycle is a great scheme to help us Reduce consumption and Reuse goods (thus avoiding the need to Recycle), the reason I'm mentioning it is that it can be a great way to kit out your garden without spending any money.

Compost bins are regularly available on Freecycle, and you may also see the occasional water butt. Paving slabs and rubble for use as hardcore are common. Lots of people have sheds and greenhouses they no longer want, but you'll probably need to dismantle them yourself. You may also get old windows, which can be cobbled together into cold frames – the height of 'Allotment Chic'.

Garden centres may be getting their act together regarding plant pot recycling, but lots of plant pots are also given away on Freecycle. During the growing season, you might be lucky enough to pick up a few plants, or spare seeds. I once collected several carrier bags of old gardening magazines from a lady who lived just down the road and was moving house.

There are also fringe benefits to Freecycling. When we first started giving things away, many of them went to a guy who lives about five houses away. Not only was collection a breeze, but we made friends with one of our neighbours. Now he takes our surplus eggs and returns the eggshells, together with shredded paper for the chicken's nest box. His daughter pops round to see the hens, and he helped us fix our guttering. Local community links like these are priceless. As we move towards sustainability we need to make as much use as we can of local knowledge, skills and resources – rather than trucking them all in from miles away.

F is for...

Fruit

A few years I fell in love with a dwarf nectarine ('Nectarella') in a catalogue. It was advertised as ideal for containers, and the photo showed beautiful pink blossom. One was soon winging its way to me. To begin with it survived in a large pot on the patio, but was never very happy – probably because I am less than enthusiastic about watering. It flowered every spring, but didn't really fruit. In the miserable summer of 2007 it set three fruits, which failed to develop and looked more like apricots than nectarines. They weren't very nice.

Now that the Grow Dome is finished, my little nectarine has a permanent home indoors. It seems to love it – it has a good crop of fruit this year, although it's too soon to know if that will translate into a good harvest.

Later I added four dwarf fruit trees – an apple, a pear, a plum and a cherry. They lived in containers for a year, but again they didn't appreciate my slapdash watering efforts. In the spring of 2006 I planted them out into the garden, a good move considering the scorching summer that followed. They are happier now, but still not exactly fruitful. I had my first apple harvest last year. There were cherries too, but the birds ate them. The pear and the plum have never fruited, and at the moment the best thing you can say about them is that the blossom is pretty and they provide some shade for the chickens.

Now I have strawberries, blackcurrants, a redcurrant, autumn fruiting rasp-berries, a jostaberry and two tayberries. Blueberries and cranberries live in pots because I don't have the acidic soil they need, and I have just invested in a fruit cage so we might be able to eat more of the blueberries this year than the blackbirds. Oh, and there are two grapevines climbing up the fence. And rhubarb. And a young fig tree.

The advantage of fruit is that it mainly grows on perennial plants that don't add much to the workload during the busy spring sowing and planting months. And there's nothing quite like tucking into a handful of home grown raspberries that are still warm from the sun.

If you don't have much space then there are still a few fruits that you can grow. Strawberries work well in containers, especially alpine strawberries – which have much smaller fruits, but pack a strawberry punch. This year I'm growing strawberry spinach, a leafy annual that grows red berries that look a little bit like strawberries. They're not supposed to have much flavour, but would bulk out a bowl of mixed berries. The leaves are edible too, so you could make an interesting salad out of the leaves and berries.

Physalis plants (AKA goldenberries, or Cape gooseberries) can be large and vigorous, but there are dwarf varieties available. They need similar conditions to tomatoes and peppers – so they will be easier to grow if you have a greenhouse, but can be grown in a sunny and sheltered spot outside.

If you're happy to move off the beaten track there are plenty of other fruiting plants to try, and you should be able to find one for any situation if you look hard enough. There are even fruiting plants that are happy in shady spots. I warn you, though, there's nothing more likely to spark a shopping frenzy then tracking down weird and wonderful fruits....

The *Alternative* Kitchen Garden

G is for...

G is for...

Garden Organic

Garden Organic is the UK's organic gardening charity. They do research into organic gardening techniques, have organic demonstration gardens that are open to the public, publish books on organic gardening and support their gardening members.

Garden Organic used to be called the HDRA (the Henry Doubleday Research Association), but went through a re-branding exercise in 2005 to make them more accessible to new members who have no clue who Henry Doubleday was. In fact he did research into the organic gardener's wonder plant, comfrey. Laurence Hills named the HDRA after him when he began the association in 1954.

I became an HDRA member shortly after I started gardening. They're a very helpful source of advice and inspiration for organic gardeners, and membership also gives you a discount with the Organic Gardening Catalogue – a wondrous online shop and mail order catalogue that carries pretty much everything an organic gardener could wish for, but may have trouble finding in their local garden centre.

In my second year of membership I also joined their Heritage Seed Library. The rules governing the sales of seed here in the UK are stacked against heritage seeds, and they are hard to come by. The Heritage Seed Library (HSL) works around the regulations by giving away heritage seeds free to its members, and by doing so allows them to conserve and maintain heritage varieties of seeds that are no longer available commercially – giving gardeners a real choice in what they grow.

Garden Organic has two gardens that are open to the public. The flagship demonstration garden is at Ryton, in Warwickshire. It's divided up into different sections, to showcase organic gardening techniques and prove that it's possible to have healthy crops and beautiful gardens without damaging the environment. There's an orchard, a huge cage of soft fruit, a model allotment, a compost demonstration garden and a display garden for some of the HSL's unusual vegetable varieties. There's a lot of fun and educational stuff for children, too, an award-winning restaurant and a big gift shop stocked with organic and environmentally friendly products as well as seeds, plants and other gardening goodies.

The latest addition to Ryton gardens is the Biodynamic garden. I've only seen it in early spring, before the growing season really started, but the idea of it is to demonstrate the use of biodynamic gardening techniques – a step beyond mere organic growing.

I've never been to Audley End kitchen garden, but it's on my To Do list. The garden is in the grounds of a stately home in Essex owned by English Heritage. The historic garden is managed organically, using techniques and varieties (as far as possible) in keeping with its heritage. There's also a 21st century garden using more modern techniques.

A visit to an organic garden can be very inspiring, allowing you to take away ideas to use at home. An idea that I've borrowed from Ryton is to try undersowing my purple sprouting broccoli plants with trefoil (a low-growing green manure). Not only will the trefoil fix nitrogen in the soil and act as a living mulch (reducing evaporation and weed growth), but apparently it should help deter cabbage white butterflies as well. The PSB isn't planted out yet, but the trefoil is certainly working well as a living mulch underneath some of my fruit bushes.

G is for...

Garlic

Garlic was one of the first things I grew. It has two advantages for kitchen gardeners. Firstly, it is usually planted in the autumn and left in the soil over winter. This means there's something growing in the dead of winter, and it relieves the gardening itch that many kitchen gardeners feel during the winter when there's not much to do outside. It's also very easy to grow, and requires almost no attention. So when life intrudes and the garden suffers, your garlic will keep going without you.

It's wise to start with proper seed garlic, bought from a garden centre or seed catalogue. It's guaranteed to be healthy stock, and also to be a variety suitable for growing in the British climate. You can plant cloves that you bought to eat, but they may well have come from abroad and be expecting better weather.

Buy a whole bulb, and leave it intact until you're ready to plant your garlic. Then break it into cloves and plant the biggest ones – just push them into the ground with your finger (or make holes with a dibber and drop them in) until they're buried. If you leave the papery tips showing above the soil it encourages birds to pull them out again (although I have no idea why). Plant them the same way up as they were in the bulb. If you have an overwintering variety than October / November is a good time, because they get settled in before winter. Spring varieties are actually planted in late winter, up until around February. Garlic isn't really fussy about soil, but if yours is very wet over winter then either choose a spring variety or plant your garlic in pots to begin with and plant it out when conditions improve.

There are two different sorts of garlic. Here in the UK we generally grow soft-necked garlic. It's a hardy plant and produces bulbs that store well. Sometimes it also produces bulbils (tiny cloves) part way up the neck. You can eat those, or plant them. If you plant them they will grow into a round, single bulb in their first year. You can treat that as a big clove, or you can replant it – and in its second year it will grow into a proper divided bulb. It's an interesting experiment, but for a big harvest it's best to stick to planting normal cloves.

Hard-necked garlic is more common in the US. It throws up flower shoots in summer, and the way that they bend gives it the name Serpent Garlic. It's impressive to watch, but these flowering shoots (scapes) divert energy away from bulb production and should be removed before they flower. They're edible, and quite garlicky. I use mine in stir-fries, but you can also use them to make garlic scape pesto or any number of other things. Hard-necked garlic is generally thought to have a superior flavour, and so is the gourmet's choice – but it doesn't store as well.

When you have your first garlic harvest, save one or two of the best bulbs as your seed for next season. Garlic has the interesting trait of rapidly adapting to its local climate – so yours will attune itself to conditions in your garden and should grow well for you each year after that. You'll only need to buy new garlic to plant if yours becomes diseased.

Although to most of us garlic is just garlic, there are in fact lots of different varieties – so if you're a garlic fan then you could develop a collection. You'll need to seek out like-minded gardeners, though, for swaps – as many of these varieties are hard to come by.

G is for...

AMARANTHUS
CAUDATUS

Grains

If you're really intrepid then there is one horizon that is rarely explored on a garden scale… grains.

Although making your own loaf from seed to flour might seem like an attractive prospect, it's not an endeavour for the faint of heart. A garden isn't going to provide all the wheat you would need for a family for a year, and it's an intensive crop that takes a lot out of your soil. Once it's mature you'll have to harvest it, thresh it, winnow it and grind it before you can start to make your bread. It would certainly give you an appreciation of life before mechanisation.

You could try barley, for brewing your own beer. And you could grow wheat and barley for their wildlife value, or for bird seed. Foodies might consider spelt, an old-fashioned grain used in artisan breads.

A soggy area in the garden, or a paddling pool, could be the ideal spot to attempt rice growing and you may get enough for a few meals. The grains are supposed to be relatively easy to rub off the stems.

If you like a nice bowl of porridge on a winter's morning then try oats – a hulless variety is perhaps the easiest conventional grain to grow and process on a small scale.

Looking further afield brings some more manageable prospects. Amaranths are sometimes grown for their leaves (used like spinach), but there are varieties bred for grain production. They make stunning plants, and the seed produced is very nutritious.

Quinoa is another grain that should grow well in the UK. The seed is full of saponins that make it soapy and need to be soaked out before the grain is used, but the advantage of this is that birds don't like eating soapy seeds either! Quinoa is a drought tolerant plant, but may suffer from moulds in a wet season.

I haven't tried any of these... yet. The diversity of grain amaranths available is enough to make me go weak at the knees. And I was tempted to try rice this year, but realistically I had already filled every available space in the garden.

There are two main rules in kitchen gardening, both regularly bent or broken by obsessive gardeners. The first is to grow only things that you are interested in eating. There's no use slavishly following a planting plan from a gardening manual and ending up with rows of Brussels sprouts if you hate them. But if you want to see how they grow, or prove that you can grow them, you may consider a few plants worthwhile.

The second rule is not to do too much – the garden in your head is larger, and much less effort to manage, than the one outside. There's no point in tracking down rare seed varieties, or raising pernickety plants, if you can't squeeze them in anywhere. Or if it means cramming plants in so tightly that they're prone to disease, hungry and stressed and you can't keep up with looking after them.

A garden can be the perfect antidote to the harried pace and instant gratification of modern life. We have to wait for seeds to germinate, and plants grow at their own pace. Even though we may be bombarded with enticing seed and plant catalogues there is no need for us to rush and try and do everything at once. The garden will be there next year, and it presents us with a blank canvas every spring.

G is for...

Greenhouses

A greenhouse is usually top of a gardener's wish list. They dream of endless tomatoes in summer, a dry place to potter around and a space for raising seedlings in spring. A greenhouse protects your plants from the weather – keeping them warm in an environment you can control.

My first greenhouse was a plastic mini-greenhouse. Something that small can be a nightmare for plants. They're not frost-proof and on a sunny day rapidly get warm enough to fry seedlings alive. And the moist environment they encourage is perfect for slugs and snails, but if it's all you've got space for then it expands your growing horizons.

My next step was a plastic greenhouse large enough for me (but not Pete) to stand up in. It came with guy ropes to secure it – an absolute necessity because plastic greenhouses act like kites in even light winds. I grew peppers and French beans and had great fun pottering around inside.

Now I have the Grow Dome, a geodesic dome on top of a wooden supporting wall. It came in kit form and it took us about two years to clear the end of the garden and erect the Grow Dome. It was a real labour of love.

A greenhouse lets you extend the growing season. In spring you can sow early crops when it's still too cold outside, but getting the timing right so that seedlings are ready to plant outside as soon as the weather is good is a real art form. Tomatoes and peppers enjoy the added heat and humidity during the summer, and hardy winter crops are more tender when grown with the benefit of some protection.

The current inhabitants of the Grow Dome include tomatoes, peppers, golden-berries, kiwano and mouse melons, taro and marigolds. I've already harvested carrots and lettuce. It will soon be time to think about what's going to be growing over the winter, but in the meantime I'm trying to keep the tomatoes under control.

Last summer, before the ponds were installed, the dry environment meant that spider mites were a problem. This year the humidity is higher and I haven't seen them so far; instead I'm having trouble with slugs.

If you have beds or borders in your greenhouse then the usual rules about rotation apply – if you grow the same crops in the same soil every year then pests and diseases build up. Following a crop rotation is easier than replacing all of the soil every couple of years, even if it means that some crops have to be grown in pots or growing bags.

The only problem with greenhouses is that they can't be left unattended. In hot weather you need to check that the vents are working and that plants have enough water. If you have clear glazing then you need to apply shade paint in summer to cut down the amount of light entering, or your plants may scorch (polycarbonate glazing diffuses light, and so doesn't have this problem). If you're going away then you'll have to set up an automatic watering system, bribe a friend to come in regularly to check the greenhouse, or resign yourself to the fact that not all of your plants will still be alive when you get home.

But in return you can be gardening pretty much year-round, harvesting fresh food all of the time and growing exotic edibles that simply won't thrive outside in the British climate.

G is for...

Green Manures

Bare soil doesn't happen often in nature — and doesn't stay bare for long. In winter, bare soil is prone to soil compaction and erosion; in spring and summer it dries out or is quickly colonised by weeds. Mulching prevents these problems, but you can also cover soil with plants.

Green manures are crops grown to benefit the soil. Some have strong root systems able to break up heavy soils. Others add nitrogen to poor soils.

Green manures also offer weed control, reduce evaporation and provide mulch or compost materials.

A green manure is usually grown for a specific amount of time, and then dug in before it flowers. The green material then rots down in the soil, adding organic matter and encouraging soil organisms. In No Dig gardens, it can be cut down and left on the soil surface as a mulch, or removed to the compost bin.

There are lots of plants that can be grown as green manures, and as each one has different requirements and offers different benefits it's important to choose the right one for your situation.

If you've got heavy clay soil then I can recommend Hungarian Grazing Rye, which is sown in late summer or autumn and left to overwinter. It's a tall plant, with strong roots that break up heavy or compacted soils. It also suppresses weed growth.

The other green manures that overwinter, field beans and winter tares, fix nitrogen in the soil and thereby feed the crops that follow them.

There's a range of green manures that can be sown in spring and summer, and the choice is made largely on how long you want the green manure to grow for and whether or not you want it to fix nitrogen. Some of these plants are from the same families as vegetables, and you need to take that into account when you're planning a crop rotation. Mustard, for example, needs to be kept with the brassicas.

And some green manures inhibit seed germination – which makes them great weed suppressors, but means you can't sow seeds directly into the soil where they grew until they've properly decomposed. You wouldn't want to use those types on your seed bed, but they don't affect transplants and can be used elsewhere in the garden.

I am experimenting with trefoil as a living mulch this year. Trefoil is a very low-growing plant, and a nitrogen-fixer. It's supposed to be good for undersowing taller plants – especially hungry ones such as fruit bushes, squashes and sweetcorn.

The trefoil that I sowed in the spring was quick to establish, and is growing well. Even in the driest weather it's lush, and so are the plants it's mulching. Some of these are fruit bushes in containers, so it seems to be doing a good job of preventing evaporation and keeping roots shaded and cool. Seeds sown in the summer, with more patchy rainfall, have found it harder to establish – I probably should have paid more attention to the watering. I'm currently trying to establish trefoil in the bed where I will be planting my purple sprouting broccoli, because according to Garden Organic trefoil helps confuse the cabbage white butterfly.

Green manures are usually cut down before they flower. Many of them self-seed, given half a chance, which adds to your weeding burden. However, some of them (particularly phacelia) have a good wildlife value if allowed to flower, although it's still worth cutting the plants down before they set seed unless it's a permanent patch.

G is for...

Goji Berries

Over the last few years we've been bombarded with messages about superfoods – usually fruits and vegetables that pack a nutritional punch and are sold as the answer to all of our ills. They contain antioxidants, flavonoids and other phytochemicals – and the application of the term superfood can send sales soaring.

Some of these 'superfoods' are cool weather crops – broccoli, watercress and spinach are easy enough to grow in the UK. Many more are exotic visitors –

including passionfruits and ginger. Last year goji berries were all the rage. Usually sold dried in health food shops, gardeners were pulled onto the superfood bandwagon and sold goji berry plants so that they could grow these wonder berries at home. I have three goji berry bushes myself, since I'm a sucker for anything unusual. They're supposed to be hardy and very easy to grow in this climate, and to start cropping when they're quite young. My gojis spent their first year in pots, but this year I planted them out into their own bed in the garden. They've put on a lot of growth, and look much happier, but I don't think they will crop this year. I've never had a goji berry; the fresh ones are reported to be much nicer than the dried ones, but I'll have to wait and see. The good thing about chickens is that they love berries and can usually be relied on to eat things we don't like!

The superfood label is pure marketing, of course. Every fruit and vegetable has its own nutritional benefits. A balanced diet is the best way to ensure that you stay healthy and get all of the nutrients you need – especially as there's still lots we don't know about phytochemicals (chemicals produced by plants) and the way they interact together.

Any fruits and vegetables you grow in your own, organic, garden can be considered to be superfoods. As they're ultra-fresh and not contaminated by chemicals you will receive the most nutritional benefit from them when you eat them. And as they're picked at their peak and fully ripe, they'll be much tastier too.

This year's superfood is the Miracle berry (*Synsepalum dulcificum*). The Miracle berry affects your tastebuds – making everything else you eat for a couple of hours taste much sweeter. You can buy granules, or fresh fruit. Although you can also buy Miracle berry plants, they're pricey. Apparently this plant is difficult to propagate, very tender and requires an acid soil to survive. This one probably isn't destined to become a kitchen garden staple.

There's also an undercurrent of interest in a British native plant, Sea Buckthorn (*Hippophae rhamnoides*). Sea buckthorn has orange berries that ripen in September, but (unusually) remain on the plant throughout the winter. They were probably an important food for our hunter-gatherer ancestors, providing a good source of vitamin C when it would otherwise have been in short supply. There are lots of health claims made about Sea buckthorn (which I am not qualified to judge), but it also has two big advantages for gardeners. Firstly it grows along the coast, and so is a good addition to a maritime kitchen garden where salt spray makes growing conditions difficult. It's also thorny, and can make a short but impenetrable hedge that adds considerably to the security of an exposed garden or allotment.

The *Alternative* Kitchen Garden

H is for...

H is for...

Happiness

It seems as though we've finally realised something that should have been self-evident – living in a concrete jungle doesn't do us any good. There are massive physical benefits to having access to green space, and particularly to kitchen gardening. Not only do you get exercise in the fresh air while you're tending your plot, but you add healthy fruit and vegetables to your diet at the same time.

But the benefits don't end there – gardening can make you happier as well.

Research shows that regular exposure to plants and green spaces reduces stress levels and improves mood. Hospitals are planting up areas so that patients can get access to green spaces, or at least have a room with a green view. And the PlantforLife campaign has even come up with a recommended daily amount (RDA) for exposure to plants – 20 minutes a day or at least a couple of hours a week.

There's even research that shows that exposure to a particular strain of soil bacteria increases happiness by boosting serotonin levels – at least in rats! And so getting your hands dirty can improve your mental health. There are regular stories in the media about celebrities who find their gardens invaluable in promoting well being, and horticultural therapy is now available to help with anything from physical and mental illness through to social deprivation and criminal behaviour.

Clearly, gardening is a happy and healthy pursuit. Everyone would benefit from tending a few plants, whether it's ornamental houseplants or an allotment full of veggies. What's going to make you happiest is a very personal thing. I enjoy trying new things in my garden, raising plants from seed and being able to eat my harvest – even if it's tiny. I love seeing the hedgehog visit, and was thrilled to watch a heron as it clambered along local rooftops. Seeing the sparrows swooping onto the patio to feed among my containers makes me smile, and so does the blackbird – although he digs through the soil and makes more of a mess! And the chickens can usually be depended on to brighten the darkest day, especially if I have a tin of sweetcorn handy.

A kitchen garden can be a lot of work, but it should never be a chore. Grow what you want to grow. Spend your time doing the gardening tasks you enjoy, and take steps to minimise the ones you don't. And if you're spending all day outside, slap on the sunscreen! Nothing puts a damper on your spirits like sunburn.

H is for...

Hardening Off

It strikes me as very odd that we refer to pathetic things as 'weedy' when, as all gardeners know, weeds are the toughest plants on the block. Anything that you really want to grow needs nurturing and protecting against these wild bullies.

Every spring, we sow seeds of tender plants indoors well before they would naturally germinate outside. It's one of the great balancing acts of gardening – sowing tender plants early enough so that they're ready to go outside the minute the weather is good enough (and they have the best chance of giving us a decent harvest) without jumping the gun and having plants that are desperately needy for light and more root space when the outside temperature is still resolutely stuck below zero.

Assuming that you get it right, and you have wonderfully healthy plants on the magical day that the soil warms up, you still need to help your plants make the transition to the outside world. At this time of year most humans wouldn't venture outside without a coat, or at least a sweater. From a plant's point of view, the weather is no better. It might be sunny, but the dim light indoors hasn't prepared them for the scorching effects of even spring sunshine. That light breeze is enough to dry out their leaves. And as for the chill as the sun goes down… brrr!

To have any chance of surviving outdoors, indoor plants need to be toughened up. The process of doing this, hardening off, is one of the gardening tasks shrouded in mystery. It's much more of an art than a science, but getting to grips with it makes gardening a much more pleasant experience.

When you're hardening off plants, a cold frame (or one of those mini greenhouses) comes in handy as a halfway house between indoors and outdoors. However, they can also be a death trap. The temperature rises rapidly inside a cold frame on a sunny day, even if it's otherwise cool. You have to check regularly to make sure your plants are still happy.

Even if you don't have a cold frame, the process of hardening off is the same. Choose a good day to start, when the temperature is comfortable and it's not too sunny or windy. It doesn't matter if it's raining, as long as it's not heavy rain that will squash little plants flat. Leave your seedlings outside in a sheltered spot for a couple of hours. Then bring them back in, definitely before night comes and the temperature drops and the slugs come out to prowl.

The following day, leave them outside for a bit longer. And a bit longer the next day. Gradually acclimatise them to the outside world. What's happening inside the plant is that the leaves are toughening up so that they lose water less rapidly and are less prone to sun scorch. The plant is changing its growth pattern, and growing more slowly and sturdily so that it's better equipped to cope with the wind. All of these invisible changes are setting the plant up for a new life outside.

The next stage is to leave the plants out all night – but if frost is forecast then you'll still have to bring them inside or give them some protection. And don't forget to get your slug defences up and running, as there's nothing quite as tasty as seedlings.

If everything goes to plan then your seedlings will transition into life outside without a check to their growth. When they're obviously growing well outside then they're ready to be planted out or potted on out in the garden. Just remember that if there's a late frost they may still need your help.

H is for...

Hardy

A hardy plant is one that can survive a frost. The US is divided up into hardiness zones (1-11) according to climate, and plants can be labelled according to which zones they can be expected to survive in without protection. Here in the UK we have a much smaller range of climates – almost everyone is in either zone 7 or zone 8 unless they live in a coastal region. So in theory it's much easier for us to decide whether or not a plant will survive in our gardens.

But you do have to take your local microclimate into account. Cornwall has such a sheltered microclimate that sub-tropical plants can survive there – there's even a tea plantation. Other parts of the country are particularly dry or wet, or cold. My own garden seems to be one of the windiest places in the country! Even within the garden there can be microclimates. There might be a frost pocket at the bottom of a slight slope, where the soil takes longer to warm up. Or a sheltered south-facing spot in the shelter of a fence where a peach tree would be more than happy. Knowing your garden well means that you can find the right spot for each plant, and take climate variations into account.

It's also worth finding out the average first and last frost dates for your area. Although they're only estimates, and not to be entirely relied upon, it will help you plan your sowing and harvesting times and give you some idea of what to expect.

Even so, there will be times when you lose plants to the weather. Sometimes it seems unfathomable. A plant that has been happily in place for several years will die one winter. It might have got too wet, or too dry. Or it may have been struggling and been killed off by a particularly nasty frost. But to balance it out you might find that you inexplicably succeed with plants that really shouldn't survive in your garden.

There are quite a few vegetables that will cope with the worst that winter throws at them. They're the traditional winter crops of kale and cabbage, Brussels sprouts and sprouting broccoli. Leeks, garlic and Japanese onions will also stand through the worst of the cold.

There are plenty more frost-tolerant plants that will survive outside, but many will be much more palatable if you can give them some shelter (in a cloche, cold frame or greenhouse) – protecting them from the worst of the wind means the leaves are much more tender. And a little bit of protection will enable you to keep cropping from plants that die back in very nasty weather (like chard and leaf beet) but spring back into life when the weather improves. Under a cloche they may keep growing right through the winter.

H is for...

Hedgehogs

When I was a kid, I developed a fascination with hedgehogs. I'd never seen one in person, but they became my favourite animal. It was probably because there was a lot in the media at the time about St. Tiggywinkles, the wildlife hospital. I collected hedgehog memorabilia, and I still have my copy of Les Stocker's outstanding work 'The Complete Hedgehog'. Hedgehogs were in the news more recently when they were culled on the island of Uist in an attempt to protect the population of wader birds (hedgehogs eat eggs, among other things) and many wildlife organizations joined together to halt the cull and relocate the hoggies to the mainland where they would be more welcome.

There are hedgehogs in most parts of the world. We have the Western hedgehog (*Erinaceus europeaus*), and our hunter-gatherer ancestors would have been as familiar with the hedgehog as we are today. In fact, it's a miracle the hedgehog has survived this long – because we used to eat them. Now of course, they face a bigger obstacle – the motor car – and we're more likely to see them squashed by the roadside than wandering about in gardens. We make the situation worse by putting out bread and milk for them. Hedgehogs are insectivores, and unsuitable snacking is likely to give them a very upset tummy.

I'm thrilled by the fact that a hedgehog visits our garden. In fact it's probably more than one. Hedgehogs roam through several gardens each night, and have quite large (and overlapping) territories. They will also have more than one nest site, and will use the closest one when daybreak comes. Although we have a fence on two sides of the garden, there's a gap under the gate where the hedgehog comes in, and we installed a ramp so that they didn't have to negotiate the large step up onto the patio and into the garden.

Hedgehogs love slugs, snails, earthworms, beetles and other creepy crawlies. If you use poisonous slug pellets in your garden then you'll be poisoning the birds and the hedgehogs as well. It's hard to tempt a hedgehog into the area if they're not already around, but if you want to feed a resident hedgehog then put out meaty food – bacon rind or dog food (or special hedgehog food) and a source of fresh water. You can buy or make special hedgehog houses for them to hibernate in, but again you may not be able to convince a hedgehog to take up residence.

If you're having a bonfire, always make sure that a hedgehog isn't hiding at the bottom of the pile, especially if it's been sitting around for a couple of days. And don't believe the old wives' tale that hedgehogs will pass on fleas to you or your pets. Although most hedgehogs are infested with fleas, the hedgehog flea is a fussy eater and won't touch any other animal.

If you have a pond in your garden then make sure there's a shallow end or somewhere that hedgehogs (and other animals) can clamber out if they fall in. Hedgehogs can swim, but will drown if they are unable to get out of the water. St. Tiggywinkle's and The British Hedgehog Preservation Society are both excellent sources of information if you want to know even more about hedgehogs.

H is for...

Hens

When Princess Layer and Hen Solo arrived they were point-of-lay: about six weeks old and mature enough to start producing eggs. A couple of weeks after they arrived, Princess Layer laid her first egg. Hen Solo was a bit more unsettled by the move, and developed a cold – requiring a trip to the vet. A short course of antibiotics sorted her out, and it wasn't long before they were both laying an egg most days.

Henny and Princess have to be kept out of the vegetable garden. Although they do lots of good – fertilizing, and eating pests – they devour anything they want and scratch up the rest. They're allowed to roam the rest of the garden when we're around to keep an eye on them. We've never seen a fox in our garden; they're more likely to fall victim to a football kicked over the fence.

Chickens each have their own character and can be endlessly entertaining. Henny is top of the pecking order, and bullies Princess – but that's normal. We make sure that Princess gets her share of treats and isn't too badly put upon. You can't have just one chicken, they're flock animals, and don't like to be separated. I think three would be ideal – Henny sometimes gets lonely when Princess is laying an egg, and makes a loud honking noise until they're reunited.

Chickens don't need much – a safe and dry place to roost at night and lay eggs, a constant supply of clean water, layers pellets and access to some greenery. Plus a source of grit to aid digestion. Ours get lots of treats – mainly poultry corn and mealworms, which is why they're on the hefty side.

They happily tuck into small slugs, and any snails they can get their beaks on. They like spiders, too, and earthworms. Centipedes are a big treat. Lettuce is their favourite green vegetable, followed by chard. If neither of those is available then they will consent to eat other greens, but it's clear that they'd much rather have grass – they make a beeline for the grassy weeds in the garden whenever I let them out.

If you really want to make your chickens jump for joy, then open a tin of (sugar and salt free) sweetcorn. It's not an everyday food (it goes straight to the thighs!) but it's the perfect chicken treat.

We have to clean the eglu out every week or so in the summer – it has a removable poo tray, so it's pretty easy to take the poo out and put it on the compost. The girls have shredded paper in the next box, and that needs changing too. In the winter they spend more time in the eglu (they go to bed at sunset and get up at sunrise) and so need cleaning out more often. Every few months we take the eglu apart and wash it down with the pressure washer, dry it off and put it back together.

Like any animals, chickens are a big responsibility. At most they can be left on their own – with a good supply of food and water – for a couple of nights. If you want to go away you'll need to arrange for someone to look after them, but it's a small price to pay for constant companionship in the garden. Let your chickens out when you're digging, and you'll find they soon wander over to help – because you're digging up tasty treats.

H is for...

Herbs

One of the first things I grew, in my little collection of patio containers, was coriander. I have the (blurry) photograph to prove it. It bolted, running to seed before we had a decent leafy harvest from it, which is what coriander likes to do. You can save the seeds and grind them to make your own coriander spice. There's no point in saving seeds from plants that have bolted, because you'll just be encouraging a certain lack of stamina in the next generation. You can buy special varieties of coriander that are bred for leaf production, and so 'slow to bolt' – but they still will. The best defence against bolting is to sow more seeds every few weeks so that you have a continuous supply of young leaves and can simply throw the older ones on the compost as and when they bolt. Other than that, make sure your plants are not stressed by lack of water.

I also had a tub of mint, grown from a little plant I bought at the garden centre. Mint smells lovely, but it was a few years before we thought of anything to do with it other than flavouring new potatoes (a distinctly seasonal event!).

Moving on from there I developed a desire for fields of parsley, the kind of harvest where you could take a hefty bunch for cooking and not make a dent in it. It took me a couple of years to manage it, but in the end I did. A number of plants (both curly and flat-leaved) growing in the edges of my raised beds performed wonderfully through one summer and into the following spring. We could have had endless bunches of parsley, but again when it came down to it I couldn't think of what to do with it all. The chickens ate some of it, but the hoverflies benefited most when the plants started to flower.

Herbs can be temperamental. In the last couple of years I've lost several rosemary plants. Two, quite mature, didn't make it through their third winter. I have no idea why. The young replacements I bought didn't make it through their first spring – they need more water than you might think when they're young! Next year I'm going to buy a packet of rosemary seeds and grow an army of rosemary plants, to ensure that some survive.

Perennial herbs (like rosemary, lavender and mint) have differing requirements and can be difficult to grow together in a herb bed. The permaculture solution is to build a herb spiral, which is essentially a mound of soil. Herbs are planted in a spiral that winds its way up the mound, which may be delineated by a row of stones or something similar. The herbs are the top are planted into the most well-drained soil. Conditions become increasingly damp as you plant down the mound, so the moisture-loving herbs are planted at the bottom. The mound itself will cast some shade – so the sun-loving herbs are planted on the south side and the shade-loving herbs on the north face. Each herb can be given just the niche is wants, following the permaculture principle of putting everything in the right place.

Growing herbs can be very moreish. If you start with a few of your favourite culinary herbs then you may well find yourself branching out into more unusual ones, and then into herbs with medicinal uses, or ones that can be used in household or beauty preparations. Most don't take up much space, and will grow in conditions that other plants would find challenging. And they add so much to the garden – pungent smells and beautiful flowers that attract a wide range of insects.

H is for...

DWARF
FRENCH BEAN
NEGRITOS
(LUCKY DIP)

NOT FOR SALE

Heritage Vegetables

If you want to start a heated discussion in a room full of gardeners, stand up and say something along the lines that you think all of the hype about heritage vegetables is nothing but claptrap, and that no one would have bothered breeding modern varieties if they weren't an improvement on the old ones. The resulting argument should go on for hours.

Back before agriculture became industrialised, seeds were prized possessions.

Local varieties of vegetables (and fruits) were nurtured and maintained for generations, with seeds being saved and passed on. Most of this grass roots seed-saving and breeding died out when commercial seed production took over.

The sale of seeds is now highly regulated, at least partly to protect consumers from false marketing claims and seeds that aren't what they're cracked up to be. There are use-by dates, and minimum germination rates. And any seed that is sold in Europe has to be registered on a national seed list.

And therein lies the problem. To register a seed variety on the national list, and maintain it there, costs money. Seed varieties that are no longer considered to be commercially viable are therefore dropped from the list, and it becomes illegal to sell it. The most commercially viable seeds are usually ones that have been bred for farm use and aren't necessarily ones that gardeners would choose for themselves.

Real Seeds get around this by making every customer a member of their exclusive seed club – so that they're only selling to members. Garden Organic's Heritage Seed Library gives seed away to its members. Association Kokopelli, a French group with an awe-inspiring seed catalogue (some of which is available to non-members) has been in trouble with the law for selling un-listed seed varieties.

Beyond these organizations (and others, all around the world) is a counter-culture of seed exchanges in which no money changes hands. Gardeners with an interest in heritage varieties are collecting them, saving their own seed and then passing them on to anyone who wants them. A lot is done in person, at seed swapping events. Still more is done on the internet. Gardeners as a group are very generous and willing to share when they have something that is different and exciting. Many pass on excess plants to friends and neighbours, and offer cuttings and divisions to gardening pals. It's even easier to pop a few seeds in an envelope and send them off.

Whilst it's true that not every heritage variety will grow well in your garden, that's true for modern varieties as well. If you have a favourite modern variety that you love and which grows well for you, then stick with it. If you're looking for new flavour sensations, or just something a little out of the ordinary, then try a few heritage varieties as well. Some people develop consuming passions for heritage French beans (which come in an unbelievable array of colours) or tomatoes. You might decide that the crimson-flowered broad bean is just the thing to liven up your spring garden, or that you really want to try achocha, one of the Lost Crops of the Incas. There's no need to make it into a political gesture, or to make a stand on either side of the argument – but if you're on a journey away from big business and rampant consumerism then growing your own heritage vegetables is a big step along the way.

The *Alternative* Kitchen Garden

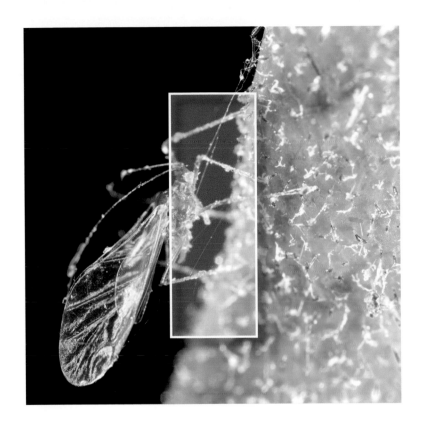

I is for...

I is for...

Impoverished Soil

Something that a lot of new gardeners have to contend with is impoverished soil. It might be that your house is relatively new, and that the builders thoughtfully buried all of their rubble under your lawn. Or that you've inherited an allotment that's been used for years by someone with a chemical fertiliser fetish, and there's not a lot of oomph left in the soil.

There's only one solution to impoverished soil, and it's not an instant fix.

You need to add organic matter, and lots of it. If you do that, and avoid the temptation to reach for the chemical fertilisers as a quick fix, then you'll gradually build up a proper soil ecosystem again and develop a garden where plants and wildlife can thrive.

That doesn't mean that you can't do some gardening and grow some crops in the meantime. There's always the option of container gardening while you're waiting for the worms to do their magic on your soil. Or you can build beds on top of the soil, by sheet mulching (also sometimes called Lasagne gardening, because the beds are built in layers). Basically you build piles of organic material on top of the soil, starting with a thick layer of cardboard or newspaper to prevent weed growth and then piling on anything you can get your hands on – grass cuttings, well rotted manure or homemade compost, leaf mould. The idea is that you use what's available locally and what you can get hold of for free. If the materials you use aren't well rotted then you'll need to leave the bed to settle for a while (try building in autumn for spring planting) but if you've got a good top layer (if you've got homemade compost then save that for the top) then you can plant into that. Vigorous plants like courgettes and potatoes thrive in these kinds of conditions, and will help break down all the materials so that you've got good soil for the next crop.

Sheet mulching is also good for reclaiming weedy ground (as long as you're dealing mainly with annual weeds) and compacted ground. It's a great project for a community garden, because it's very quick if you've got a lot of people helping out and you can get growing almost immediately without the back-breaking ground clearance that scares most people off.

Sheet mulch gardens gradually rot down and sink into the soil. If you've got more permanent issues (such as bad drainage or very shallow or stony soil) or even no soil at all then consider permanent raised beds – they're also great for people who want to avoid too much bending.

I is for...

Inbreeding

In human terms, inbreeding is generally frowned upon. It leads to all sorts of complications that are best avoided. But things are different in the plant world and there are many plants that are inbreeders – naturally self-pollinating.

Vegetable plants that nearly always self-pollinate include lettuce, French beans and peas. Species that will happily do so include tomatoes, peppers and aubergines. They have a couple of advantages. The first is that they can be grown easily undercover, because they don't need insects or the wind to pollinate them. They make great crops for polytunnels and greenhouses, or sunny windowsills.

The other advantage is that it's very easy to save seed from inbreeders. Since they don't easily cross-pollinate with other varieties, the seed you save will have the same genetic characteristics as the parent plants – it will 'come true' (providing it doesn't come from an F1 hybrid). You don't have to worry about trying to keep different varieties physically separate, or a certain distance apart. By coincidence, these plants generally have seed that is easy to collect, clean and store – they're great plants to start with if you want to try out seed-saving.

Outbreeders are plants that normally cross-pollinate. Fertilization will normally only take place when there are other plants of the same species around and flowering at the same time. In some cases, male and female flowers grow on different plants (like holly).

Some plants are considerably more promiscuous than others. If you have more than one type of courgette growing in the garden, for example, you would have to go to great lengths to keep them separate if you wanted to save seeds that come true. If you don't mind experiments and surprises then you could save seeds anyway and see what happens – you'll get some odd shaped courgettes next year, most likely, but you might find one that's ultra-tasty.

I is for...

Indoor Edibles

Offices are quite dull places, often made more habitable by the addition of a few houseplants here and there. They do a lot for the air quality, as well, with some plants in particular being very good at filtering out toxins, bacteria and moulds. Although most people aren't lucky enough to sit by a window, health and safety standards ensure that offices are pretty brightly lit – and the constant temperatures mean that they can be great places for growing a few edible plants.

I caused quite a stir when I added sweet peppers to the list of plants growing in the office where I used to work. If you've got a sunny windowsill they thrive – they love the warmth and as much light you can give them – and because peppers are self-pollinating they will fruit. (You can encourage heavier crops by helping out with a little manual pollination as well.) You can get dwarf plants, and peppers are very ornamental – especially some of the chillies – with their pretty flowers and fruits that ripen from one colour to another. If you've got a prime location then aubergines should be even more impressive. Depending on the nature of your office, you may have to contend with a few fruits going missing – but gardening in a shared space is always about give and take.

There are plenty of plants that would enjoy a shadier spot, too – including salads and herbs. I had one colleague who kept a basil plant alive for several years, pinching off a few leaves to liven up his sandwiches every day. When it looked like it was about to flower it got a more brutal pruning, and then just kept going. You could have your own 'living lettuce' on your desk, or a communal 'salad bar' container. Many herbs are happy in pots and would also thrive in suitable indoor locations.

If you work for a really forward-thinking company then you could even have a dwarf peach tree in the lobby, a fig, or citrus bushes, rather than the traditional yucca. You have to be a little bit sensitive to people with allergies, and not choose something that sprays pollen all over the place, but I didn't have any complaints about my indoor garden.

Suitable conditions at home are most often found on windowsills. I currently have several citrus plants (lemons and clementines, grown from seed), young pomegranates and peppers enjoying my sunniest windowsill. I've also got plenty of aloe vera, which we don't eat but it's a very useful plant. There's also a dragon fruit cactus (very spiny!), growing quite slowly. One day I might try growing my own coffee beans or peppercorns. If you like ginger then it also makes a good indoor specimen – the advantage being that we keep our houses at a comfortable temperature all year round, and so there's no need to go to the expense of heating a greenhouse. However, bear in mind that during the winter low light levels can be a problem.

I is for...

Insecticide

Every gardener has a gardening nemesis – whether it's slugs, red spider mite, cabbage white butterflies or aphids – that can send them over the edge.

The problem with reaching for insecticides, pesticides and fungicides is that they affect the natural balance of the garden ecosystem and make the problem worse in the long term. In the short term they can save a crop that you'd like to eat, but do you really want to eat something that's been sprayed with chemicals?

In an organic garden, the solutions to pest and disease problems involve starting from the ground up - improving your soil so that plants are healthy and fight off pests and diseases. Crop rotation prevents pests and diseases building up; growing a wide variety of plants helps to prevent them zeroing in on any one crop. Encouraging wildlife works wonders in keeping pest populations under control. Choosing plant varieties with in-built pest and disease resistance also helps.

The next line of defence is physical, preventing pests from getting to your crops. Fruit cages keep birds out; mesh tunnels keep all kinds of insects out; slugs can be deterred from approaching their favourite crops, or manoeuvred into traps. Traps and barriers can be very effective, especially if you experiment to find which ones work best in your garden.

Eternal vigilance helps to keep pest problems under control – if you spot aphid populations while they're small then it's easy enough to blast them off with a jet of water from the hose, or pinch out the tips of the plants they're growing on.

Biological controls are populations of predators you release into the garden. Some are obvious – you can buy ladybirds or ladybird larvae to control aphids. Others are almost invisible, but go to work on pests and keep their numbers down. The range of biological controls is increasing, but you need to remember that these are living creatures. Always buy from a reputable supplier, and it's probably better to buy mail order to guarantee fresh supplies. Read the instructions carefully, as biological controls are only effective within specific temperature ranges.

Even after you've religiously followed a crop rotation, planted companion herbs, encouraged wildlife, chosen pest-resistant varieties and set up your defences, you may have problems. And they will be different year on year. A wet summer last year caused a slug boom this year, and this year's damp summer isn't helping.

In these situations you may find it acceptable to reach for one of the insecticides that has 'qualified acceptance' in the organic guidelines. 'Qualified acceptance' means that ideally you wouldn't have to use them, but in the event that it's an insecticide or crop failure then you use them as a last resort. Even so, they're not completely benign and you should follow the instructions carefully to minimise collateral damage to wildlife.

You may also come across recipes for home-made pesticides. The assumption is that anything home-made is bound to be safe, but unfortunately that's not the case. Some of the things you could concoct in the garden are toxic, to you and the local wildlife – which is why home-made pesticides are illegal in the UK.

Most of us can afford to lose a few of our crops. In the event that something becomes badly infested or diseased, dispose of it, try to understand what went wrong and plant something else in the space instead.

I is for...

Intercropping

Intercropping, undercropping, catch cropping and double cropping are all slightly different ways of doing the same thing – growing more than one crop in the same space and thereby increasing harvests.

Intercropping is using the space between plants that will eventually become large, like brassicas or squash. While the main crop is small, fast-growing plants like lettuce or radishes are sown in the spaces between. By the time the larger crop grows into the space, the intercrop will have been harvested and eaten.

Undercropping relies on the fact that some plants like a bit of shade. Growing shade-loving crops (like lettuce) underneath taller plants gives them a little bit of shade, and acts as a living mulch for the taller plants.

Catch cropping fills the gap between harvesting one crop and planting the next. If you've got a little patch of ground that isn't due to be used for a couple of weeks then you've got enough time to grow radishes, lettuce and salad or some of the fast-growing Oriental vegetables. When it's time to sow or plant out the next main crop, you'll have young and tasty salad vegetables to harvest.

And double cropping involves growing two vegetables in exactly the same place, and relies on different growth rates. The classic example is that of sowing radish and parsnips in the same rows. Parsnips are notoriously slow to germinate, and the radishes will quickly sprout and mark the rows – making weeding in between a doddle. By the time the parsnips make an appearance, it will be time to harvest the radishes and the parsnips can have the space to themselves.

The Native Americans had an intercropping technique known as the Three Sisters. They planted squash, sweetcorn and beans in the same beds. The sweetcorn provides tall stems for the beans to climb up; the beans fix nitrogen in the soil to feed all three crops; and the squash rambles along the ground as a living mulch. The Three Sisters is undergoing a resurgence among organic gardeners, although I haven't tried it myself yet.

Intercropping is a great way to prevent monocultures and the pest and disease problems they encourage. You could even try planting two different varieties of the same crop (with different disease resistance) together. But the golden rule with all of these techniques is to avoid a situation where growing a second crop interferes with the main crop. If you try and cram too much into the space you'll be making problems for yourself, increasing the need to water and cutting down on the air flow between plants that is essential to prevent fungal diseases.

I is for...

Internet

Before I became a full time Garden Geek, I was a plain old geeky geek – working with computers. I had a blog (online diary) before I had a garden, but once I started gardening it quickly became a gardening blog and these days covers very little beyond my garden and some wider gardening and environmental issues.

A garden journal is a fantastically useful tool, recording what happens in your garden. It's great to be able to look back and find out that your garlic didn't send up any shoots until February last year either. Or to be able to work out what it was you sowed in that bed where the odd looking plants come up. And it's lovely to be able to look back at past harvests and successes when it won't stop raining and the slugs have eaten all your lettuces. If you're electronically inclined then a gardening blog is a great way to keep a gardening journal.

And once you have a gardening blog then you automatically become part of the online gardening community. There are all kinds of gardeners around the world who have gardening blogs and websites, and you're bound to find some kindred spirits. People who will celebrate your successes and sympathise with your failures abound, and for the most part online gardeners are lovely people and avoid the bad behaviour apparent in other areas of the internet.

In the autumn, when things are winding down in the northern hemisphere, the days are just starting to get longer in the southern hemisphere, and you'll have a fresh bunch of gardeners sharing their gardening stories to tide you through the long, dark days of winter.

If you like to chat then there are hundreds of gardening forums, including several dedicated to allotments and kitchen gardening. And gardening topics make an appearance in other sorts of websites as well, including those dedicated to environmental causes and simple living. In spring, many sites organise a seed swap, which is a great way of expanding your seed collection (and getting rid of your surplus seed) without spending much money.

There are an increasing number of commercial sites aimed at gardeners. Most seed catalogues now have an online shop, and it's an easy way for smaller companies to reach a larger audience. That means that you can source seeds, plants and sundries on the internet that you would have trouble buying in your local area.

And, of course, you can listen to podcasts online and watch gardening videos. Now that the TV companies are catching up with the online trends, you can even watch tv gardening shows online.

If it wasn't for the internet then the Alternative Kitchen Garden wouldn't exist. The blog would never have been written, the podcast would never have been recorded, and it would have been much harder for me to track down all the unusual seeds that I love so much. And my life would have been much poorer as a result, especially as I've made some fabulous friends in the online gardening community.

I is for...

Inspiration

In the early days, all of my inspiration came from gardening books. One of the first was *The Edible Container Garden* by Michael Guerra. It's a lovely book that encourages everyone to grow as much of their own food as possible, however tiny their space. There's a reference section at the back about the size of container you'll need for each type of vegetable, and the beautiful photos are inspiring.

Urban Eden (by Adam and James Caplin) has a similar intent, and more photos of beautiful gardens that flourish in the tiniest of spaces. It has a recipe section in the back.

Plants for a Future, by Ken Fern, is crammed full of plants that are edible, medicinal or otherwise useful. This is the book for you if you want to know which plants can be used as coffee substitutes, or for herbal teas. Or for oil, paint, charcoal, dyes and fibres.

Simon Hickmott's *Growing Unusual Vegetables* is a lighter read. It covers less than 100 plants, but it gives you detailed cultivation and harvesting information for some of the unusual edibles that are likely to do well in the UK.

Window-box Allotment by Penelope Bennett looks at gardening on a different scale. There are tiny miracles on each page, from detailed accounts of seed germination to ant farms and wormeries. The book follows a tiny, window box garden from January to December and is so full of wonders you won't ever want to put it down – even if you have a huge garden.

There are many more wonderful books on my shelf, but these five are the most inspiring. I've read them all several times, and each one has the power to make me wish I was outside in the garden, and fills me with the joy of gardening all over again.

At some point I moved onto gardening magazines, and I've had subscriptions to most of them. They all have their own personality, but most suffer from having to repeat the same things at the same time each year. There's only so many articles about how to grow the perfect tomato, or avoid a courgette glut, that most people can stomach. Try *Permaculture Magazine* for a fresh approach.

Visiting gardens is a great way to get ideas. Take a camera, or at least a notepad, so that you can jot down the names of plants that catch your eye. Personally I find the big horticultural shows to be too crowded and too commercial to be very inspiring. I know there are lot of gardeners who love them, though. If you're going to go, get yourself one of those little crates on wheels (or make your own!) with a long handle to help you cart your purchases around. Unless it's a cactus show. If you want to look like you belong at a cactus show then you need a plastic tool tray, one of the ones with a carry handle in the middle. It's perfect for carrying around prickly little plants.

These days much of my inspiration comes from the internet. Gardener bloggers are an inventive and resourceful bunch of people, with no shortage of ideas.

Of course, the best source of inspiration is always the garden itself. Take the time to sit outside and experience your garden. Relax and ponder what's good, what could be better and possible solutions to any problems. And if inspiration doesn't strike, you can do the same thing again tomorrow!

The *Alternative* Kitchen Garden

J is for...

J is for...

Jam & Juice

If you've got an allotment, or a large garden, then you may have problems with gluts. A glut is an overly large harvest, more than you can eat fresh. It's possible to avoid most gluts (I've never really had one, I grow too many different things). It starts with planning – thinking about how much you like to eat certain fruits and vegetables and the probable yield of your plants allows you to guestimate how many plants you need in the garden. Or you can cheat and look up how many plants the experts recommend for a household of your size.

Successional sowing of fast-growing crops (mainly salads) means that, by sowing small numbers of seeds several times throughout the season, you have a continuous supply of plants ready to harvest, but not a big glut all in one go.

If your garden is producing more of one thing than you can cope with, there are several possibilities. The first is sharing – giving part of your harvest to family and friends, or work colleagues. In the event that you have too many courgette plants, you may even find yourself trying to persuade complete strangers to take the excess off your hands. It's helpful to be a pillar of the local community, because it means endless school / church / charity fetes with produce stands that can sell your overflow.

Animals can be useful too – my chickens will eat their way through quite a lot of things (courgettes and achocha included) if they're chopped up small enough and their favourites aren't on the menu. And of course you could pull up the offending plants and replace them with something else, although for some reason many people find that a disturbing idea ('wasteful', or something!).

Preserving harvests is also making a come-back. If you have a large freezer then it makes sense to freeze some of your harvests for later, although in some cases it means making up meals and sauces in advance as some vegetables don't freeze well raw. However, although buying a second freezer would help to make you self-sufficient it won't do much for your carbon footprint.

Which is why more and more people are preserving food in other, older ways. Drying, pickling and bottling (called canning in the US) are all relatively easy – although you have to be careful with hygiene if you don't want to poison yourself later on. If you've got a sweet tooth than jam is a popular option; chutney is a similar process for more savoury preserves. You can also juice fruit (I juice all of my tomatoes – I have the juice and the chickens eat the pulp) and make cordials. Or wine.

You may not feel you're a true kitchen gardener until you've got strings of onions, sacks of potatoes and a windowsill of cured pumpkins stored for the winter. You may even go to the lengths of building a clamp to store your root vegetables for the winter. It really depends on what your goals are, and how much space you've got. Some of us are happy just to freeze a few raspberries, for a taste of summer in the middle of winter. And the rest of us are happy to scoff them all while they're still warm!

J is for...

Jelly Melons

My name is Emma, and I'm a Seed Addict. In recent years I have had more time (and energy!) for armchair gardening than the real thing, with the result that I have a large collection of seeds – far more than I could hope to sow in the garden in the course of one year. Or several. My seed buying habit is now under control, but I'm still tempted by the seed catalogues that come out each spring and parade their new and exciting plant varieties (or old and exciting) under my nose.

The fact that I have such a large collection of seeds, and can rarely now justify adding anything new, gives me a slight problem each autumn when Garden Organic's Heritage Seed Library sends out their catalogue to members. The catalogue comes out in December, making an HSL membership an ideal Christmas present for a gardener, although you can join at any time of the year.

The HSL catalogue is full of heritage varieties of beans, peas, tomatoes, carrots, beetroot and more. All of the common garden vegetables are covered, and you can find varieties inside that would be all but extinct if it wasn't for kitchen gardeners. Being a member entitles you to six packets of seed from the catalogue, on a first come first served basis – so if there's something in particular that you really want then it pays to get your request in early.

My overflowing seed box means that I find it hard to pick six varieties – although, of course, there's nothing compelling me to choose anything! I've got plenty of peas and beans and far too many carrots. I don't have room for any really big squash, and I'm not the world's biggest fan of tomatoes. And so I keep my eye out for anything really unusual.

My first achocha seeds came from the HSL, a few years ago now. Last year I picked sorrel, although I didn't grow any until this year. This year's new arrival was the African Horned Cucumber, also commonly known as kiwano. I prefer one of it's other names – the jelly melon. It's Latin name is *Cucumis metuliferus*.

The jelly melon is a common crop in the tropics, and likes warmth. Here in the UK it's grown in the same way as regular cucumbers. Mine are growing in the Grow Dome, clambering up bamboo canes with garden twine twirled around them for extra grip. Since they're still growing, all I can say about them is that they're vigorous and healthy plants with hairy stems. They're currently growing much faster than the Mexican Gherkins (*Melotria scabra*, also known as Mouse Melons!) I'm also trying. They're supposed to produce the most adorable mini-cucumbers, perfect for pickling or for lunch boxes.

If the jelly melons fruit, the fruit will have soft 'horns'. When young then can be eaten like cucumbers. Once they've ripened to their mature bright orange(!) they're sweeter and the ripe flesh can be scooped out with a spoon and eaten raw. Or you can cook them like marrows. Apparently the fruits don't keep well and need to be eaten fresh, so you're unlikely to see one in the supermarket any time soon.

J is for...

Jerusalem Artichokes

Although Jerusalem artichokes are rarely found in supermarkets and aren't the most popular of vegetables, they are commonly grown on allotments – probably because they're very vigorous and almost impossible to kill.

Jerusalem artichokes make an intriguingly creamy soup and you would never believe that it doesn't have oodles of fat in it. They have a mild, slightly smoky flavour that blends well with other things. Try carrot and artichoke soup, or artichoke and sweet potato. They can also be eaten in much the same way as potatoes – mashed, baked, roasted or fried.

I decided to try growing Jerusalem artichokes in containers, and planted up some tubs in the winter. They sat on the patio all summer. When they wilted, I watered them. I didn't feed them. The following January I tipped the pots out and there was a decent harvest of tubers in each one (they grow in a similar way to potatoes). Each tuber had turned into enough for a portion of soup. As I harvested each tub (leave Jerusalem artichokes in the ground until you want them – they keep best in the soil) I picked one medium-sized tuber and replanted it straight away. Jerusalem artichokes are very hardy, and mine have never failed to grow, although you can plant them right into spring.

I'm into my third year now, replanting my own tubers in large pots that I picked up for free because they were being thrown away on a building site that was being landscaped. I refill the pots with home-made compost each year and I can't think of a better example of permaculture – creating a harvest with barely any inputs.

Jerusalem artichokes are related to sunflowers and have a similar growth pattern, being tall and quite leafy. In a good year they might even flower, although I've never seen it (and it's probably unlikely in containers). They're so vigorous that they're often recommended as a seasonal windbreak. In containers they tend to be shorter; if you pinch out the tops of the stems then you can encourage them to be bushy.

I could get a larger harvest if I planted the tubers in one of my raised beds, but there are issues. Although we love artichoke soup, we wouldn't want to eat it every day. And there are flatulence concerns that make it an unwise choice for a dinner party starter. Like potatoes, Jerusalem artichoke will grow from any small tubers that are left in the ground – making them problematic to eradicate once you have them. And they would take up space that I would rather use for something else.

Although Jerusalem artichokes haven't been popular in recent times, they're undergoing a resurgence. This is partly because allotments are becoming more popular again, and Jerusalem artichokes work really well on allotments.

But there's another reason. The starch in Jerusalem artichokes is inulin, which we can't digest - making Jerusalem artichokes a low calorie food. They're satisfying to eat, but won't pile on the pounds. Inulin makes it through to the gut undigested, and is fed upon by the bacteria – making it a prebiotic that encourages a healthy population of bacteria in the gut.

That's also the reason for the flatulence, of course. The effect differs from person to person. Some people can eat them without any trouble; others suffer from incredibly painful wind and have to avoid them. So try them first, before you plant up a whole bed!

J is for...

Jostaberries

When I made my big move into fruit, I chose a jostaberry because it's a dual purpose fruit. The jostaberry is a cross between a blackcurrant and gooseberry. It's a thornless, vigorous plant with good disease resistance and when the berries are young you can cook and eat them like gooseberries. When they're fully mature they're just like big blackcurrants and can be eaten raw (or made into pies and jam).

   You don't see many jostaberries about, and there's certainly not much written about them. Mine spent its first year in a very large container, and did fine. But when I saw the one growing in the RISC roof garden I realised that it was going to become quite a large plant. In fact they can grow up to three metres tall and two metres wide. The container clearly wasn't a good idea, so this spring I planted the jostaberry out into the garden. It seems happy enough, especially as it is now in the fruit cage, and has produced a small harvest of fruits.

It doesn't seem to need much pruning, so it should be an easy plant to keep happy and will fruit for many years to come.

The *Alternative* Kitchen Garden

K is for...

K is for...

K (Potassium)

There are three major plant nutrients (also sometimes called macronutrients) – referred to on fertiliser packets as N, P and K. N is for nitrogen, P for phosphorus and K for potassium (also known to gardeners as potash).

Potassium encourages fruiting and flowering in plants. Liquid feeds for tomatoes (and peppers and aubergines) are high in potassium. Potassium also promotes healthy growth, toughening plants up and increasing their ability to cope with stresses like drought in the summer and cold weather in the winter.

The main problem with potassium is that it tends to form water-soluble compounds, meaning that it can easily be leached out of soil (particularly sandy soils) in wet weather.

Comfrey is a great source of potassium-rich fertiliser, and you can turn comfrey into a liquid feed for your tomatoes and peppers or use it to pep up your home-made compost. Other readily available sources include banana skins and wood ash, which was used by gardeners during WWII when fertilisers were in short supply.

K is for...

Kale

Kale is the darling of the food industry these days – tiny dark green or red-tinged frilly leaves are packed in puffed up bags of salad, and grace the plates in fancy restaurants. It's a far cry from the days when kale, the hardiest of winter vegetables, was a tough and strongly-flavoured vegetable that most people steered clear of.

Kale is another one of those plants that thrives on allotments. It will quite happily stand right through the worst of the winter weather, and is practically indestructible

– although the pigeons might tuck in if they get hungry enough. Because it grows through the winter it makes good use of otherwise empty spaces, avoids many of the pest problems that plague brassicas in the summer, and provides fresh greens through the darkest days and into the 'hungry gap' in April when stored harvests are running out but the veggie patch isn't providing much new growth.

If you want a trendy kale then try 'Nero di Toscano', which is very dark in colour but has long, thin, very bobbled leaves. 'Pentland Brig' produces side shoots a bit like sprouting broccoli. You can also get dwarf green curly kale, kale with red leaf veins and the heritage variety 'Asparagus' has flower shoots reputed to taste like … yes, asparagus. You can even get kale that grows so tall that you can use the stem as a walking stick.

In short, there's a kale out there to suit everybody (except, perhaps, those with a lingering phobia of cabbage from one too many school dinners). Like most winter vegetables, growing kale is a long-term commitment. You really need to sow seeds in April or May for the plants to reach their full potential. You can start taking young leaves from November onwards, and you'll be pulling up the plants in late spring to make room for new crops. Although kale is entirely hardy, if you want baby leaves for salads through the winter then you'll get more tender leaves if you can give it some protection.

K is for...

Kitchen Gardens

It used to be that people cultivated kitchen gardens for purely economic reasons – they needed to grow their own food, medicines and useful plants. Although that's still true in some parts of the world, it's not true here – but there are plenty of people who find that a kitchen garden makes a valuable contribution to the household budget.

Kitchen gardening these days is more likely to be seen as a hobby, complete with many health benefits, or a political statement.

As I write this, we're in the midst of the Credit Crunch – with food and fuel prices rising rapidly. More and more people are turning to growing some of their own food to save money. When you look at the prices of items like organic herbs and chilli peppers, it's easy to see that even a few pots on the windowsill can help make a frugal life a bit tastier.

I've already mentioned my reason for starting a kitchen garden – a concern about food miles. With a scientific consensus that we're causing climate change, and the consequent responsibility for us to do something about it, environmental issues are another reason for people to turn to a kitchen garden. There's also growing awareness of a problem that we've ignored for a long time – fossil fuels are non-renewable resources and they will run out. Many people now believe that we have reached, or will soon reach, Peak Oil – the time after which our oil supply will begin to dwindle and we will be faced with the choice of developing more sustainable lifestyles or fighting endless wars for scarce resources.

There's also a movement towards simpler lifestyles and against globalization and rampant consumerism. And against waste – the food waste produced by our industrial food system (as well as by households who have lost the ability to plan and cook meals and make the most of leftovers) and the mounds of waste caused by the packaging in processed food.

In the US there have been several big food scares in recent years, focusing on fruits and vegetables. Here in the UK our food scares usually revolve around meat and animal products, but we're also concerned about pesticide residues in our food – driving consumers to buy organic if they can.

Demand is increasing for growing space and for vegetable seeds and plants. If there was just one reason behind the renaissance of kitchen gardens then it could be written off as a quaint trend, soon to be forgotten. But hopefully, with so many good reasons to grow your own food, kitchen gardens are here to stay.

K is for...

Kiwis

When I was a kid the kiwi fruit was the exotic star of the fruit bowl. They've become almost common place now, but I still love them, and so I was interested to see them growing at the RISC roof garden. They're climbing plants, and were growing up the trellis at the edge of the roof garden, making good use of the vertical spaces.

The most commonly grown kiwis are *Actinidia deliciosa*. In their natural state, plants are either male or female — so you need two plants if you want them to fruit. One male can successfully pollinate about eight females, although you'd need a lot of space to grow nine kiwi plants! If you only have space for one then you can also get self-fertile varieties, with 'Jenny' being the most commonly available, although the fruits will be smaller.

You can also get Siberian kiwis (*Actinidia arguta*); the self-fertile variety is usually 'Issai'. The fruits are smaller, but sweeter, and smooth rather than hairy.

Kiwis are relatively hardy and should survive a British winter, but they will appreciate a sheltered spot. They don't like wind, which will damage their stems and leaves. In theory they will do fine in a pot, given plenty of water in the summer.

I'm on my fourth kiwi. The first three were cheap plants, and very young. Two were 'Jenny' and one was 'Issai'. I couldn't keep any of them alive long enough to plant them out. And so I have just splashed out a little bit more money (there's a lesson in there somewhere!) for a well-grown plant at a proper garden centre. It's another Jenny, and it's beautiful. The stems are covered in red hairs, giving it a lovely red tinge as the sun shines through it. Not to mention it looks like a soft toy version of a plant (kiwis are sometimes grown as ornamental plants). It's growing in a large pot on the patio, where I can tie it into the trellis. So far it's doing well and has settled in nicely and started to grow.

It seems as though a certain amount of luck is involved with growing kiwis. I know people who have had plants for several years and not had any fruit. I've heard stories of people who have so many fruits that they give them away in buckets. I'm hoping that my little Jenny will prove to be vigorous and fruitful, so I can be one of the latter.

K is for...

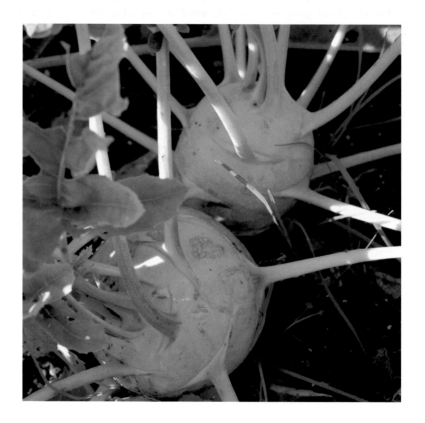

Kohl Rabi

If you've got kids then you might be able to encourage them into the garden by growing space aliens. Kohl rabi is certainly one of the oddest-looking vegetables around, a bit like tennis balls with leaves growing out of them. They even come in a range of colours, from white or pale green right through to purple and red.

The part we usually eat is the swollen stem, which forms what looks like a bulb that grows above ground. But the leaves are edible too. Kohl rabi is in the brassica family, and the leaves taste like cabbage and the swollen stems taste like turnips. So not everybody's favourite flavour! The advantage of kohl rabi is that they're fast-growing, but you have to pick them while they're young or you run into the same problem that turnips have – they go all woody and horrible. Make sure they get plenty of water, too.

I've grown them once, and wouldn't rush to again, but if you're a fan of the cabbage tribe in general then you'll probably like them.

The *Alternative* Kitchen Garden

L is for...

L is for...

Ladybirds

We're all familiar with red ladybirds, but there are 46 native species of ladybirds in the UK and they come in a variety of colours. Many eat aphids and lay eggs that hatch into an aphid's worst nightmare – ladybird larvae.

Ladybird larvae look a bit like tiny crocodiles. They're black, with orange patches on their backs, and eat their way through as many aphids as they can find. They grow rapidly until they're ready to pupate into adults. You can buy ladybirds or ladybird larvae to release into your garden – although if conditions aren't right they won't stay.

Ladybirds hibernate through the winter in tufts of long grass or hollow stems, and leaving dead plant material around helps them find suitable hibernation sites. You can also make hibernation hotels by stuffing a plastic container with straw, making a few holes in the lid (use something the size of a pencil, to allow for easy access) and then popping the whole thing in a sheltered spot.

Also consider leaving a patch of nettles to grow. Nettles provide food for the earliest aphids to emerge in spring. Without a source of food any ladybirds that emerge from hibernation leave your garden to find something to eat; those early aphids on your nettles could persuade ladybirds to stay in your garden and feed on the aphids that affect your crop plants later on.

You might spot an exotic visitor in your garden. The Harlequin ladybird arrived here in 2004 and is gradually spreading throughout the country. The Harlequin is larger than our native species, up to 7 mm long, and comes in different colours. They eat aphids too, but if aphids are in short supply they snack on other things – including fruit, butterfly eggs, caterpillars, lacewing larvae and other ladybirds. Because the Harlequin ladybird eats a range of food it is out-competing our native ladybird species.

A few weeks ago I found several ladybird larvae that had spines or tufts of hair on the orange patches on their backs, rather than being smooth. I sent a photo off to the Harlequin Ladybird Survey, and they confirmed that these were Harlequin ladybird larvae. Since they I have spotted adults in the garden as well. There's no reason to panic if you find Harlequin ladybirds in your garden. The Harlequin Ladybird Survey is monitoring their spread across the country, and you might like to report your find, but at the moment they do not recommend any action.

Other garden heroes that prey on aphids include hoverfly larvae. Hoverflies look a bit like wasps, but are far more timid and can hover in mid-air. The adults feed on nectar and pollen, so to encourage hoverflies into the garden, grow more flowers.

Lacewings are graceful insects with transparent green wings, and both the adults and larvae eat aphids and are worth encouraging. You can make a lacewing hibernation hotel out of a plastic bottle and some corrugated cardboard. Leave the lid on the bottle, but cut the bottom away. Roll up the cardboard and stuff it into the bottle. You might need some tape or a paperclip to keep it inside. Hang the bottle up by its neck outdoors in late summer. When the nights turn cold, put the bottle somewhere sheltered – in the shed, if you have one. In spring, bring it out again. Any lacewings that found their way inside emerge in spring, ready and willing to tackle your aphid problems.

L is for...

Leaf Beet

One of the first plants that I grew, in my container garden, was leaf beet. The packet said that it grows well in containers and is good in stir-fries. It was right on both counts and leaf beet is one of the most successful crops in the garden each year. It has taken on a new significance since we got the chickens, because they love it as well and it can provide them with fresh greens pretty much all year round.

Leaf beet has several names, including perpetual spinach and spinach beet.

It's in the beetroot family, along with its larger relative chard.

Leaf beet is a small plant, growing about 30 cm tall. It has relatively soft green leaves with thin green stalks. The flavour is quite bland, making small leaves great in salads. Larger leaves can be cooked in the same ways as spinach – they wilt nicely with brief cooking.

If you sow seeds in spring then you'll be able to harvest leaves (a few at a time from each plant) all through the summer. Sow seeds in late summer and you'll have leaves through the autumn and well into the winter. With protection they will stand through the worst of the weather, although they tend not to grow much, and spring back into life as soon as the days start to get longer in February. In bad weather the plants may die back, but they will usually reappear when the weather improves.

Although seedlings are prone to slug attack, leaf beet is generally quite pest-free and easy to grow. You might find that your plants get attacked by leaf miners that eat their way through the inner part of the leaves and leave translucent trails. If one or two leaves are affected then you can cut them off and compost them (or feed them to chickens!). If a plant is badly infested then you can cut all of the leaves off. By the time new leaves emerge, the pests have usually moved on.

Occasionally plants are affected by mildew. Make sure that they're not overcrowded, so that there's room for good air flow, and that plants are getting enough water and are not stressed.

Chard is a much larger plant, growing to 60 cm and more. The leaves are larger, and a glossy dark green. The stems are so thick that they have to be cooked separately. Chard varieties have coloured stems and leaf ribs. The classic Swiss chard has white stems and ribs; they're red in rhubarb chard (the flavour remains the same) and you can get mixed colours in rainbow chard – including yellow and orange.

Chard is used in much the same way as leaf beet. Small leaves can be added to salads, larger leaves are best cooked. They can be harvested a few at a time and the plants can provide leaves nearly all year round.

Leaf beet and chard are both biennial plants, meaning that (providing they are not overly stressed by drought) they will flower and set seed in their second year.

In common with the rest of the beetroot family, what we think of as the seeds are actually fruit clusters containing more than one seed. The big 'seeds' are very easy to sow (and are pretty reliable, and quick, so would be a good choice for children) and generally produce at least two seedlings. They are happy in containers but if you sow them in the ground, you will find that they grow much more impressive root systems – perhaps not surprising in a vegetable that's related to a root crop. As with all leaf vegetables, a good supply of water and nutrients is important to keep the plants growing rapidly and producing a good harvest of tender leaves.

L is for...

Leaf Mould

Falling leaves can be a real problem for gardeners. If they fall into ponds then they foul the water. Left on the lawn they'll cause bleached patches, and on paths they can rot down into a slippery, slimy mess. Gathering them up becomes an autumn chore in gardens with (or surrounded by) trees, and many of them get bagged up and sent off to landfill with the rubbish.

Sending organic matter off to landfill is not a good idea. It has a tendency to rot down anaerobically (without air) and produce methane – a flammable gas that also contributes to climate change. Although some landfill sites can collect methane for use as a fuel, it would still be better if they didn't produce it. And by composting our organic matter at home we can also save the fuel needed to transport it off to landfill, while at the same time turning it into something useful for the garden and saving ourselves money.

If you only have a few fallen leaves then you can mix them in to your regular compost heap – they're 'browns' and help to balance out grass cuttings and kitchen waste, although they can be slow to rot down (it depends on the tree they come from).

If you've got lots then it's better to use them to make leaf mould – compost made only from leaves. They rot down most quickly when they're exposed to the weather, and so leaf mould bins are open to the elements. You can make a really simple one out of four posts and some chicken wire.

Or you can collect your leaves in plastic bags, tie the bag up, make a few holes in it (a couple of sharp prods with a garden fork should do the trick) and then leave it out of the way at the end of the garden.

Leaf mould takes longer to make than regular compost. After a year, you'll have partially rotted leaves that make a great mulch or soil improver (it's called a low fertility soil improver because it doesn't add many nutrients). If you leave them for two (or even three) years then you'll end up with something lovely and crumbly that makes an ideal addition to home-made potting mixes.

You can speed up the process slightly if you chop the leaves up first (if they're on the lawn then you can run the mower over them). And if you're making leaf mould in plastic bags then it works best if the leaves are wet when you bag them up.

Leaf mould is such great stuff that you may find yourself searching out more leaves. If you have an allotment then you might find that the local council delivers loads of leaves that it has collected from parks. You should try and avoid leaves that have been contaminated with road dirt, because you don't want to add toxic chemicals to the garden. And you should never collect leaves from woodland as you'll be interfering with the local ecosystem. Keep an eye out instead for neighbours who are still putting their leaves out with the rubbish, or for people who might appreciate some help keeping their garden free from fallen leaves.

If you've got bare soil in the garden over the winter then you can use fallen leaves as a winter cover. They can also be piled up against plants that might appreciate a bit of winter protection – but in both cases you'll be collecting them up again in spring.

L is for...

Leeks

Leeks are another traditional winter vegetable. You can sow leeks for harvests in late summer or early autumn, and/ or for harvesting right through the winter and into the following spring. The winter varieties will happily withstand the nastiest winter weather. But again, this is another crop that involves a considerable time investment. Leek seeds are sown in spring, and depending on the variety could stay in the ground until the following spring.

Leeks are a member of the onion tribe, which means that you can control the size of the finished article by changing the spacing between plants. If you want baby leeks then you can cram them in so that they're only two centimetres apart. For large mature leeks they need 15 cm spacing. But if you pop them in too close together initially, you can harvest some as baby leeks and then leave the rest to grow nice and fat. And they don't need to take up space in the veg. patch all year – leeks are normally sown in a seed bed (or a container) and then planted out as seedlings about the size of a pencil.

Of course, given that they're alliums, leeks are prone to the same set of diseases as their relatives onion and garlic. Leeks are also prone to rust, a fungal disease that leaves them with orange spots on the outside leaves. A serious infection can kill them off, but a mild case is not so devastating. Make sure that you keep your leeks with the other alliums, and rotate them around your plot each year.

L is for...

Lemon Balm

At some point in the last few years I developed more of an interest in herbs and bought some little herb plants from the garden centre. There were some unusual flavours of mint and sage (none of which survived the following winter), lavender and thyme, and two lemon balms – one plain green and one variegated with green and gold leaves.

Lemon balm (*Melissa officinalis*) is in the same plant family as mint, and needs to be grown in the same way — i.e. with an eye to keeping it under control. The green variety likes full sun; the variegated variety prefers partial sun as its paler leaves can be burned if the sun is too strong. There are other varieties, too, and they will all be happier and more productive with a decent supply of water.

I forgot about my lemon balm plants, but they survived and settled in nicely. In fact they're quite rampant, and regularly need cutting back. The leaves have a lovely lemony scent, and when I looked for ways to use them in the kitchen I came across the idea of lemon balm tea.

Lemon balm makes an incredibly healthy tea — just steep around five leaves per person in water that's just off the boil, for around 10 minutes. The plant has antibacterial and antifungal properties, making the tea ideal if you're feeling a bit under the weather. It's also incredibly soothing, and can help with headaches and stomach aches. And, as if that wasn't enough, it's supposed to help improve your memory as well.

Lemon balm has other uses — you can use it to flavour syrups or fruit salads, or add it to baking — wherever you want to add a bit of a lemony kick.

Lemon balm is a perennial plant, growing up to 75cm tall. The plain green variety can be grown from seed, but if you want one of the others then you have to propagate them vegetatively — buy a plant, or take a cutting or a division from an existing specimen. Cuttings are taken in summer; division can be done in autumn or in spring, although it's quite a tough job with a well-established plant.

L is for...

Lemons

Lemons are the hardiest of the citrus plants, and hence the easiest to grow in our not-exactly-Mediterranean climate. Citrus plants have to be several years old to fruit, and hence the specimens you can buy are generally quite expensive.

Having said that, if you've got the patience then you can try growing your own lemon from seed. Although the ones that are sold are named varieties, in truth most lemons taste so similar that you'd have a hard time telling them apart.

A year ago, I sowed some lemon seeds that came out of a lemon wedge in a salad garnish from an Indian take away. I potted them up, put a clear lid over the top and then pretty much forgot about them. They didn't germinate quickly, it took several weeks, but they did germinate. They spent the winter on a sunny windowsill, and a year on they're nice healthy plants. It will no doubt be at least a couple more years before they're old enough to fruit, but if I can keep them alive then I've grown some lemon bushes entirely for free.

The one slight issue with growing your own lemons from seed is that they have a tendency to be spiny – a characteristic bred out of most of the named varieties. A little bit of caution when harvesting your lemons would be a good idea!

The situation is more complicated with the rest of the citrus family. Although they may still grow easily from seed, a lot of the resulting plants will be more difficult to care for and the quality of the fruit can be highly variable. It will be several years before the plants fruit and you find out whether the fruits are nice to eat or not. But citrus plants are ornamental anyway, with glossy leaves and nicely scented flowers, so many people would consider it worth attempting.

Some citrus species have a tendency to produce polyembryonic seeds – seeds from which more than one seedling emerges. One of these seedlings will be a true seedling, and hence genetically different from the parent plant. The others are formed differently, vegetatively, and are essentially clones. So if you sow one citrus seed and more than one seedling comes up, you're pretty much guaranteed that one of them will grow into a plant that produces nice fruit like its parent did. The only problem is that you won't know which one – you'll have to grow them all on until they're mature and then find out which is the nicest. Limes and tangerines are the citrus species that produce the highest proportion of polyembryonic seeds, according to *The Pip Book* (by Keith Mossman, currently out of print but well worth hunting down if you want to try growing plants from pips and stones).

L is for...

Lettuce

Lettuce used to be the boring old leaf that bulked out summer salads and was a mainstay for dieters. The hip, modern lettuce comes in a multitude of different guises – especially if you choose to grow your own.

Butterhead lettuces have floppy leaves. They form compact hearts, so they're lettuces that you would harvest all in one go. If you choose a couple of different varieties then you can have butterhead lettuce pretty much all year round.

Cos lettuces (romaine) have longer, crispier leaves and a loose heart in the centre. Iceberg lettuces are crisphead varieties that form a solid heart, with the outer leaves removed. Batavia lettuces are crispy like icebergs, but grow more openly.

Loose leaf lettuces don't form hearts at all. They're also called cut-and-come again lettuces because you can harvest a few leaves whenever you want, and leave the plant to continue growing. Loose leaf lettuces are great for small spaces and containers, and ideal for fast harvests. They can be very decorative, with frilly or even frizzy leaves.

There's even special varieties of lettuce that grow in the winter. You sow the seeds in late summer or early autumn, for harvests in late autumn and into winter. If you can give them some protection then you can grow lettuce right through the winter and have early crops in spring.

The only aspect you don't get much choice over is the colour: lettuce only comes in green or red. I'm sure someone is working on it, and that soon we'll be eating lettuce in all colours of the rainbow.

Lettuce can be tricky to grow. It's a pest magnet, and it's prone to diseases. Cramming too many lettuces into a small space is guaranteed to make them mildewy – they need breathing room. In hot weather they suffer from drought and appreciate a good mulch and some shade.

Sowing a lot of lettuce seeds in one go is an easy way to create a glut. They will all be ready at about the same time, and lettuce bolts (goes to seed) quite quickly, rendering your harvest inedible. The easy way to avoid this, and to have a continuous supply of lettuce, is to sow successionally. Sow a few seeds, and when they germinate, sow a few more. Sowing in batches also means you've always got new plants coming on to replace ones that have died or been munched.

I'm not a big lettuce fan myself. Pete likes the occasional iceberg, but the real lettuce eaters in our household are the chickens. They're not demanding consumers – they'll happily eat lettuce that has been slug-munched (in fact they're overjoyed if it still has the slugs in it!) and they don't mind if it has bolted.

It's easy to break away from lettuce and into a wide variety of salad plants. Salads get a lot of space in seed catalogues, and you can choose from rocket, baby leaf beet/ spinach leaves, Oriental vegetables, herbs and even dandelions. If you want leafy vegetables for a stir-fry then you've got an even bigger selection. And you can even eat leaves from vegetables that are usually used for other purposes – including beetroot, turnips, radishes and peas. If you can't choose then you can buy ready-made salad or stir-fry seed mixes. A packet of seeds costs about as much as one of those pre-washed salads in the supermarket, but keeps you in salad all summer.

The *Alternative* Kitchen Garden

M is for...

M is for...

Marigolds

I have never found marigolds (*Tagetes*) to be the most attractive of flowers. They come in a range of 'hot' colours – reds, oranges and yellows – and for the most part I'm a very 'cool' person. They're a bit frilly, and they have a very pungent smell.

And yet I grow them in my garden every single year. The reason I grow them is that they make great companion plants. Among other things, they deter whitefly and I use them to stop whitefly from bothering my tomato plants. It works in my garden – I've never seen whitefly on the tomatoes! This year they're growing in the Grow Dome, and in my the window boxes on the front of the house – where visitors can appreciate the splash of colour they produce.

Whichever marigolds you choose for your garden, you only need to buy seeds once. Although the plants need dead-heading to keep them looking nice and producing more blooms, you can let some go to seed at the end of the season. You don't need too many, as each flower produces a lot of seeds. Once the flowers are dry, it's easy enough to separate the seeds as they're large. Keep them dry and you'll have more than enough seeds for your garden next year.

The only word of warning I will give with marigolds is that you need to check the height of the variety you choose. My first attempt at using marigolds as companion plants for peppers failed miserably when the marigolds grew rapidly and towered over the slower pepper plants. These days I only have dwarf marigolds in the garden!

M is for...

Master Composters

Gardening is a great hobby. It benefits the environment, keeps you fit and even makes you more cheerful. It has a tendency to be a solitary pursuit, however, although gardeners enjoy getting together to swap tips and seeds and show off their giant vegetables.

So when I found out about my local Master Composter scheme, I jumped at the chance of being involved. Master Composters are trained volunteers who go out into their community to get people composting and solve their composting problems.

There are similar schemes all over the world, but here in the UK the Master Composter schemes are usually run by the local council together with WRAP and Garden Organic. WRAP are the Waste and Resources Action Programme, a government-funded body with the sole aim of reducing waste and increasing recycling.

I was one of the first Master Composters here in Oxfordshire. Twenty of us attended a two day training course. The first day covered the details of the scheme in the morning, with a trip to a commercial composting site in the afternoon. The composting site was impressive – an enormous, steaming compost heap that deals with garden waste and cardboard collected from households. Waste is shredded, piled in mounds that heat up to a least 70°C, turned several times and then sieved. Any large pieces left go round again. Some of the finished compost is given to the farmer who owns the land, as part of the rent. The rest is sold to landscapers.

The site has a concrete base that collects the run-off (called leachate) from the compost. Leachate is rich in nutrients, and would cause havoc in the local environment if it was left to wash away (because of the scale of the site – on a garden scale, leachate is harmless). The leachate is collected in an underground tank and used to damp down the compost piles in dry weather.

The second day of the course was held at Ryton Organic Gardens (Garden Organic's HQ) and concentrated on the basics of cold composting. We saw slides of compost critters, tried to guess which materials are compostable and which are not, and trooped outside (in the rain) to check out the various composters that Garden Organic have on display.

Trained Master Composters are provided with access to resources (games, signs, leaflets and display compost bins) and then complete a certain number of hours of voluntary work during the year. How you fill your hours is up to you – you might be good at giving talks, help out with composting at the local community garden, hand out leaflets at shows and fetes or just field composting questions from your loved ones and neighbours. So far I have written several articles, visited a local science park to help with a compost display, stood outside the local garden centre to answer queries and answered a few email queries passed on to me by the council.

Schemes that distribute free compost bins – or offer discounted ones – really encourage people to compost at home. However, some people encounter problems and stop composting as a result. Once they've stopped composting, it's hard to get them started again, because of their bad experience. The goal of Master Composters is to get people composting, and to keep them composting – so if you've cracked composting, why not see if there's a similar scheme near you and sign up to help other people?

M is for...

Mint

I can't imagine that there are many gardens without a mint plant. Mint grows just about anywhere – from sunny to shady, wet to dry, and in any type of soil. In fact, the problem is frequently to stop it growing. Mint spreads via underground stems, and is so vigorous it will out compete any unfortunate plant that gets in its way. It really is a tough nut and a garden thug.

   The trick to keeping it under control really lies in preventing these underground stems from spreading. If you want to plant your mint in the ground then you can bury it in a bucket or a large pot. Make sure the rim is just above the soil surface, so it has no chance of escaping. At Ryton I saw a selection of mints planted into tall chimney pots, which looked very nice. Of course you can just keep your mints in containers above ground, and since they don't mind shady spots they can make great plants for difficult areas.

There are lots of different mints, from the common peppermint and spearmint (my personal favourite) through to chocolate mint and pineapple mint. You can't even grow mints together – they'll set out to strangle each other, and will mingle together. And some of the more exotic mints are not as hardy, and will need some shelter to survive the winter.

Mints in pots get very unhappy after a couple of years, when their roots reach the sides of the pot and can't spread. To keep them happy, you need to divide them. Literally tip them out of the pot, break them into chunks, and replant one of the chunks in the pot. The other chunks can be potted up and either brought inside for winter mint supplies, or passed on to friends. Dividing plants this way can be a tough job – if the plant is big then you might need to use a spade to slice through – and you shouldn't feel the need to be gentle. Division should be done in autumn, or in spring.

We had mint in the garden for years without really finding a use for it. The new potato season is short, and doesn't use that much mint. We're not big fans of mint tea. However, there's a bar near us that serves the most divine non-alcoholic cocktail. You take elderflower cordial, a handful of mint, ice cubes and water and shake the whole lot in a cocktail shaker. You have to really bruise the mint to get the flavour out – and you'll need to drink it through a straw to avoid straining mint through your teeth - but it's a heavenly and very refreshing combination. Of course, if you prefer alcoholic drinks then a boisterous mint plant makes a lot of mojitos! And if you've got a good pea harvest then you can try pea and mint soup as well.

M is for...

Mulch

In a natural ecosystem, plant material falls to the ground and stays there – covering the surface of the soil until it is broken down and incorporated - in the garden, we can approximate this process by adding a mulch to the surface of the soil. A mulch is simply a layer of material on top of the soil – and it can be organic or non-organic.

Mulch has many advantages. It protects the soil surface from heavy rains that can damage the soil structure. prevents rapid evaporation from the soil surface, and helps to keep plant roots cool and dark – both of which mean less watering is necessary, even in the height of summer. If the mulch is thick enough to prevent light from reaching the soil surface then it prevents weed seeds germinating as well.

If you use an organic mulch (e.g. compost, cardboard, shredded paper, bark chips, grass cuttings) then the mulch will break down into the soil over time and add nutrients. If you're using an inorganic mulch (e.g. plastic sheeting, pebbles or gravel) then you won't be adding nutrients to the soil, but you won't have to keep topping up the mulch.

You can even use plants as a living mulch. Trefoil, a green manure, is very low-growing and makes a good living mulch under larger plants. Trefoil grows quite fast, but our chickens love eating it and prevent it getting out of hand.

Whatever you choose to use as a mulch, there are several golden rules to bear in mind. The first is that you should never mulch dry soil – because the mulch may slow down water penetration. So water first, then mulch. Likewise, if you need to add fertilisers or soil improvers, do that first.

The mulched area needs to be free from perennial weeds, which a mulch won't stop (unless you use black plastic sheeting, or weed control fabric). If you're using a mulch to control annual weeds then it needs to be pretty thick to prevent germination.

You can use clear plastic sheeting to warm up cold soil in the spring, but in general you should only apply mulches once the soil has warmed up – because they stop light from reaching the soil and heating it up.

Leave gaps around your crop plants, as most will not enjoy having their stems crowded by mulch. A lack of air flow encourages rots and other diseases, and a handy place to hide out means that your crop plants will be prey to more pests as well. On the plus side, a nice place to hide out also helps beneficial predators and keeps the ecosystem in balance.

If you want to sow seeds in an area that has been mulched, you'll need to clear the mulch away so that the seeds can germinate in the soil and get established.

Mulches are great for containers as well. They have the same benefits - helping to prevent evaporation, keeping roots cool and stopping weeds from taking root. For long-term plantings, a decorative mulch of gravel (which comes in some spectacular colours) is perfect. For one season containers I generally use an organic mulch (mini bark chips) because recovering the gravel from the top and cleaning it up is a chore. With bark chips you can just throw the whole lot on the compost heap when you're clearing out the old plants.

As I didn't have any money for bark chips this year, I have been experimenting with using shredded paper as a mulch. It's great in the Grow Dome, and is gradually melding together like papier-mâché. Outside it would have been more problematic as it would be difficult to stop it blowing around.

M is for...

Mushrooms

Mushrooms are not plants. Fungi are a completely different branch on the tree of life, and hence grow and live differently. Even so, they're often on the menu for an adventurous kitchen gardener.

There are lots of different mushrooms, in all shapes and sizes. They all grow mycelium, roughly the mushroom equivalent of plant roots, through the soil or other organic matter. Mycelium are much thinner threads than plant roots, which is one reason why plants form relationships with fungi. It's more efficient for mycelium to spread out over long distances and find scarce resources, and then share them with the plant in return for sugars, than for the plant to grow roots over similar distances. The mushrooms we see above ground are just the fruiting bodies of the fungus.

Fungi are one of nature's decomposers – they can break down and feed on the tough and woody plant material that nothing else can digest. They don't need light to function, because they don't photosynthesise, and they thrive in dark and damp conditions. There are two stages to growing mushrooms. The first is to help the mycelium to become well-established. Once they are, the second stage it to encourage them to fruit.

The easiest place to start with mushrooms is with a kit that you can use indoors. Button mushrooms grow on a special compost. When you get your kit you have to spread out the mushroom spores (that often look like mouldy grains of cereal), cover them with the compost and keep them damp and warm while the mycelium grow. Then you have to reduce the temperature slightly to encourage them to fruit. A kit like this will provide a couple of 'flushes' of mushrooms before it becomes exhausted, although you may find more mushrooms grow outside if you put the tired compost in the garden.

My experiences with button mushroom kits are not good. They have a tendency to attract fungus gnats (which adore living in the warm, damp organic matter as much as the mushrooms) and end up being thrown on the compost heap. It's depressing, as I love button mushrooms!

Other types of mushrooms grow on different materials. Oyster mushrooms can be grown in bags of straw, or even on toilet rolls – as can the unappetizingly named slime mushroom. More and more kits are becoming available as demand increases.

A lower maintenance option is to buy a mushroom log for the garden. These are freshly sawn logs, impregnated with mushroom spawn and then left to their own devices in a suitable location outside. You can also buy impregnated dowels if you want to insert them into your own logs (although you should stick to one type of mushroom per log). A mushroom log will usually fruit periodically over several years – the outdoor conditions will trigger fruiting as and when the mycelium think it's time. The price you pay for longevity is erratic harvests.

If you want to be very fancy then you could try growing your own truffles. Truffles are underground fungi. They grow in the roots of live trees, and so to grow one you buy a suitable tree that has already been inoculated with the fungal mycelium. Growing truffles is a long term endeavour; it will be at least four years before the truffles start to grow. And then of course you have the problem of finding them!

M is for...

Mould

Moulds and rots play a role in breaking down organic matter in the garden. We're surrounded by fungal spores, and they're not something we have any hope of eradicating. But generally, moulds don't come to a gardener's attention until they're infecting plants.

Plants can fall prey to fungal diseases at any stage in their life. Seedlings can be literally mowed down by 'damping off'. Many mature plants have their own fungal diseases – including leek rust, broad bean chocolate spot, onion downy mildew and parsnip canker. And there are many more that will attack a wide range of plants. Reading about fungal plant infections is enough to give anyone the heebie-jeebies.

Keeping fungal diseases at bay in an organic garden focuses on keeping your plants healthy. Build up the soil so that plants grow well, and deal quickly with any stress factors – such as drought or pest attack. Companion planting can help as well, especially with chamomile, which is known as the 'Doctor Plant' and can help improve the health of its near neighbours.

Make sure that plants have enough space, so that there's air flow around the leaves. Fungal spores can only take hold when there's moisture around, so they're much more of a problem in warm and humid weather. Try to water at the base of plants, to keep leaves drier, and avoid splashing soil up onto the lower leaves.

Bordeaux mixture is used by some organic gardeners to prevent fungal diseases (it is not a cure) – especially on high risk crops such as tomatoes and potatoes. In a blight-ridden summer it may save your crop, but it's not something I have ever used.

Try choosing plant varieties with in-bred resistance to fungal diseases, and time sowings so that plants are not in the ground when they are most vulnerable. Early potatoes generally escape blight because they miss the most humid weather.

Keep up with your crop rotation, to prevent diseases building up in the soil, and remove crop residues at the end of the growing season so that they don't provide a host for the fungus over the winter. Be careful about bringing foreign soil into your garden. A devastating disease of brassicas, club root, is soil borne and can be spread by walking on infected soil and then wearing the same boots in your garden. Or by accepting plants from an infected garden. It's almost impossible to eradicate, so good hygiene is key.

At the end of the season, a lot of plants succumb to powdery mildew as they lose their vigour. Courgettes and squash are very good at this, and although they look messy they may well carry on producing edible fruit. If it hits early on in the summer then check that the plants are getting enough water and fertiliser.

Rots are the enemy of gardeners who want to store produce. When you've got a good crop and want to keep some of it for later, make sure that you only store the best specimens. Anything that has been damaged should be eaten straight away. Once you have stored your crop, make sure to keep checking that none of it has started to rot – because the rot will quickly spread. Removing and disposing of rotting produce will help the rest to keep for longer.

The *Alternative* Kitchen Garden

N is for...

N is for...

Nasturtiums

Nasturtiums are another annual flower that comes in a range of bright, 'hot' colours. They're spectacularly easy to grow, and vigorous. You can get dwarf, trailing and climbing varieties, so they're easy to fit into any available space – although they prefer a sunny position and well-drained soil. They're good in containers and hanging baskets and can really brighten the place up.

Nasturtiums flower all summer, and the leaves and the flowers are edible

– if you're in the mood for a fancy salad with a peppery bite then add a few to the bowl, but they're probably best as a minor component.

As well as being edible, nasturtium flowers will attract beneficial insects into your vegetable garden. They'll also attract pests – nasturtiums are notorious for being attacked by blackfly and other aphids, and they also provide food for cabbage white butterflies. In fact, they're so tasty to pests that you can use nasturtiums as a trap crop – plant them next to your vegetables and the pests will eat them in preference. Once the plants are well and truly infested, you can pull them up and compost them.

Nasturtiums have large seeds, about the same size as peas. It's easy to spot when they're ripe (they turn from a lush green to a dry brown) and they're very easy to collect – even if they fall to the floor they're easy to pick up. And so nasturtiums are another flower for which you only have to buy seeds once – you can save your own from there on in. And they'll even self-seed if you don't pick all of the seeds up. My nasturtiums this year are entirely self-sown (they're 'volunteers'), but if they spring up in awkward places then they're very easy to weed out.

And at the end of the season, you'll have plenty of plant material to compost – nasturtiums make big plants with fleshy stems. But don't feed them too much of your compost in return, because they flower better in poor soil. Too many nutrients will make them grow leaves rather than flowers.

N is for...

Native

Most of the vegetables that we plant in our kitchen gardens came from other parts of the world, and have been in cultivation for a long time. Onions, for example, don't exist in the wild – and were grown way back in 3000 BC. Leeks were brought here by the Romans. There are some familiar plants that grow wild in the British Isles, including raspberries and blackberries and sea kale, but for the most part the vegetable garden is not the place to look for native plants.

There are two reasons that people grow native plants. The first is to conserve them – many of our native plants are threatened, mainly by us encroaching on their habitats – and if you have the space (for a wildflower meadow, for example) then that is a worthwhile endeavour.

The other reason is that many people believe that native plants are much better for wildlife than exotic aliens. It seems a sensible idea, but the truth is that most wildlife species are actually less than fussy about what they eat. A few have very specific dietary requirements, but for the rest a tree is a tree and a flower is a flower. Highly bred, showy domesticated species of flowers may well not be a good source of nectar and pollen for bees, but simple flowers will be – wherever they happen to come from.

In fact, it's quite difficult to determine whether or not a plant is a British native – i.e. one which arrived here without any human assistance. Even plants that have been here since the Bronze Age may have been deliberately or accidentally introduced by our ancestors. And since we've only be separate from Europe for around 10,000 years (since the end of the last Ice Age), the plants that grow here aren't that different from those on the mainland anyway.

So if you have an interest in native plants, by all means seek them out and grow them in the garden (but don't take them from the wild to do so, that's naughty). But if wildlife is what you're after, then where your plants came from is one factor that you don't have to take into account.

N is for...

Nectarine

Peaches and nectarines may seem like exotic, sun-loving species, but if you've been to visit a walled kitchen garden then you'll know that the Victorians regularly grew them in this country. Some were kept indoors, in heated greenhouses, but they also grow well if they're trained up a south-facing wall. The aspect provides them with the sun they need, and the wall behind them takes in heat during the day and keeps them warm at night. So if you've got a sunny spot, or a greenhouse, then you can grow a peach or a nectarine.

The problem is that peaches and nectarines make big trees – around 4.5 metres tall if they're grown as a bush, they'll need at least 3.5 m of space if you're going to fan train them. You can get special dwarf varieties (sometimes called patio or terrace varieties) that will do well in a smaller space and even in a container garden. They don't need much pruning, so in that sense they make a great tree for a beginner.

The only disease that really bothers peaches and nectarines is peach leaf curl. It's a fungal disease that latches onto leaves as it is splashed up from the soil during winter rains. Peach leaf curl is obvious, because it makes the leaves curl up. You can remove affected leaves, but in a bad case the tree might be defoliated. I had a mild case on my little nectarine one spring, but it survived (although it didn't fruit). The only way to avoid leaf curl completely is to keep your tree covered up. Fan trained trees can be covered with clear plastic from November right through to May; container grown trees can be brought under cover. But you'll have to make sure that pollinating insects have access to the flowers on bright days, or do the pollination yourself.

Hand pollination isn't actually that tricky, although you have to get the timing right. You just need something soft (a rabbit's tail is traditional, but you can use a soft paintbrush or a cotton wool ball) to transfer pollen from one flower to another. Do it more than once, a few days apart, for a better shot at getting it right.

Once the flowers start the fade, the tree begins to leaf up, but you'll still be able to spot tiny fruits swelling if you look closely.

As to pests, well an outdoor tree may well attract aphids, and there are some caterpillars that will try to attack the fruits (as might wasps, in late summer). Indoors you're most likely to be hit with red spider mite. Red spider mites cause leaves to develop tiny gold spots, and you'll probably see that before you see the mites themselves – travelling between leaves and plants in the webs they produce. You can buy biological controls for spider mites, or use a fatty acid spray. In a greenhouse they're almost unavoidable in hot weather, but you can deter them by keeping things nice and humid – give plants plenty of water and 'damp down' the floor of the greenhouse with water on hot days.

If you get a lot of fruits forming then you'll need to thin them down to give the tree a chance to ripen some of them fully. Always thin fruits in two stages. Early on you can thin fruits down to 10 cm apart, and remove any that look odd. Later on they need to be thinned down to 20 cm apart. Leave the best-shaped fruits to mature.

And if you succeed with peaches and nectarines, why not try apricots (which need more heat and should be grown under cover) or even almonds (which flower earlier in the year and will need frost protection for the blooms if they are to set fruit)?

N is for...

Nettles

Nettles are wonderful things. They have had a long association with humans and have been used for everything from food and medicine to clothing and dyes.

Early in the spring, when not much else is growing, nettles will be sending out shoots of tender green leaves that can be made into tea and cordial and soup. If it weren't for the sting, we'd probably welcome nettles into our vegetable gardens.

And what a sting – it's a masterpiece of natural engineering. A hollow hair, stiffened by silica, is so brittle that it breaks at the slightest touch – injecting the aggressor with an acid in a way that's very similar to a hypodermic needle. The acid causes a burning sting, enough to deter even the most determined of predators. The sting is sharp enough to work its way through thin gloves, too – as I know to my cost!

The theory is that if you handle nettles firmly then you'll break the stings before they jab you, but for most of us suitable gloves are a much better option. Nettle tips should be harvested from February to June – after which they get tough.

Although the sting disappears completely in cooked nettles, there are still plenty of people who aren't convinced they would be good to eat. Even so, they're worth encouraging at the end of the garden. Nettles provide a source of food for the early aphid populations, and so encourage ladybirds to stay in your garden when they wake up from hibernation. They support more than 40 species of insect, so they have a good wildlife value, and there are also birds that eat nettle seeds and the aphids that live on nettles. They do have other uses as well. You can pack fruit in nettle leaves to help prevent mould, and dried nettles can be added to animal fodder, for a vitamin boost.

But for gardeners, the best use for nettles is to turn them into compost or liquid feed. They accumulate nutrients (including a lot of nitrogen) that will be useful elsewhere in the garden. Nettle tops can be harvested a couple of times a year without harming the plants. If you want to compost them, harvest them before they flower and set seed and then mix them in with plenty of 'brown' materials for nutritious compost.

If you want to turn nettles into liquid feed then it won't matter when you harvest them – but you might want to choose a time when you know your closest neighbours are going away. Stuff the leaves into a bucket with a lid, cover them with water, put the lid on and leave them to rot down. You'll know when the liquid feed is ready because the stench will be wafting down the garden. I read (on an internet forum) an idea that adding scented herbs to the mixture cut down on the odour. I tried it with lavender and it didn't work. After a week I tipped the whole lot onto the compost heap to get rid of the smell!

I have a patch of nettles at the bottom of the garden which I encourage, to the extent that I don't try to remove them. I do cut them back for compost material, and I do try to keep them under control. If you do have nettles in your garden that you want to remove then you'll have to cut the foliage back and then try and dig the roots out, because they spread by rhizomes (creeping horizontal stems). They'll also grow from seed, so cut them back before they flower if you don't want them springing up all over the garden. It might be hard work, but as you'll also be getting compost/ mulch / liquid feed material, animal fodder or a green vegetable, it will be worth it.

N is for...

Nitrogen

If they've got enough of it, plants use nitrogen to build lush, green growth – so a plentiful supply helps green vegetables to grow quickly and provide plentiful and tender harvests. Sweetcorn likes a healthy supply of nitrogen as well.

But too much nitrogen can be a problem as well. It can promote leafy growth at times when it's not want you want. Fruiting plants like tomatoes and peppers are a perfect example – give them too much nitrogen and they'll grow tall and leafy, but won't set many fruits. Too much nitrogen in the autumn can cause plants to grow lush, tender growth that won't survive the winter weather.

Outside of the kitchen garden, nitrogen can be a real pain. Nitrogen can be found in soluble and insoluble forms – and the soluble form can be washed out of the soil in heavy rain. It leaches out into the environment, and run-off from agriculture and other industrial processes finds its way into rivers and streams where it encourages the growth of algae that use up all of the oxygen in the water and cause fish and other animals to suffocate if they can't move on.

Farms using chemical fertilisers aren't the only source of nitrogen in the ecosystem – we're to blame as well. Human urine contains quite a lot of nitrogen, and removing it at the water treatment plant is expensive. When this source of nitrogen makes its way into rivers, it causes the same problems.

The best way to ensure that the plants in your kitchen garden get the right amount of nitrogen is to make sure your soil is healthy. Make and use compost, avoid walking on your soil (which destroys the soil structure) and consider including a nitrogen-fixing green manure in your crop rotation. Instead of using chemical fertilisers, make your own liquid feeds and make sure that you understand which of your plants are likely to need more nitrogen – and at which stage in their growth. If you apply nitrogen at the wrong time, the best case scenario is that you're wasting your time. At worst you could be encouraging the wrong sort of growth, or polluting the environment.

Be aware that adding a carbon-rich mulch to the soil surface (or incorporating a carbon-rich material) into the soil can cause a temporary lack of nitrogen in the soil as the soil organisms use up the available nitrogen as they're breaking down all that carbon. To avoid this, compost the material and use the compost as a mulch.

The *Alternative* Kitchen Garden

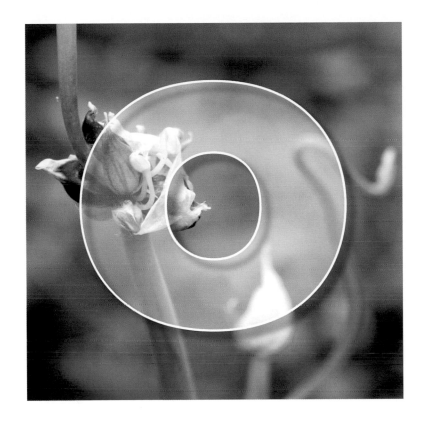

O is for...

O is for...

Red oca

Oca

One of the joys of globalization is that your garden can become a smorgasbord of plants from all over the world. You can have a bed of Oriental vegetables next to one filled with the Lost Crops of the Incas and no one will bat an eyelid. In fact we're all doing it anyway – potatoes, tomatoes, peppers and aubergines all hail from South America, sunflowers and Jerusalem artichokes have travelled from North America and beetroot, radishes and cabbage were domesticated in the Mediterranean region.

I've already said that achocha is known as one of the Lost Crops of the Incas (there are some people who think that it was deliberately misplaced, such is its vigour), but there are others. There are some nice root crops from South America to try, including mashua, yacon and oca.

My mashua plants didn't thrive this year, and yacon is on the list for next year, but the oca seems to be doing well. The problem with root crops, of course, is that you don't really know whether they've thrived until you dig up your harvest. The proof of the carrots is in the digging.

I can really see Oca catching on with kitchen gardeners in temperate zones. For a start, the tubers are beautiful. They come in a rainbow of colours. I'm growing two – pearly white and brilliant red. They're knobbly tubers, like Chinese artichokes, and they need a long season to grow. The tubers don't start to form until after the summer solstice, so if you can protect them from early autumn frosts you stand a better chance of a decent harvest. They're supposed to be like lemony potatoes, but I can neither confirm or deny that until later this year!

What I can say is that the plants have lovely and unusual foliage. They have divided leaves, a bit like four-leaved clover, held on thick stems – the growth pattern is (not surprisingly, perhaps) a bit reminiscent of potatoes. They seem to be fairly resilient, although the leaves tend to curl in on themselves a bit when they weather is hot. The only pest problem I've had is with blackfly – but they're been infesting everything this year.

My oca are all growing in containers, so (like other tubers) I may get limited yields, but the tubers store very well so once you have oca you can save your own tubers and replant them each year without having to buy new seed.

Another unusual Incan tuba you could try is Ulluco. Ulluco is even less well known and even more colourful – each tuber is multicoloured. At this stage, ulluco is another plant that forms tubers late in the season, and so is currently marginal as a crop without protection – although the same was true of potatoes when they were first brought back from South America, and selective breeding has given us the heavy croppers we rely on today.

Of course, to refer to these botanical gems as 'Lost Crops' is somewhat disingenuous – they're still staple crops in South America, it's just that agribusiness has never bothered to develop them to the point where they grow well in monocultures and have the right characteristics to withstand an industrialised food distribution system.

O is for...

Onions

In 2006 I grew so many onions that we were eating them for a year. I chopped them up and froze them in batches to use in cooking. It was immensely convenient – once I'd gone through the eye-watering job of chopping them up. And it really was eye-watering. I don't know whether it's the variety (Radar), the fact that I don't bother watering them, or because they're grown organically – but my onions are strong!

In 2007 I planted fewer sets, and poor weather led to a poor harvest. We missed the onions. Even though they're a run-of-the-mill vegetable, and available everywhere, it meant something to me that we'd provided our own onions for a year.

So last autumn I planted two bags of onion sets – Radar (white onions) and Electric (red) - and we've just had another bumper onion harvest. They're drying indoors, as the weather is wet, and I'll soon have to start the mammoth task of chopping and freezing.

I grow Japanese (also know as overwintering) onions because they grow through the winter, and I like having full beds rather than empty soil. They mature about a month before spring-planted onions, but you can start harvesting them earlier. They don't store as well – hence me freezing them rather than plaiting them into strings and hanging them in the garage. Plaiting onions and garlic is a skill you must learn, by the way, because your skill as a vegetable gardener will be unfairly judged on your ability to form a good string of onions.

Onions can be grown from seeds, or from sets. Sets are baby onions, dug up when they're young and stored until onion growing season. Plant them with the root end downwards – a simple enough task as it's obvious that the pointy end is the top. However, I guarantee you that no matter how careful you are when you plant your onion sets you will come back a week or two later and find a couple that are growing the wrong way up and sending pasty white roots out into the air while the green shoot digs down deeply. Just pull them out and put them back in the right way up.

You might find that some of your onion sets mysteriously re-appear on the surface shortly after you've planted them. Apparently this is due to birds – they love pulling on the papery skins that poke through the soil surface. I've never seen them do it, but its widely thought that you should remove any loose papery skins to avoid attracting avian attention.

Onions hate competing with weeds, so keep the soil around them clear. In my garden the leaves tend to be munched by snails, but it's not a big problem, and certainly not beyond the trouble-shooting skills of Princess Layer and Hen Solo. Onions can fall prey to some nasty diseases – onion white rot being particularly unpleasant – and you should be strict with your crop rotation (onions are in the same plant family as leeks, garlic and chives).

Onions sometimes bolt, sending up flower stems before the bulbs are ready. Cut the flower stems off to save the bulbs, but they won't store well, so eat those first.

Spring onions are great in salads and stir fries. There are also some perennial onions – including Walking Onions that form little bulbs at the top of tall stems that arch down and plant the bulbs in the soil.

O is for...

Oranges

I thought I would try growing oranges. The little oranges that you see in garden centres are frequently the Calamondin orange – they're easy to grow, but produce very bitter oranges that are only edible once they've been turned into marmalade. Pete likes marmalade, so perhaps I should get one, but my preference would be for an eating orange.

The oranges most likely to grow well from seed are the small ones – the mandarins, tangerines, satsumas and clementines. Fortunately Pete likes them all, so I had a reasonable supply of pips to choose from. Unfortunately, due to a labelling drama, I'm not entirely sure which pips grew. They should be relatively cold hardy. The tangerine is the one most likely to have polyembryonic seeds and hence give you the best chance of growing a plant with nice fruit. Personally I can't tell the difference between them all anyway, so I have to go by the labels in the supermarket. But whatever you have, small orange-wise, at the very least you'll have a bushy little plant with beautiful flowers and a lovely scent – and perhaps it will grow oranges that you can turn into marmalade and perhaps it will grow oranges you can add to the fruit bowl.

According to my records (and records are very handy things to have), I sowed my lemon and orange pips on the same day at the beginning of July last year. And the first seeds of each germinated on the same day – in the middle of September. So you can see, they're not the speediest of seeds and it would be easy to decide that they weren't going to germinate when in fact they're just taking their time. I didn't identify any polyembryonic seedlings, so I will have to take pot-luck with the plants when they mature. Spurred on by the success of my seedlings I tried sowing some pink grapefruit seeds in February – and they really didn't germinate, even though I left them to it for months. In each case I did the same thing – I sowed the seeds in little pots, gave them a plastic lid (the ones that come on large yoghurt pots are ideal) and put them on the windowsill where they would receive sporadic attention. That meant that they were watered occasionally, but otherwise forgotten until they showed signs of life. It meant that I really didn't worry that they took so long to germinate, because mostly I'd forgotten they were there.

I've just remembered that there's a lime in the fridge (Pete is experimenting with summer cocktails)… I must go and see whether it has any pips.

O is for...

Organic

If a company wants to use the term 'organic' on one of their products then they have to have certification from one of the official certifying bodies (there are several here in the UK, and more in Europe). Each certifying body has its own guidelines that companies have to follow, but the idea is the same – that a high percentage of the ingredients are grown without chemical pesticides and fertilisers, on ground that hasn't been used for conventional farming for several years, and that the product doesn't contain any ingredients that have been prohibited under the guidelines. For farmers wanting to go organic, there is a conversion period during which they have to farm organically but cannot claim organic certification.

'Organics' is now big business, and large companies are getting into organic products where beforehand it was the realm of small, often local, companies and a minority market. The rise in the status of organics has advantages and disadvantages. Organic products can command a price premium, making organic farming a viable option for economically-pressured farmers. Organic products are still becoming cheaper and more widely available – which means that more people have the option of choosing more environmentally friendly food and other goods.

But there has also been a backlash against organics, and there is continual discussion about what the word should and should not stand for. There are people who believe that the involvement of big business undermines the ethical component of organic products. The Soil Association was involved in a very big discussion about whether air freighted produce (with its significant contribution to climate change) should be considered organic.

There are regular media stories quoting scientific research that 'proves' that organic food is either better for you or a complete waste of money – but the truth is that we're all walking storehouses of pesticide residues (as well as other nasties) and there is a growing number of people who prefer to avoid ingesting any more.

Within the gardening community, there are similar divides. There are organic purists but the people who are more commonly represented in the media are the ones who admit to being 'mostly organic' – which means they're happy to reach for the slug pellets when their crops are threatened, or the weedkiller when faced with a new allotment site that's got so many weeds is could qualify as a Site of Special Scientific Interest.

I am happy to admit that I have fallen off the organic bandwagon once during the six or seven years I have been gardening. There were two apple trees in the garden when we arrived, both old and neglected and horrible specimens. We cut them down but we couldn't dig out the stumps and one of the trees kept sending up new shoots in a valiant attempt to cling to life, so I resorted to a chemical stump killer. Now that stump is gradually breaking down and enriching the soil in the goji bed while I find the other one makes a handy place to put a bucket down.

For some people, organic gardening will be a journey as they adjust to gardening without chemicals (and when our oil supply runs out we will all have to do just that). For me it comes down to a simple question – if you're holding a packet of pesticide and it says on it that you need to wear protective clothing, is that really something you want to spray on plants you're going to eat?

O is for...

Oriental Vegetables

The first Oriental vegetable I grew was mizuna. I've grown it several times since, but mine never looks as lush and leafy as the picture on the packet. I have far more luck with garlic chives. Instead of the tight purple flower heads of standard chives, they have a loose collection of white, star-shaped flowers. And the leaves are slightly wider and have a slightly more garlicky taste.

There's an enormous array of Oriental brassicas, but they're generally smaller plants than the brassicas we're familiar with, and grow faster. If you don't have room for purple sprouting broccoli then you can find some similar (but smaller) plants in the Oriental vegetable section of the seed catalogue. In fact, most Oriental brassicas have edible flower heads, and you should get used to that idea now because Oriental brassicas are prone to bolting and you'll have endless plants that flower before you're ready to eat them.

There are two factors at work here. Most Oriental vegetables are cool weather crops and aren't happy as the temperature climbs. Some are also day-length sensitive, so it's important to sow seeds at the right time.

Last year I sowed Chinese cabbage, pak choi and tatsoi in mid-September, to overwinter in the Grow Dome. They were all very successful, providing fresh greens all through the winter and spring.

If you want to try a few Oriental leaves to find out which ones you like, then the mixed packets of stir-fry leaves are ideal – although it's not always easy to identify the resulting plants!

Moving on from leafy vegetables... If you're a fan of beans then you could try Lablab beans, or the impressive Yard long bean, but they're not likely to do well in a cool English summer. The same goes for most of the Oriental cucurbits (squashes, melons and cucumbers).

Chinese artichokes are on my list of things to try. They're grown in a similar way to Jerusalem artichokes, but are members of the mint family – both of which should be ringing alarm bells about invasive plants. If you don't manage to dig up all the tubers then you'll have volunteer plants next year, which makes them problematic to remove. But they can be used as a home-grown substitute for water chestnuts in Oriental dishes.

There's an impressive choice of radishes (we're back to brassicas!), especially the winter radishes (including Mooli and Daikon) that grow so much larger than the summer salad radishes we're used to. They're usually used for cooking, and come in some stunning colours. Mantanghong is a cylindrical radish with crimson flesh – very impressive in salads or stir-fries.

You can also get radishes that are grown for their leaves, and one, the Rat's Tail radish, which is grown for its seed pods. In fact all radish seed pods are edible, so if your radishes run to seed then you can try the pods and see whether you like them. The heat will depend on the variety, and they've got a good crunch to them.

If you've got a lot of radish seed you can consider sowing them as a seedling crop – a bit like mustard and cress, although again the heat depends on the variety.

With a handful of Oriental greens, a few spring onions, Chinese artichokes and radishes and you'll be knee-deep in stir-fry veg all season.

O is for...

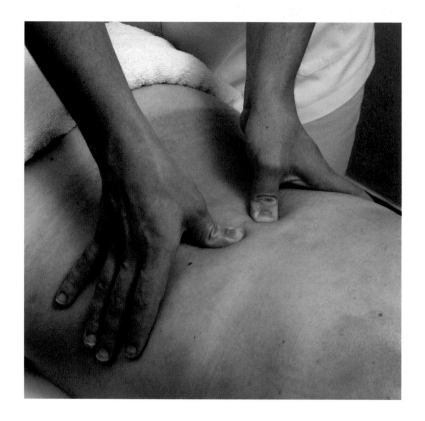

Osteopath

Gardening is a very British hobby, seen as peaceful and stress-free and possibly somewhat middle-aged. But in truth gardening can be very hard work, and not a little dangerous.

Early in the year, thousands of vegetable gardeners troop out to their plot in cool weather and dig, dig, dig – trying to get their seed beds into a 'fine tilth' for the sowing season. And no doubt a large proportion of them will strain their backs, stick a fork through their foot or slip in the mud and fall over.

If you want to avoid a series of visits to the osteopath then the trick is not to take on too much at once, not to overdo it and don't do anything that hurts. Personally I do very little digging, as I do my gardening in raised beds – but any good gardening manual will be able to show you the best technique for digging without injuring yourself. You should also look on gardening as a form of exercise, and make sure that you're warmed up and stretched before you take on anything strenuous – like moving that overlarge flower pot.

Don't do the same thing for too long, especially if it's bending or kneeling. Wear the proper gear for the job – sturdy boots if you're going to be digging and gloves for anything that might hurt your hands. Shorts and sandals is not the right attire for anything other than relaxing in the garden.

Put your tools away properly, so they're not lying around where they can be trodden on (you'll also extend the life of your tools if you treat them well). And if you must use power tools (the only one we have is a hedge trimmer) then make sure you've got one of those gizmos that cuts the power if you slice through the cable.

And a note from personal experience – if you have to tackle brambles and you don't want to be stabbed with the thorns then you need leather gauntlets. Nothing else will cut it – they'll find a way through. And if they're long enough then you might want to consider safety goggles – because they have an alarming habit of waving around at eye level as you chop them down.

P is for...

P is for...

Parsley

Legend has it that parsley seeds take forever to germinate, but as I always sow mine indoors I've never had any trouble. In fact, there's lots of folk lore about parsley – including that the seeds have to go to hell and back several times before they germinate, that it should never be transplanted (for fear of bad luck) and that only the wicked can grow it well.

Despite that, parsley is pretty easy to grow and a useful plant to have in the garden. It copes well with inclement weather, meaning that you can harvest leaves from it over a long period. A few leaves can perk up a salad, garnish a plate or a bowl of soup – and a generous handful can become the star of the meal if you like tabbouleh. Parsley is a very healthy plant, rarely bothered by pests and diseases. The curly variety is so pretty that it's often used as a decorative edging for beds. The flavour of the flat leaved variety is better, though, if you want a purely culinary herb. I started growing it because I'm a real fan of parsley sauce, although ironically I hardly ever make it now that I've got a continuous supply of parsley to hand. I should make more of an effort.

Parsley likes more water than some other herbs, and if you're harvesting a lot of leaves then an occasional feed will help it to stay green and lush.

Parsley is a biennial plant, so it won't normally flower until its second season. It's an umbellifer, which means it has flower heads that look like umbrellas – made up of hundreds of tiny blooms. Insects go mad for umbellifers, so if your parsley flowers it's worth leaving it for a while if you don't need the space for something else. The hoverflies will thank you for it by breeding large families of larvae to eat all your aphids. You'll also be able to save some seed for next year, if you want to.

When you come to dig up your parsley plants you'll be amazed at the chunky tap roots they grow. They look like root vegetables – and in fact there is a type of parsley (Hamburg parsley) that's grown for its edible roots, although it's more common in mainland Europe than here in the UK. Seeds are easy enough to come by, though, if you fancy giving it a try. And par-cel is a herb that grows like parsley, but tastes like celery.

Parsley is in the same family as carrots, celery and parsnips, so bear that in mind when you're planning your crop rotation. Sow seeds early in the year for spring and summer harvests and sow a second batch in late summer for autumn and winter harvests. Parsley is pretty hardy, but you might want to bring a pot indoors to guarantee a supply through the worst of the winter weather. The parsley probably won't mind being under a foot of snow, but you won't want to go outside and harvest it if you're likely to be buried in a snow drift.

P is for...

Peas

There are two opposing opinions on growing your own peas – the first is that they give very low yields for the space they take up and are not worth the effort. The second is that eating peas fresh from the pod is one of life's most rewarding experiences and should not be missed. I attempt to grow peas most years, but I've yet to reap more than a handful of pods for my efforts.

It's likely that my lack of success is partly due to low levels of rhizobia bacteria, as mine is a relatively new garden and I have used a lot of bagged potting compost in the past. If that's the case then harvests should suddenly improve as the right rhizobia take up residence.

Modern varieties of pea tend to be dwarf ones and happily scramble up 'twiggy sticks' if you can get hold of such things. Heritage varieties can be very tall indeed and need a more beefy support. Peas also come in 'wrinkled' or 'round'. Wrinkled peas are sown from spring onwards. Round varieties are hardier and can be sown in the autumn or early in the year for earlier harvests and tend to be slightly starchier and less sweet.

It's also possible to find varieties with coloured pods that make harvesting easier as the pods stand out against the foliage. And there's always mangetout and snap peas if you want to eat the whole pod. If you grow peas to shell then there's no need to waste all the flavour in the pods, as you can use them to make vegetable stock for soups. Or wine!

If you have problems with mice eating pea seeds sown in the ground then try sowing them in a length of guttering. When they're ready to plant out, water the compost well and slide the plants out into a ready-prepared trench (there's a knack to it and you might need to practice). If you sow in modules then it's best to plant out peas when they're on the young side, as they start to tangle into each other. Don't bother trying to unwind plant tendrils – they only curl up once. It's quicker to snip through them, and the plant will grow some more.

In the autumn and winter, when gardening activities are few and far between, you might want to try growing pea shoots. Fill a tray with a shallow layer of compost, sow as many pea seeds as you can fit in and lightly cover them with compost. Keep them indoors and the peas will start to grow. When they are a couple of inches high you can pinch out the tips and use them in salad or stir-fries. They're eaten a lot in China, but if you see them here they cost a fortune.

After the first harvest the peas branch out and grow more shoots and you can keep harvesting every few days. When the plants get tired throw the whole lot on the compost and start again.

My personal experience is that shorter varieties of pea make better candidates for pea shoot harvests, because they grow into stockier plants with less of a tendency to tangle. Douce Provence is my favourite variety to date. When you're growing peas outdoors then you can pinch out the tips of shoots and use those – as long as you don't go mad you won't affect your pea pod harvest.

P is for...

Peat

Peat bogs are a valuable wildlife habitat, and yet we're digging them up at a frightening rate to use the peat for potting compost. It makes good potting compost, and people love using it, but peat bogs all over the world are now in danger and it's time we stopped extracting peat and used something else.

If you buy a bag of compost that doesn't say it's 'peat free', then it isn't. The cheap bags of multipurpose compost at the garden centre are likely to be largely peat.

It can be difficult to find a suitable substitute, but due to consumer pressure there are now more brands of peat-free compost available – and they're getting better.

The problem is that peat-free potting compost is different to peat-based potting compost, so if you're used to growing in peat then you're going to have a period of adjustment before you get used to your new composts. They need watering differently, and feeding at different rates. My current favourite is New Horizon, which works well for me but isn't always available.

A lot of peat-free composts are made from waste materials, like composed bark. You could also investigate whether your local council collects green waste for composting and then makes it available to gardeners. Of course, the more compost you can make, then the less you'll need to resort to bought in supplies anyway.

There are some plants that will only grow in peat-based composts, because that's what they naturally grow in. I have some carnivorous plants in the bathroom (they eat bugs – the sticky leaves of the sundews are particularly good at dealing with pesky fungus gnats) and they need to be planted in peat. But you can actually get eco-friendly peat compost if you really need it. There's a brand called Moorland Gold that is made from particles of peat that are caught in filters as water from the hills flows down into reservoirs. Rather than treating this peat as a waste product, it becomes a valuable resource. I bought a sack for my carnivorous plants, and they think it's great. You're unlikely to find it locally though, and will probably have to buy it mail order. It's expensive, but (apart from the compost miles) guilt-free.

Something else you can try is coir – made from the waste bits of coconuts. That means, of course, that it comes with built-in 'coir miles', but it's a valuable trade commodity for the countries that produce it. You can get little coir pots that can be planted out into the soil (which prevents root disturbance when transplanting), or a coir version of the Jiffy-7 modules that lots of people use for seed sowing. And you can get big bricks of coir that you soak in water and break up into a planting medium. It's commonly supplied as the bedding for the worms when you get a new wormery.

I've never had much luck with coir. I've never managed to get the biodegradable pots to biodegrade (they even seem to survive a few months on the compost heap!) and likewise the big blocks don't seem to break down into a nice growing medium for me. But you can find coir-based composts, which might be easier to use.

So, to recap: make as much of your own compost as possible, experiment with peat-free composts as necessary and leave peat where it belongs – in the ground.

P is for...

Peppers

Peppers are my favourite plants. We like eating sweet peppers, and whatever I harvest is quickly scoffed. They're easy to grow indoors (if you have a sunny window-sill) and very decorative – star-shaped flowers give way to fruits that change colour as they mature. Some chilli peppers are even more decorative. I have Trifetti growing this year, as its variegated leaves and purple fruits were too pretty to resist.

Peppers come in all the colours under the sun and fruits tend to start off one colour and change to another when they're ripe – although they're edible at any stage. They also come in different sizes, from tiny pickling peppers through to enormous ones that are great for stuffing. But the larger the fruit, the harder it is to get them to ripen successfully in our climate.

You'll find it easier to get a crop with some protection, and peppers make ideal greenhouse plants, but a plant in a sunny spot on the patio will fruit well. The problem comes in the autumn, when you have unripe fruits. If you can move the plant under-cover then they continue to ripen, otherwise you'll have to be content with green peppers.

Plants need to be kept warm throughout their life, and the seeds need quite a high temperature to germinate. A heated propagator is often recommended, but I've never had any problems germinating seeds without one, although they take longer to germinate without extra heat.

Slugs like pepper seedlings, but once past that all you have to worry about is aphids and red spider mite if you're growing them indoors. Peppers like a potassium-rich feed from when they start to flower, and plenty of water. Indoors you can encourage pollination (although they are naturally self-fertile) by shaking the branches or gently running your finger over the inside of the flowers.

With a continuous supply of light and a warm temperature, peppers survive for years and fruit more abundantly as they mature. But peppers can be difficult to overwinter – the low light levels here in the UK are problematic, and peppers frequently drop their leaves as the short days wear on. They look horrendous, but most spring back into life when the days get longer. An overwintered pepper crops earlier in the year than a new plant sown from seed in February.

Pepper seedlings in sunny spots grow faster, which gave me the idea that pepper seedlings may overwinter better than mature plants – they adjust their growth to the available light, rather than finding themselves with more leaves than they can support. To test my theory, last September I sowed pepper seeds and kept them on a sunny windowsill. By December, the seedlings were thriving. By April they were growing fruits. These were fully ripe at the beginning of June, so this technique does give earlier crops.

Most peppers grown in gardens are *Capsicum annum*. Aji peppers are *Capsicum baccatum*, much taller plants. The only one I've grown is the sweet aji from Real Seeds – which tastes like a chilli pepper, but doesn't have the heat. *Capsicum chinense* varieties are common in the Caribbean and the Tabasco pepper is *Capsicum frutescens*, requiring long hot summers to ripen fruit. An unusual pepper I would like to try is *Capsicum pubescens*. It's a native of the Andes, and hence used to cooler conditions, with furry leaves and purple flowers. You'd need two plants to guarantee fruit as this species is not self-fertile.

P is for...

Permaculture

Permaculture is a topic that's close to my heart because it's about sustainable living and gardening. Many permaculture principles are easy to grasp and put into practice – and to an organic gardener they make a lot of sense.

Permaculture is all about designing systems that are sustainable by modelling them on natural processes. It can be applied on any scale, from a singe household upwards to towns and cities, and is often used to design productive gardens.

The idea is to get the largest possible output from minimal inputs and to make the best use of what we have.

One of the most recognisable permaculture projects is the herb spiral. A mound of soil is built up and herbs are planted upwards in a spiral. The mound creates microclimates so that each herb can be given the conditions it prefers. On the north side of the mound, at the bottom where the soil is wettest, plants like mint and sorrel will be happy. On the sunny side, at the top where the soil is driest, Mediterranean herbs like rosemary and thyme will thrive. Putting each plant in the right place cuts down on maintenance – one of the biggest inputs in a garden! In permaculture, productive areas are divided into zones.

* Zone 1 is closest to the house (Zone 0 is indoors) and is the place to plant crops that need a lot of attention – salads, strawberries and things that need regular harvesting. It's also the ideal place for compost bins and the green-house – if you've got space. Zone 1 could be a patio, or it could be a porch or a window box, depending on the space you have.

* Zone 2 is a little bit further away – maybe the end of the back garden. Here you can grow plants that can take care of themselves for longer, e.g. fruit bushes and perennial herbs.

* Zone 3 is where the bulk of food production takes place, so it could be your vegetable patch or an allotment. This is a place you visit once or twice a week.

* Zone 4 is semi-wild, places where you can find wild food (like blackberries) and that might be used for timber production. A coppiced woodland would fall into this category.

* Zone 5 is wilderness, space to be enjoyed but not tampered with. Wild ecosystems should be left alone, but can be observed and appreciated.

In reality, most of us can't divide our spaces up into zones that easily – but the underlying concept is sound. Put the things that need most attention close to where you live so that you can visit them often. Things that are a bit more robust can be further away.

Composting, recycling and reusing resources are all part of the perma-culture idea – as is getting what you need from the local community rather than transporting it in from elsewhere. You could organise a local seed swap, or find people nearby who could help you deal with your vegetable glut, and might even help you to dig your garden in return.

There's a lot more to permaculture, and many people more qualified to write about it, so I will leave it to them (have a look in the *Recommended Reading* section at the end of this book and subscribe to *Permaculture Magazine*).

P is for...

pH

As you might remember from your school days, pH is a measurement of the acidity of something. The pH of your garden soil depends on the underlying rocks and geography – and there's not much you can do to change it because there's so much of it. However, you can adapt your planting to your conditions, and manage the pH in small areas of the garden.

The problem lies in the fact that the pH of your soil affects the soil chemistry and hence the availability of nutrients for your plants. At extremes of the pH scale (and it runs from 1 (very acid) to 14 (very alkaline), different nutrients will be almost completely unavailable to plants, and plants have adapted to these growing conditions – and won't thrive at different pH levels as a result.

Most garden vegetables like a soil that's roughly in the middle – between about 6 and 8 – and 7 is a neutral soil that is neither acidic nor alkaline. You can measure the pH of your soil using either a meter with a metal probe, or a little chemistry set. It's possible that the pH of the soil varies in different places in your garden, so it's worth taking a series of measurements to see what's what.

Plants that like alkaline soil are known as 'lime-loving' or calcicole plants. They include brassicas. Plants that like acid soil are known as 'lime-hating' or calcifuge. Blueberries are a prime example – you can only grow them in acid soil.

If you follow a traditional crop rotation then you will be applying lime (a source of calcium) to one of your beds each year. Lime is also used to balance the pH of compost heaps and to help manage heavy soils. Since I have a very alkaline soil it's not something I've ever had to do.

Whatever type of soil you have, adding organic matter can help to keep a plentiful supply of nutrients available for plants.

Lowering the pH of your soil (i.e. making it more acid) is difficult to do on any scale. You can add compost and sulphur chips, but you'll have to use rainwater to water your plants because the chances are if you have alkaline soil then you have alkaline tap water as well (essentially hard water). You'll have to keep checking that the pH of your soil isn't rising – which is exactly what I have to do to keep the blueberries I grow in containers happy. I also had to start off with acidic (ericaceous) compost.

The best thing to do is to only manage the pH of the soil in the kitchen garden, and then only gently – growing anything that doesn't like your soil (and yet you must have) in containers. In the ornamental garden, let nature take its course and grow the plants that are suitable for your soil conditions. Sneak a peek over the fence and see what's growing well in your neighbour's garden and grow those too – if you ask nicely they might even give you some cuttings!

P is for...

Phosphorus

Phosphorus is the final macronutrient in the NPK trio. It's important for root growth and healthy growth generally, and needs to be available throughout a plant's life. It comes from the rocks in the garden, and how much of the phosphorus in your garden is available to your plants depends on lots of factors including soil health and pH. Plants often rely on soil bacteria and fungi to help them collect enough phosphorus.

Phosphorus in organic fertilisers comes either from rock phosphate or bonemeal. If you make your own comfrey liquid feed then it has reasonable levels of phosphorus – it's quite a balanced diet for plants, with plenty of potassium for fruiting vegetables.

Phosphorus deficiencies can be difficult to diagnose in your plants – they're by no means as obvious as a nitrogen deficiency – and so your best bet is to make sure that your soil is healthy, to use a balanced fertiliser as and when necessary and to grow plants that are happy in your soil (in terms of the pH range they will grow in).

Beyond NPK there are lots of minerals that plants need in smaller quantities – micronutrients – that aren't generally included in chemical fertilisers (which is one reason that they're problematic). If you add plenty of homemade compost to your soil then you shouldn't have problems with micronutrient deficiencies. For plants in containers, or if you suspect a mineral deficiency, then try using a seaweed based liquid feed. Seaweed feeds are a godsend to organic gardeners, because they are essentially a pick-me-up for plants, containing lots and lots of different nutrients. They can be applied to the soil as a liquid feed, or directly to leaves as a foliar feed – which has the advantage of working very quickly if you have a plant that is sickly. They smell a little bit fishy, but that wears off quickly and it might even deter some sap sucking insects who think your plants taste funny.

P is for...

Potatoes

Potatoes are easy to grow, nutritious and versatile, and the 'humble spud' has become a firm favourite. If you've got the space then you can grow enough potatoes to be self-sufficient, but even in a small garden it's worth growing a few to experience home-grown potatoes. They're like the best new potatoes, only better.

If you've only got space for a few potatoes, perhaps in a container, plant an early variety or a salad potato. They mature more quickly and you'll get enough baby spuds for several portions.

Potatoes in containers need a lot more water than you'd imagine. They're also a magnet for slugs – get your slug defences in place before the leaves emerge. In the ground plants tend to grow away from slug and snail damage.

Potatoes are tubers and grow from the stem of the plant. Burying the stem means that more potatoes grow – 'earthing up' involves shovelling soil or compost onto the plants as the leaves show, to end up with potatoes in mounds. Earthing up also protects tubers from sunlight, which turns them green and poisonous. You can achieve the same effect with a deep mulch.

Potato plants flower and produce little fruits that look tomatoes but are poisonous. It's recommended to remove them, but early potatoes are ready once the flowers fade.

The main problem with potatoes is blight, a fungal disease that attacks during humid weather. It spreads quickly, causing dark splotches on the leaves before the whole plant collapses. It's difficult to control – removing affected leaves slows it down, but the best course of action is to cut down and remove the foliage when you realise there is a problem. Leaving the tubers underground for a couple of weeks helps to protect them, but you'll have to be prepared for them not to store. Blight-infected tubers rot, so eat them while you can.

Early varieties ('earlies') mature before the blight season and are rarely affected, and you can now get blight resistant varieties of potato.

Conventional wisdom is that, to help prevent blight, you should not put potato peelings or foliage onto the compost heap. Given that blight is everywhere, and spread by rain and wind, I don't really follow the logic – but if you have blight problems you might want to bear it in mind. Diseased foliage of any description should be kept off the compost heap unless you're a hot composter and you know that your heap gets warm enough to kill plant diseases. What you will find, if you add potato peelings or rotten potatoes to your compost heap, is that they often start growing. It depends a bit on the weather conditions. It's quite disconcerting to find a large triffid emerging from the compost heap (especially when it's a wormery!), but they tend to die off by themselves, as there's very little light, and then compost down properly.

If you don't manage to dig up all the potatoes they grow again next season. These 'volunteer' potatoes can spread pests and diseases and should be removed. You should also buy fresh seed potatoes each year unless you've got a heritage variety that's only available as microplants. With those you save your own seed potatoes, to increase your stock, but you have to be vigilant for disease problems. The up-side is that you can try coloured potatoes. The colours may not survive being boiled, but you can steam your spuds for a rainbow dinner.

The *Alternative* Kitchen Garden

Q is for...

Q is for...

Qing dou

If you look through the index in any gardening book, you'll find that topics beginning with Q are few and far between (and I mentioned quinoa earlier on) – in fact some books don't list any subjects under Q at all. So I'm having to be a little bit creative, and borrow from Chinese for this one. Qing dou means (I believe) 'green beans' and refers to green soy beans – what's known as edamame in Japan.

Pete came back from a trip to London one day, raving about the edamame he'd been served as a snack with a drink in a bar there. I did a bit of investigation, and soya beans got added to the growing list last year.

Soya beans, although commonly grown around the world, aren't common here. There's pretty much only one variety available to UK gardeners, Ustie. Ustie has been bred to be day-length neutral and hence perfect for the British climate. The plants are self-pollinating and start to set pods in September. The pods are described as 'weather proof', whatever that means, and this variety is GM-free.

At the end of the growing season, many garden centres sell off their leftover seeds at a discount. I was in a garden centre in the autumn of 2007 and I bought (among other things) a packet of Ustie seeds. I sowed them early in May 2008 and waited – and nothing happened. Towards the end of May I tried sprouting some in a sprouting jar as a germination test, and they all went mouldy before they germinated. The seed wasn't viable.

It could be that they weren't viable because they weren't stored well in the garden centre. Seeds need to be kept at a fairly constant temperature – large fluctuations will kill them off – and in some garden centres that's difficult to achieve. Seeds bought mail order are more likely to have been stored in good conditions because they don't have to be kept on display. It's something to bear in mind if you're shopping for bargain seeds as the end of the year – the germination rates might not be up to expectations.

There's another possibility. Garden Organic ran an experiment in 2005 in which they gave members Ustie seeds to trial in their gardens. The results were not good, with most people reporting problems with germination. When Garden Organic tried germinating the seeds themselves, they found that only around a quarter of them germinated at all – and that many of those that did germinate were abnormal and would not have grown into mature plants. So it seems that there might be a general problem with the seed supply.

Hopefully some more varieties will become available, or you could look further afield for seeds if you really want to try it. But in the event that you do manage to grow some soy beans, remember that they have to be thoroughly cooked to be edible.

Q is for...

Quamash

Quamash (*Camassia quamash*, also commonly called Camassia) is an edible bulb, a staple food of native Americans. I can't now remember why I decided to try and grow it, but I do remember seeing some growing at the RISC roof garden in Reading. They have pretty blue flowers, a bit like bluebells.

The seed needs a period of winter cold to germinate, so I sowed mine in a pot last autumn and put it in the cold frame. It sat outside all winter, and the seeds burst into life in spring. The seedlings were tiny, single-leaved things.

Unfortunately I got engrossed in other things in spring, and when I checked on them one day the quamash seedlings were dead. It's a shame when something like that happens, because it's a whole year before you get the chance to try again.

However, I have since read that it takes rather a lot of cooking to make the bulbs edible. They would have been cooked in large fire pits by the native Americans, something which few of us would be able to replicate today – even if we had enough bulbs to make it worth the effort. If I grow quamash again next year, it may well become one of the plants in the garden that – although technically edible – is grown for its interest and ornamental value.

Q is for...

Quick Return

In the 1930s, Maye Emily Bruce developed (through trial and error and a knowledge of biodynamic compost making) the Quick Return compost method. The idea behind it was to make high-quality compost for gardeners and farmers, without using animal manure. The compost method involved building heaps in layers, and paying attention to both heat retention and drainage. It also involved the application of plant essences that act as an activator.

It became a very popular method of making compost.

The activator was later mass-produced by Chase Organics – the company behind the modern *Organic Gardening Catalogue* – and is still on sale today. All you do is dilute the mixture with water and then add it to the compost.

Compost activators in general are quite popular because they speed up the composting process. They work by supplying minerals and trace elements that are necessary for composting to take place but might be in short supply in the materials to be composted. As such they can help heaps to heat up, or simply to rot down. A lot of organic compost activators are seaweed based because (as previously mentioned), seaweed contains a lot of micronutrients. Those nutrients will then be available in the finished compost.

Although compost activators have their place, they're not necessary and your compost will rot down without them – it might just take a little bit longer. It's far more important to get the balance of materials right in your compost so that both 'browns' and 'greens' are available to the microbes that feed on them. They also need enough air and a reasonable water supply – so bone dry heaps and sopping piles are both equally unlikely to compost well.

It doesn't pay to rush your compost too much. However you choose to make it, compost that has been allowed to age will be finer and more suitable for using in potting mixes. It may well also have less weed seeds, even if it's a cold heap, as recent research (reported in the US magazine *Organic Gardening*) seems to suggest that weed seed germination drops off sharply as compost sits in a heap, and drops to nearly zero after five months. It could be that the composting process kills the seeds, or that they germinate in the heap and then die.

The *Alternative* Kitchen Garden

R is for...

R is for...

Raised Beds

I have raised beds in my garden for several reasons. The first is that this garden hadn't been looked after for years, and was a mass of weeds – bindweed being the hardest to control. When I made the original raised beds, I put weed control fabric underneath them to stop it growing up through the compost. The bindweed is under control, but not eradicated. The brambles are confined to the bottom of the garden, and so not an issue for the main vegetable patch (although they keep trying to find a way into the Grow Dome). The soil here is very heavy clay – another reason not to try and grow anything directly into it, especially as it had been heavily compacted by feet of various shapes and sizes. The final reason is that I'm not a big fan of digging, and if you avoid walking on your soil and compacting it then you can get away with very little digging, or even none at all.

My main raised beds are made out of big concrete blocks – the ones with two holes in. The idea was that I can use those smaller holes around the edge as extra planting holes. After a couple of years of trial and error, I can recommend that anyone doing the same confines their use to short-lived plants that are low and don't flower too profusely. If you fill them with compost then the volume drops over the course of the year, taking the plants with them. Perennial plants are quite happy in the holes, but become very difficult to remove as they sink down. Anything too tall makes it difficult to reach into the bed beyond, and flowers that attract bees make life very hazardous. Welsh onions are therefore a terrible choice on all counts.

This year I also have a couple of temporary raised beds, made of wooden frames (two halves of an old wooden crate) filled with compost. They're home to my courgettes, which seem quite happy. They can root into the soil beneath in search of water, although since it has been a wet summer that's not the advantage it would have been in a drought.

Raised beds don't have to have permanent sides – which are often time consuming or expensive to make. You can make beds with simple earth sides, and mound up the soil from paths onto the beds for extra depth. You can also just build them up in layers on top of the soil, using anything that will rot down – from cardboard and newspaper at the bottom for weed suppression to homemade compost and a straw mulch on the top.

Another advantage of raised beds is that they allow for more intensive cultivation. The added depth (even if it's only a couple of inches) of good soil keeps plant roots happy and means that you can plant them closer together. You can concentrate soil improvers, water and effort on the areas where plants are growing (one of the underlying principles of Square Foot Gardening), and can make spaces for trailing plants.

The golden rule for raised beds is that they shouldn't be wider than around 1.2 metres, so that you can always reach into the middle from the edge. They shouldn't be too long either, or you'll be tempted to take a short cut by walking over the middle rather than go round the long way.

Raised beds are great for people who don't want to do too much bending, and you can built them up as high as you want – or create them on frames with legs so that you have table top gardens.

R is for...

Raspberries

One of the stories that's frequently told in our family is of the day when I discovered a little worm in my bowl of raspberries. It was pale, with a black head and it was standing upright and waving its head around. Needless to say, I didn't finish my raspberries, especially when my brother (he's older than me) start making his forefinger wiggle like a crawling worm! It's surprising that I'm not scared for life, but I do like raspberries as long as they're fresh and juicy, so I am growing my own.

Raspberries grow on quite tall, fruiting canes. They're usually tied into a supporting structure of wires, and you prune the canes after they have fruited as they fruit more abundantly on the new canes that grow each year. Those are summer-fruiting raspberries; you can also get ones that fruit later in the season, called autumn-fruiting raspberries, that are treated slightly differently – the old canes are cut down early in the year rather than immediately after fruiting.

Autumn-fruiting raspberries are more self-supporting too, and can be grown in a container (as long as it's a large enough one). I have two large tubs, each with five canes of Autumn Bliss raspberries, and they've fruited well this year – in fact they and the blueberries are the reason that I bought the fruit cage. They all looked like they would fruit well this year, and I didn't want the blackbirds to beat me to all the fruit!

And it is true that there's nothing like home grown raspberries, eaten fresh off the bush while they're still warm. Pete bought a punnet of raspberries home from the supermarket earlier in the summer, tried one and decided he wasn't going to eat them. I thought he was just being fussy – but then he threw them into the chicken run and the chickens wouldn't eat them either! They must have been very nasty, as Hen Solo in particular is a soft fruit junkie. She thinks nothing of wandering around the garden and pinching ripe raspberries off the canes that she can reach (although she can't reach very high because the container is quite tall). She's been very lucky this year as the tayberry (a cross between a blackberry and a raspberry) has started fruiting, and it has berries much nearer the ground.

Although the majority of raspberry varieties are the classic red colour, there are also some golden ones. And, I've just discovered, you can get some that are almost black as well. And there's even an arctic raspberry (*Rubus arcticus*), the raspberry equivalent of the alpine strawberry, that's a much more low growing plant with pretty pink flowers. It doesn't mind cold weather, and could be used as a ground cover plant in a forest garden. Needless to say, I've added one to my Wants list!

I do have a *Rubus tricolor*, the creeping bramble that I've planted as groundcover between the two tayberries. It has settled in well, but has yet to fruit – so I don't know whether they're fruits for the humans of the family, or ones that the chickens will be allowed to munch. It's called 'tricolor' because of its glossy green leaves, white flowers and red fruits, and apparently its ornamental value is such that it is used in flower arranging.

R is for...

Real Seeds

More and more consumers are searching out truly ethical businesses, ones which clearly state their ethical code and try and reduce their impact on the planet. Gardeners are just the same, and as we regularly buy seeds for the garden it's nice to know that we can do so with as little impact as possible.

And so rather than worry about creating profits for agribusiness, GM seeds or F1 hybrids, and our disappearing vegetable heritage, people are turning to heritage seed suppliers (like the HSL) and ethical seed businesses.

Real Seeds is a very small seed company, run by Ben and Kate from a community-based farm in Wales. They only sell varieties that they have grown and tried themselves, and so they don't stock seeds that don't grow well in our climate.

They also only offer open-pollinated seed for sale, which means that you can save your own seeds and never need to buy that variety again. In fact, they actively encourage you to do so. Each packet of seed comes with full growing instructions, seed-saving information and even some hints and tips on using your harvest. All of the seeds are grown on the farm itself, or by a network of seed growers – none of whom use any chemicals on their land (although many of the seeds are not officially certified organic because of the costs involved in certification).

The catalogue is extensive, with all of the common vegetables represented. You can also find more unusual varieties, including sweet peppers that have been specially chosen because they crop well in our cool climate, achocha and its relative the exploding cucumber, unusual tubers (including oca and ulluco), an enormous selection of 'greens' and some grains to try if you've got the space. And if you're a chilli fiend then they've got plenty of those to choose from too. Try buying from Real Seeds, and experience guilt-free shopping!

R is for...

Recycling

We can't go on cutting down trees and not replacing them. We don't have endless deposits of metals to mine. Even synthetic materials are made from natural resources, with limited supplies.

We're also running out of places to throw away our waste – we're gradually coming around to the idea that 'away' doesn't exist and that we're cluttering up the planet (and even the space surrounding it). Burning rubbish causes atmospheric pollution, and although we can recover some energy from the process, the resources we've burned are gone for good.

Recycling is still in its infancy. We struggle to collect, sort and process a limited number of items. In the UK the recycling facilities available depend on where you live, as each local council negotiates its own waste contracts. Many of our waste materials are reprocessed into lower quality materials – like office paper being recycled into toilet roll or cardboard. We haven't caught on to the idea of upcycling, where materials are reprocessed into something of equal or greater value. And we haven't made much progress on designing items with recycling in mind – which means that many consumer products are impossible to recycle.

A garden gives you almost endless opportunities for recycling at home. The compost heap is a great start, and gobbles up any paper and cardboard you can't recycle as well as kitchen and garden waste. Shredded paper is problematic for recycling collections, but makes great compost material. Newspaper and cardboard both make great mulch materials, and if you're into origami then you can make your own biodegradable plant pots out of newspaper.

Clear plastic bottles can be used as cloches, once you've carefully cut the bottom off. They even come with their own ventilation system – you can leave the lid on or take it off, depending on the weather. Small bottles make good cane toppers, protecting you from poking your eye out on canes as you're bending over to look at the plants. Or you can sink bottomless bottles into the soil and water into them so that water goes to the roots where it really needs to be rather than evaporating from the soil surface.

Plastic milk bottles, especially ones with handles, are endlessly useful as watering cans, or (if you cut the bottom off) compost scoops. You can slice them horizontally from the bottom right up to the neck so that they hinge open and can be closed over swelling corn cobs to protect them from birds. Use them to store your liquid feeds – but remember not to put anything poisonous into a bottle that could be mistaken as a drink. You can even store dry goods in bottles to keep them dry – one holds my supply of soap flakes, only needed when there's a major aphid attack. You can turn bottles into slug pubs or bird feeders or lacewing hotels... the list is almost endless.

Plastic food trays make great seed trays for small batches of seeds, and clear ones can be used as propagating lids. Yoghurt pots can be used for growing seedlings and anything that holds compost and has drainage holes can be used as a planter.

I'm not a person who squirrels away anything that might eventually be useful – we don't have the space – but I'm always open to ideas about how to reuse or recycle so that I can save money and help the planet at the same time.

R is for...

RISC Roof Garden

A few years ago a community centre in the heart of Reading – RISC, the Reading International Solidarity Centre – had a leaking roof and no funds to replace it. They put together an exciting bid for lottery funding and the roof garden was born.

The roof garden is a forest garden, designed along permaculture principles. All of the plants are edible or useful and they come from temperate zones all over the world. And all the plants are growing in one foot of soil.

The garden has a solar panel, a wind turbine and a rainwater tank. Green cone composters take vegetable waste from the café and paper waste from the office. In return, the garden provides herbs for the kitchen and flowers for the café tables. Nettles and comfrey planted around the base of the composters are used for making liquid feeds, and many of the hard landscaping materials are recycled.

A winding path means that you can't see one end of the garden from the other. Around each bend you'll find amazing plants. The golden hop is one making use of vertical space. It's used to flavour beer, can be used as a relaxing filling for pillows and has vines suitable for basketry. It also has an ornamental value as well as a lovely scent.

The spiny pepper plant has long spines and aromatic foliage and grows little red peppercorns. You can drop them into a bottle of olive oil to make a salad dressing with a kick, and if you chew them they make your gums numb – giving this plant its alternative name of the 'toothache tree'.

Emmer wheat was one of the early sources of carbohydrate for Western civilization, brought to Britain by the Celts about 6000 years ago. The Chilean guava (*Ugni molinae*) is a myrtle from South America and makes a good hedging plant with tasty berries that ripen in October.

The medlar used to be a popular tree and has the most beautiful white flowers in May, followed by fruits that look like apples wearing crowns. They're left to ripen on the tree, and then after harvesting the fruits are stored and allowed to 'blet' (rot, essentially) until they're almost fermenting – at which point they are soft enough to be eaten with a spoon and taste like spiced fruit.

The roof garden crams over 160 different plants into a space 30 metres by 6 metres. As you can imagine, it is a haven for wildlife. There are goldfinches and a sparrowhawk, and blackbirds that manage to beat the human visitors to most of the berry crops. There are lots of butterflies and other insects, and no doubt the soil is teeming with mini beasts as well.

As to the problems of growing on a rooftop... well, slugs and snails don't seem to make it up the stairs, but there are rats. It can be windy up on the roof, and some plants struggle to get enough water.

The roof garden is open to visitors under the National Gardens Scheme (see www.risc.org.uk/garden for details). You could spend all day here without running out of plants with interesting stories, and there are plenty of ideas to take home. The designers have created a garden that is productive, and yet almost maintenance free. It's a complete change from the low maintenance gardens you see on garden makeover shows, completely sustainable and hopefully something that will really catch on.

R is for...

Rotation

The ideas underlying crop rotation are simple. Firstly, growing the same vegetable in the same place is a bad idea –they become magnets for the pests and diseases. Secondly, plants belong to families, and plants in the same family tend to have similar requirements and similar vulnerabilities and should be kept together.

Put those two ideas together and you've got the essence of crop rotations – plants are grouped together with their relations and moved around so that they don't grow in the same place each year. If you stop there, that's good enough in most cases. The three and four year rotations laid out in gardening manuals also factor in soil amendments such as digging in manure, or applying lime, at the right time in the rotation so that brassicas have a nice high pH and potatoes don't go hungry.

The pumpkin (*Cucurbitaceae*) family includes courgettes, squash, cucumbers and melons, and so gets split between the garden and the greenhouse. They all like rich soil and plenty of water, and they all take up a lot of space. Some of the more exotic edibles are in this family, including achocha, watermelons and kiwano.

Peas and beans are in the same family (*Fabaceae*, but still referred to as legumes), together with soya beans, chickpeas, peanuts and many others. They all form symbiotic relationships with rhizobia bacteria, which enables them to take nitrogen from the air and 'fix' it into the soil. Different legumes need different strains of bacteria though, they don't share.

Over-represented in my garden is the onion family (*Alliaceae*). I've got two different varieties of garlic, two varieties of bulb onion, two sorts of chives and two unusual onions – the clumping Welsh onion and a top-setting onion. There are also leeks, shallots and spring onions. Alliums are fairly pest-resistant (although the snails here seem to love their leaves) but prone to a nasty set of diseases.

At first glance, the members of the potato family (*Solanaceae*) don't seem to have much in common. The potato is the only root crop – all of the others bear edible fruit, including tomatoes, peppers and aubergines. The goji berry is in this family, too, along with physalis, huckleberries and tomatillos. It's when they flower that you can see the resemblance.

Carrots are members of the *Apiaceae*, often known as umbellifers. They're joined by celery and celeriac, parsnips and parsley, fennel and some of the more unusual roots such as skirret and Hamburg parsley. They can all be bothered by the carrot root fly, and again it's when they're allowed to flower that you can see the relationship between them.

Beetroot is the only root crop in the *Chenopodiaceae* family – its relations are spinach, chard and leaf beet, quinoa and Good King Henry. There are less commonly grown plants, too, such as strawberry spinach, orach and the common weed Fat Hen.

Lettuce is often one of the oddities in a crop rotation, but the *Asteraceae* family also includes chicory and endive, Jerusalem artichokes (and sunflowers) and the root crops salsify and scorzonera. Cardoons and globe artichokes make extremely large plants.

Plenty of plants don't fall into one of these families, including sweetcorn. Many herbs are unrelated to the main vegetables, as are some unusual crops – tiger nuts, for example, are in the papyrus family! It's worth trying to find out which family a plant belongs to, but generally unusual edibles are less prone to common pests and diseases.

The *Alternative* Kitchen Garden

S is for...

S is for...

Saffron

Saffron used to be grown in this country (hence Saffron Waldon), but these days it's mostly grown in countries around the Mediterranean and India. It's the world's most expensive spice, because it is very labour intensive to grow. The saffron crocus flowers grow three red stigmas – and it's these that are harvested by hand and dried to make saffron spice. The saffron crocus has been domesticated for so long that its flowers are sterile, and it can only reproduce via its corms.

Saffron is an oddity in the kitchen garden because it dies back and lies dormant in the summer, when in its native lands there would be a shortage of water. As the days get shorter (and wetter!) it bursts into leaf and flowers in the autumn.

In 2005 I ordered half a dozen saffron corms (*Crocus sativus*, be sure to get the right variety as some of the other Crocuses are poisonous) from eBay. I planted them up in pots and then pretty much forgot about them. They sent up spindly leaves, but didn't flower, and then in the summer they died back – which isn't an advantage in a container plant because I have a tendency to think they've died. But I'd labelled the saffron pots, so I just ignored them. In the autumn of 2007 I remembered them, and planted them into the raised bed in the Grow Dome, where they should be much happier. They've got nice deep soil (and they like to be planted deeply) and will be drier – which will keep them dormant in the summer and stop them from rotting away in the winter. True to form, they died back at the beginning of the summer and I'm just waiting to see whether they will survive and thrive in the autumn.

When you consider that the most I'm likely to get for my troubles is less than a handful of saffron each year (and saffron is notoriously picky about whether it flowers in gardens), it might seem like a waste of time. But I'm growing them for the interest value, and a handful of home grown saffron would be the icing on the cake. They're not exactly labour intensive plants, and they don't need any care at all when everything else in the garden is growing and demanding my attention, because they're asleep.

S is for...

Seeds

If you've never grown anything from seed then you may believe that it's difficult, but in actual fact seeds are designed to grow and growing plants from seed is easy. It's also a fascinating process. If you've never done it before then kit yourself out with a packet of cress seeds and some damp kitchen paper and watch a whole new world unfurl before your eyes. Caring for cress also gives you a crash-course in looking after seedlings as cress is very dependent on regular watering.

Most seedlings, grown in a shallow layer of compost, are a doddle if you can keep cress alive for several days.

The important thing with seeds is to sow them according to the instructions on the packet. They won't grow well at the wrong time of year or at the wrong temperature – especially if you're sowing them directly outside. They also won't grow well if you plant them at the wrong depth. Some need light to germinate (start growing), and some need darkness.

Unless you've got an allotment, a packet of vegetable seeds contains far more seeds that you can hope to use in one season. Most will keep, although some seeds are notoriously short-lived, including parsnips. Others stay healthy for years – leaf beet seed seems to be particularly indestructible, as are tomato seeds. You could always find someone to share with, or try and swap your spares for something else. Store your seeds somewhere dry and where the temperature doesn't fluctuate too much – so not in the greenhouse – and in a rodent-proof container.

I sow as many seeds as I can into modules, for two reasons. The first is that their roots are kept separate, which means that they're much easier to separate when it comes to planting out. The second is that I don't enjoy thinning out, which is the process whereby you decide which seedlings in your over-crowded seed tray are going to live, and which ones have to go on the compost. The temptation is always to try and save far more seedlings than you need, which just makes life harder down the line when you have to plant them out and care for them. Better to sow as few as possible and spare yourself the pain.

The main problem with raising plants from seed is a fungal disease called 'damping off'. It tends to affect seedlings growing in seed trays, especially if they're overcrowded. You'll check on them one morning and find that some have fallen over, with their stems rotting. If you don't remove them straight away then the others in the tray will follow suit. The only way to save your remaining seedlings is to prick them out - carefully lift each one out by its leaves and replant it in a new container with fresh compost and fewer neighbours.

To avoid damping off, use clean pots and seed trays and water your seedlings with tap water - let it warm up to room temperature first though, as they don't like cold showers. You can also use sterilised seed compost, although I never have. I have a secret weapon against damping off – I water my seedlings with weak (and cold!) chamomile tea. Chamomile has anti-fungal properties and helps to keep seedlings in fine fettle until they're past their vulnerable stage. I use organic chamomile tea bags to make the tea, but if you grow your own chamomile you can use the flowers.

S is for...

Seed Saving

A lot of gardeners save seeds from their ornamental plants. It's easy enough, you just shake the seed loose from the flower heads late in the year and either sow it straight away (for hardy annuals) or keep it dry until spring. It's a handy way of getting free plants, just like taking cuttings or dividing perennials.

Seed saving largely died out in kitchen gardens when seed became readily available from seed companies, but it's now making a comeback, and in many cases is not hard to do. By saving your own seeds you can save money, conserve heritage varieties and pass on your favourites to friends and neighbours. You'll have a supply of your chosen varieties even if the seed company stops selling them.

There are several factors to take into account if you want to save seed. The first is whether your plants are annual or biennial. Annual plants grow from seed, flower and set seed in one year; biennials overwinter and flower and set seed in their second year.

The second important factor is whether the plant is an inbreeder or an outbreeder. Inbreeders are naturally self-fertile, and generally pollinate themselves rather than attempting to cross-pollinate with other plants. As such, seeds from inbreeders are likely to grow into reliable copies of the parent plants. In some cases you need to take minimal precautions to protect inbreeders from cross-pollinating, but overall they're pretty easy.

Outbreeders are more problematic, especially if you're growing them somewhere where they are surrounded by other varieties (like on an allotment) as they'll cross-pollinate given half a chance and leave you with seeds that grow into very variable plants. They either need to be physically isolated and hand-pollinated, or separated from other varieties by large distances. You'll also need to save seeds from more plants to guarantee a decent gene pool.

The other considerations are how much space plants take up and how long you have to leave them in place – very important if you're trying to make the most of a small garden – and how easy the seeds are to extract, clean and store. Seeds range from tiny, fiddly things to enormous bean seeds. Some are produced dry, clean and ready to store and some of them have to be extracted from fleshy pulp or threshed from stems.

Although it might seem daunting, it doesn't have to be. A lot of seed saving can be done from happy accidents – radishes and brassicas that have run to seed, or flowers that you've forgotten to dead head. The first seeds I saved were from my achocha, which has hard, black seeds that are easy to remove. They were followed by the Welsh onions (hang them upside down in a paper bag to catch the seeds as they dry out) and the dwarf marigolds. In most cases you will have plenty of seed to share.

Seed swaps usually run at the beginning of the year, in February or March. Rules vary, but entry is often free if you have seed to swap, and then you can take home pretty much anything you want to. Sometimes there's an entry fee for people without seeds to swap. Some swaps only want home-saved seeds, others will accept anything – so check the rules before you go. If there isn't a seed swap near you then you could try running your own, perhaps at work or at the local fete.

S is for...

Shallots

Shallots are like little onions, used in stews and for pickling. They're often a gourmet choice for chefs and keen cooks. In the kitchen garden they're often grown from sets, just like onions, planted in the spring. Each shallot set will grow into a clump of shallots, rather than one big onion. You can also grow shallots from seed, but then each seed grows into one shallot.

I haven't mastered shallots yet. I've got some prized banana shallot seed that I found in a seed swap. Banana shallots have a longer shape than normal shallots, and are supposed to be even tastier. Seed is hard to find, sets non-existent and banana shallots in the supermarket are usually imported from France. I did sow some of the seed this year, and it germinated without any problems, but in the spring rush I forgot to plant them out and so they dwindled in their seed tray. My plan is to try again next year, grow plenty and let some run to seed so that I can pass on banana shallot seed to anyone who is having trouble tracking some down!

S is for...

Slugs and Snails

Standard slug pellets are horrible. Once they've poisoned the slugs they work their way up the food chain, poisoning anything that eats slugs. They're not safe for humans or pets and don't encourage a healthy set of beasties in the soil. It's easy to reach for them when the slugs have driven you to distraction, but it's better to control slugs in other ways to preserve the natural order in the garden.

Whenever I go outside I generally find a couple of intrepid snails that obviously haven't heard the stories…. We feed snails to the chickens. If they're too large we stamp on them first. Snails beware! The chickens eat small slugs, too. But even with two chickens on patrol, slugs still get the upper hand at times.

Ducks can be equally effective at munching their way through slugs, but if you don't have the space for livestock encourage wildlife into your garden – birds, hedgehogs, frogs, toads and slow worms will all be happy to feed on your pests. If you seem to be a little short on animal helpers then mobilise the human troops – there's nothing like a good slug hunt on a damp evening or early in the morning, although it does leave you with a slug disposal problem. Some people salt them, others take them down to the local duck pond as a treat for the ducks. The ones the chickens won't eat I tend to incarcerate in the compost bin, where they can do some good.

There are plenty of barriers you can try to prevent the slugs from getting to your plants. Broken eggshells, soot, sand, coffee grounds or cat litter – anything that's either uncomfortable for them to cross or sucks them dry. Copper barriers give slugs an electric shock when they try to cross them. You can also buy copper hand tools, the use of which is supposed to deter slugs generally.

You could also try protecting your plants (especially seedlings) with cloches, or surrounding them with a moat. Or use diversionary tactics and set up slug pubs – just sink a yoghurt pot into the ground and put some old beer (or milk, or yeast extract) in the bottom. The slugs go in, and they don't come out. Just remember to leave the rim of the pot slightly above the soil surface so that beneficial creatures don't fall in as well.

Try persuading your slugs to eat something else. A ring of bran around vulnerable plants seems to work, or wilted comfrey leaves, or you could try planting sacrificial crops – something the slugs love so much that they'll leave your vegetables alone. These 'trap' crops work well with hand collections, because you know where the slugs will be.

If slugs still get out of control and you want to play a more active role in killing them then you can get a biological control that is watered onto the soil in spring. It only kills young slugs, but it gives you a head start. It has to be applied when the weather conditions are right, because you're using living creatures that have their own needs.

Last of all, when you're tearing your hair out, you can resort to environmentally friendly slug pellets. They're used in the same way as the nasty ones, but they're safe for wildlife, humans and pets. When you're shopping for safe slug pellets, make sure you don't pick up the nasty ones by mistake.

S is for...

Squash

The only squash on the traditional British menu is marrow, and in most kitchen gardens marrows are only grown by accident – they're what you get when you go away on holiday and the neighbours don't keep up with harvesting your courgettes. To be fair, there are people who love marrow as a vegetable, but I've been put off by the horror stories of watery, over-boiled marrow that are part of our family history.

However, there is much more to squash than marrow. Summer squash (essentially oddly shaped courgettes) include patty pan squashes, which look like flying saucers and come in white, green or bright yellow. And there are oddly bobbly crookneck squashes, but in truth most squash can be eaten when they're young and treated as summer squash.

Winter squash are allowed to grow to their full size and have hard skins that mean they'll keep for months. We're not fond of winter squash in the UK, as a rule, and tend only to grow big, orange pumpkins for Halloween, and then throw the innards away. But more and more people are cottoning on to the joys of squash, from the mellow goodness of the butternut to the improbably named Uchiki Kuri.

Winter squash are big plants. Most of them trail and rapidly take over a small garden if you're not careful. You can encourage them to grow up a support – the best ones I've seen look like sturdy step ladders. Summer squash can be big plants too, but there are compact versions that can be grown in a large container.

Squash seeds are sown outside after the risk of frost has passed, or started indoors and planted out when the weather warms up. They need plenty of food and water to perform at their best, and if you're trying to grow a mammoth pumpkin for Halloween then you need to restrict the plant to one or two fruits.

If you have the space then it's easy to develop a squash obsession. Like French beans, there is a considerable weight of heritage varieties – all of which have their own unique charms. I fell for one that had pink fruits, with a smooth skin when they came off the plant that turned all bumpy and warty in storage. That was according to the packet, through, as I didn't manage to get one to fruit. I don't have the space for winter squash now, although they're still tempting.

It's easy to save seed from squashes as they have large seeds that are easily removed (as long as the fruit was ripe when it was harvested). Sometimes the seeds even start to grow inside the fruit. But squash plants are the floosies of the plant world – they'll happily swap pollen with any others within a large radius. If you want to be sure that your seeds grow true you'll have to isolate your squash plant to prevent bees from pollinating the flowers, and then pollinate them yourself.

Pollinating squash flowers is pretty easy. You should be able to identify female flowers because they have small fruits growing behind them. The male flowers don't, so you just pull off one of the male flowers and smoosh it into any female flowers you've found to transfer the pollen. Early on in the season it's quite normal to find that your plants are only growing male flowers. They'll sort themselves out over time, and then start to fruit.

S is for...

Strawberries

There can't be many things more evocative of a British summer than strawberries. Growing their own is a goal for many kitchen gardeners, but the problem with strawberries is that they're a magnet for all of the pests in the garden. Slugs and snails love them. Once they've damaged the skin the woodlice take over. Birds peck at them too, and when the weather turns wet (as it invariably does) then fruits rot, or grow that horrible fluffy grey mould.

If you do manage to grow a nice crop, it's worth it – strawberries picked fresh and ripe taste so much like strawberries that you'll start to wonder what those red fruits in supermarket punnets actually are.

One way to avoid slug and snail damage is to grow strawberries in containers. Strawberries make great container plants because they don't take up much room, and they're very attractive with lovely white flowers and trailing fruits. If you can keep up with the watering then you can even grow them in hanging baskets.

Those little strawberry pots with the holes in the sides are very pretty, but I've never found them much use for growing strawberries. You can get larger ones, called strawberry towers, which are even worse – it's almost impossible to get enough water to the plants at the bottom. If you're seriously into strawberry growing then you might want to investigate buying or making one of those contraptions that holds two or three growing bags up off the floor, protecting the fruits from slugs, snails and rots and making picking a doddle.

Traditional gardening wisdom states that you should replace your strawberry plants every three years, because they become tired and disease-ridden. In the first year you allow the plants to grow runners, and you can pot up those runners for a continuous supply of new plants without spending any more money. In their second and third year plants fruit well, and then you dig them up.

And at the end of each growing season you have to cut off all of the leaves and clear away all the plant debris so that the plants grow fresh, healthy leaves in the autumn.

I'm not a strawberry expert by any means, but I will let you into a secret – the healthiest strawberry plants I ever saw weren't grown like this. They were part of the ground cover planting in the RISC roof garden, and they were the original strawberries, planted when the garden was created. They'd been there for five years, left to their own devices, and looked beautiful (although I was there too early in the year for there to be any fruit) and have never been bothered by disease.

It is possible to grow strawberries from seed, although the only varieties I've seen are F1 hybrids and alpine strawberries. Strawberry seed is tiny, really fiddly, and it's a big challenge to sow it where you want it to grow. I have three different varieties of strawberry grown from seed (two F1 hybrids and one alpine) growing as ground cover in the goji bed, and they're settling in very well.

Alpine strawberries are nearer to being wild strawberries, with tiny fruits that grow a few at a time rather than all in one go. They make up for that by being very strongly flavoured, and a few go a long way. They don't spread by runners, so they're easy to keep under control.

The *Alternative* Kitchen Garden

T is for...

T is for...

Tea

Being quintessentially English, I do love a nice cup of tea. And these days I buy organic or fair trade, but that doesn't quite make up for the fact that it has travelled half way around the world. There is at least one tea plantation in Cornwall (where the mild microclimate suits the bushes) and in 2007 the people who make Yorkshire Tea were in the news for starting a plantation in Harrogate, but realistically we could never grow enough tea (*Camellia sinensis*) to keep up with demand.

However, we can supply our own herbs for herbal 'tea' (strictly speaking they're tisanes or infusions, not tea). The important thing to note about herbal tea is that it's usually made with boiled water that has been allowed to cool slightly before it's poured over the herbs – which stops too many of the essential oils (the good bits) from evaporating. Then you leave them to steep for 5-10 minutes, much longer than real tea unless you like it so strong you can stand a spoon up in it.

You may have to try a few different herbal teas to find one that you like. Mint (made with spearmint leaves) is very popular, as is chamomile, although neither of them appeal much to me. If you like them then they're very good for your stomach if you've eaten a large meal. My personal preference is for lemon balm, which makes a mild lemony tea that is good for soothing tummies, headaches and nerves and is nice if you've got a cold.

There are lots of other herbs that can be used for tea, which I have never tried. Rosemary tea is supposed to be good for hangovers, and you can use lemon grass for another lemony tea – although lemon grass is not hardy so you'll need to keep it under cover in the winter. You can also mix and match herbs, or add them to real green or black tea, until you find a blend that you enjoy. For most tea herbs you'll need to bring pots inside in the winter for a continuous supply, or dry the excess harvests over the summer.

On hot days you can make herbal teas without turning on the kettle, although it will take a while. Put your herb leaves into a clean, clear glass jar with a lid. Fill it with water, put the lid on, and leave it in the sun for a few hours – after which you'll have about the laziest cuppa you've ever made!

T is for...

Thigmomorphogenesis

I was listening to an old Radio 4 programme one morning, and I came across a new word – thigmomorphogenesis. It has to be one of the longest horticultural terms I've come across. I know some people are intimidated by long words, but I love this one, and it describes a very simple (and possibly common sense) principle – namely that plants grow differently when they're not exposed to the wind.

It's more of an issue in commercial greenhouses, where there's very little air movement, but in the absence of anything touching their leaves (usually the wind, but also rain and passing animals), plants grow taller and less strong. When the movement is replaced – by creating air currents, or lightly brushing plants – they grow shorter and stockier.

The only time when it might be a handy thing for a gardener to know is in the early spring, when you're raising lots of seedlings indoors. In the event that there's not much airflow, you might want to gently blow on your seedlings, or brush them with a piece of card, so that they grow up nice and big and strong. Your friends will think you're nuts, of course, but if you're there talking to your plants anyway, give them a bit of a workout at the same time!

T is for...

Thrive

Thrive is a UK charity that believes the benefits of gardening should be available to everyone, and that gardening can make a real difference in people's lives. Thrive runs three of their own horticultural therapy gardens, where people with special needs or who are recovering from illness or accidents, or who are just going through a rough period in their lives, can get their hands dirty and nurture plants.

They also offer advice and practical assistance to other therapeutic gardening projects, and to the general public – they have a special website dedicated to easier gardening, for people who find conventional gardening techniques difficult or hard work. They promote things like raised beds, table top gardens, and No Dig gardening.

If you're in the mood for fundraising, Thrive is a very worthwhile charity to support. When my seed box gets too full to close and I have to clear out my excess seeds, I always send them to the Thrive head office, as they can make use of spare seeds at all their gardening projects.

T is for...

Tiger Nuts

One of last year's experiments was Tiger Nuts (*Cyperus esculentus*), an edible tuber in the same plant family as papyrus. Tiger nuts were sometimes seen as a substitute for sweets during the Second World War, as they are small and quite sweet. They're not so easy to find nowadays, but you might be able to get some in the local health food shop. And as the tubers seem to be pretty much indestructible, the chances are you can get them to sprout if you want to try growing your own crop. You might also come across them in fishing tackle shops, as they can be used as carp bait.

I grew mine in two large pots. They're not frost hardy, so they have to be planted indoors, or outdoors only once the weather has warmed up. They're about the size of a pea and need to be planted about 5cm deep and about 15 cm apart. They don't mind being sown in modules and transplanted later. I tried pre-soaking my tiger nut tubers (as they looked pretty dry and wrinkled), but that had no obvious effect and it's probably not worth trying unless you're having trouble encouraging them to sprout.

Tiger nuts like being wet. If you've got a boggy patch in the garden then you could try growing them outdoors. I just popped plant saucers underneath my pots, and kept them topped up with water. They make quite vigorous plants, growing up to 60cm tall. If you like grasses then they're quite ornamental, although they rarely flower. They like quite fertile soil, but don't give them extra fertiliser as that encourages leafy growth rather than tuber production.

Tiger nuts are ready for harvesting when the leaves turn yellow or are cut down by frost. Growing them in containers makes harvesting much easier, as you can just tip them out – hunting around in cold wet mud for tiny tiger nut tubers doesn't sound like it would be much fun. The tubers are hard, very reminiscent of small pebbles.

From my two containers, I got what looked like a reasonable harvest of tiger nuts (about 200g in total). However, they were very hard and not at all sweet. They were fiddly to clean and not at all tasty. I don't know what went wrong, because tiger nuts are supposed to be nice (the Spanish grind them up and turn them into a drink called horchata), but they're not something I will be rushing to try again! I suppose they could be a handy crop if you're a carp fisherman…

T is for...

Tomatoes

If people only grow one vegetable then it tends to be tomatoes (although, botanically speaking tomatoes are fruit). I'm not a big fan of raw tomatoes, although judging by the horror on people's faces, every time I say that a fairy dies. In previous years I've grown a few cherry tomatoes, juiced them and fed the pulp to the chickens. Cherry tomatoes make very good container plants, even in window boxes and hanging baskets, because they're compact and bushy.

Cherry tomatoes also fruit earlier and more prolifically than their larger relatives.

Tomato plants are either determinate (bushy) or indeterminate. Indeterminate tomatoes are usually grown as cordons – essentially one tall stem from which fruiting trusses appear. To keep them growing as cordons, you have to support them and remove the side-shoots that appear between the main stem and the side branches. Side-shoots are vigorous, and unless you remove them when they're small they'll take over. You want the plant to concentrate on making and ripening tomatoes, not growing side-shoots.

The maintenance involved in cordon tomatoes is the main reason I never bother to grow any, but this year I've been involved in a Garden Organic experiment and I'm growing two different cordon tomatoes in the Grow Dome. One is Yellow Submarine (a modern variety) and the other is Yellow Queen (an older variety). So far the Yellow Submarine is fruiting more prolifically, but it's also a real thug of a plant, sending out side-shoots all over the place. I can't keep up with them and I'm starting to avoid the Grow Dome as a result. The Yellow Queens are far more well-behaved.

It's often recommended that you pinch out the growing tips of cordon tomatoes when they've set four trusses of fruit because later trusses of fruit don't stand much chance of ripening in an English summer, even if the plants aren't cut down by blight.

Blight is a fungal disease, rampant in warm, humid summers. Tomatoes grown outdoors are the first to succumb. Dark patches on the leaves quickly spread and plants collapse. You may be able to save some of the fruit, but it won't keep for long. Plants grown indoors survive for longer because they have drier leaves and aren't as exposed to the fungal spores, but even so they may not escape completely. Removing affected leaves as soon as you see them can help slow down the disease's progress, but there is no cure.

Cherry tomatoes often escape, and even if they do eventually become infected, it's easier to get a good crop of small tomatoes before blight really sets in (on humid days in late summer, usually).

Although they grow well in containers, tomatoes are thirsty and hungry plants. They like a continuous supply of water, especially when they're fruiting. An irregular water supply causes blossom end rot (where the bottom of the fruit starts to rot) and splitting. Tomatoes need a good supply of potassium to encourage fruiting, and so need a tomato feed, or your own comfrey liquid feed, regularly.

Tomatoes are another vegetable for which there is a huge range of varieties. They come in all shapes and sizes, from tiny cherries to huge beefsteaks (although they're more difficult to grow in our climate) and lots of different colours from white through to almost black. Seeds are easy to save, at least in small quantities, so if you discover something special you can carry on growing it every year.

T is for...

Tubers

Tubers are plant storage organs, generally underground, that keep plants alive when they're dormant and allow them to burst into life and grow leaves. They're formed out of modified plant stems, as are rhizomes (creeping underground stems) and corms. Other storage organs are formed from fleshy roots (e.g. carrots) and bulbs (made from modified leaves).

The most commonly grown, and easily recognisable, tuber is the potato.

Jerusalem and Chinese artichokes are also tubers, easy to grow although not as easy to find in the shops.

Many kitchen gardeners try their hands at sweet potatoes, which are tubers but from a different plant family from the common potato and hence not susceptible to blight. They need warmer conditions, however, and can be tricky in a poor summer if you don't have a greenhouse or polytunnel. Sweet potatoes are often grown in raised mounds covered in black plastic to soak up heat and help keep them warm. And they're grown from slips – essentially shoots – rather than seed potatoes.

There are several interesting tubers that are commonly grown in South America, but not here. I'm growing oca this year, and I also tried mashua (but the plants died). Ulluco and yacon are still on the list of things to try.

If you want something more oriental then you could try the Chinese yam or the water chestnut, both commonly grown in Asia but unusual here.

If you like surprises then tubers and root crops are great – because you rarely know how well they've done until it's time to dig them up! And there are plenty of unusual varieties to try.

With root crops you could go for one of the colourful varieties of carrot that are becoming more popular – the carrot was not orange when it was originally domesticated, and you can get everything from white through to purple and even packets of seeds in mixed colours. You can also get different colours of beetroot, white or yellow or even stripy, and beetroot varieties with very long roots instead of the usual spheres. I've already mentioned the huge variety of radishes available, and the unusual root Hamburg parsley.

For people with an interest in history, there's salsify and scorzonera – two long, dark roots that were more commonly grown in the past than they are now. Or you could try skirret, which was very popular in the 16th century

The *Alternative* Kitchen Garden

U is for...

U is for...

Umbellifers

Umbellifers are the family of plants that grow big heads of little flowers, in the shape of umbrellas. There are lots of them in the vegetable patch, but you won't normally see them flower, because they're biennials and we eat them before they get that far.

Carrots, parsnips and Hamburg parsley are all umbellifers, and we eat their roots. You'll only see them flower if you want to save seed, and leave them in the ground for a second season. Celery and celeriac are in the same family, and we eat their stems.

The ones you're more likely to see flower are the herb relatives – including parsley, angelica and fennel. It's easy to leave parsley in the ground long enough for it to flower, as it's a useful plant that will survive most winters to provide fresh herbs year round. By the time it flowers and runs to see, this year's plants will be well on the way. I've never grown fennel. It's a tall, very ornamental plant (it even comes in two colours – green and bronze). I don't have space for something that statuesque, and we don't like eating it anyway.

There are good reasons why you might want to let some umbellifers flower in your veg patch. Not only are they very ornamental (in fact, there are plenty of flowers in the umbellifer family), but their collections of small flowers are insect magnets. They'll be buzzing with garden helpers all summer long, and you might even spot some soldier beetles.

In fact, the umbellifer family (know formally known as the *Apiaceae*), are so numerous and varied that it would be hard to have any kind of garden without them.

U is for...

Undercover

Undercover gardening sounds like a lot of fun, doesn't it? Clandestine gardening in the dead of night, leaving flowerbeds that mysteriously seem to have blossomed overnight – amazing passing commuters. It's called Guerrilla Gardening. Guerrilla gardeners take responsibility for neglected spaces, planting shrubs and bulbs, weeding and removing litter. It is technically illegal but in public spaces it's unlikely to do more than raise an eyebrow. On vacant lots though you could be arrested for trespass, which is why some guerrilla gardeners use seed bombs, throwing them over fences so that 'waste' land can bloom again.

Fascinating though guerrilla gardening is, that wasn't what I meant by under-cover gardening. I meant the joys of having a sheltered space in which to grow your plants. Whether it's a greenhouse, polytunnel, or kitchen windowsill, undercover gardening allows you far more control over your growing environment.

The advantages are that you have somewhere nice and dry (if not warm) where you can garden when it's raining. I mean really raining, if it's just spitting then that's not enough to keep you indoors – it's refreshing. Just think of those cosmetic companies who try and sell you a bottle of water to spritz on our face to get the same effect. And you have somewhere where the rain won't drown your seedlings, the wind won't shred them and the local cats won't stomp all over them. The slugs may still get them, though. If we ever colonise other planets, we'll have problems with slugs in our hydroponic systems.

I raise almost all of my seedlings under cover. I've got some indoors now (in August, but in my defence it has been raining all month), for winter salads. In here I can keep an eye on them, make sure they're happy. Outside I have a tendency to forget about them, and they have to take their chances. After years of selective breeding, vegetables aren't really used to going it on their own. The problem is that I've developed a slight phobia of sowing seeds outside. I can't imagine that they will survive. I have tried. An entire bed of carrot seedlings disappeared (slugs). The camassia seedlings, as previously mentioned, were neglected to death.

Which leads me to the point I'm trying to make. Undercover gardening is great. I love my greenhouse, and I love watching seedlings unfurl indoors. But undercover gardening is no substitute for the real thing. There's no pleasure in having a greenhouse, but no garden. You can't watch the seasons unfold in the same way. You won't have the wildlife, and any bees you hear buzzing will be butting their heads against the glass, trying to find a way out.

We live very indoor lives, and it can be hard to break the habit and go outside as often as we should. But more importantly, we need to let go of the feeling that we have to be in control of everything. That nothing happens on the planet without human interference. That everything in the garden has to be perfect, or it's not worth the effort. We need to appreciate that the weather is unpredictable, that it's not possible for all of our crops to be perfect every year, and that some of our treasured seedlings might not make it. When we let go of our (apparent) control, we open ourselves up to randomness and chance. Those aren't very positive words in our vocabulary, so I'll try a different one – serendipity. Poke your head outside, relax your control over the garden, and watch it develop in its own serendipitous way.

U is for...

Undersowing

Undersowing is simply sowing seeds of a low growing plant underneath a taller one. It happens naturally in woodlands, with small plants making use of the light that filters through the leafy canopy – even if it's only for part of the year.

In garden terms it's most often used to describe the use of a living mulch under a crop. When there's more than one crop involved, people tend to use the term undercropping instead.

A living mulch has all the benefits of any other kind of mulch – it protects soil structure by covering bare soil, prevents nutrient leaching heavy rain and slows evaporation in dry weather. A living mulch also hinders weed growth, and can add to the fertility of the soil (particularly if it's a nitrogen-fixing plant).

There's also possible benefits from avoiding a monoculture – confusing pests and diseases so that they don't find the crop as easy a target.

The important thing with undersowing is not to let the mulch interfere with the growth of the crop. Orchards are often grassed over, with the grass effectively undersowing the fruit trees, but the grass has to be managed so that it doesn't steal all the nutrients and compete with the trees. If you've got sheep then they can be allowed to graze in the orchard and return some of the fertility to the soil; if you haven't then you'll have to get the mower out, and leave the grass cuttings as a mulch. In gardens, trees are more often grown with a ring of mulched soil around them to the drip line (the point to which the leaf canopy extends), to avoid competition with the grass.

In the vegetable garden, trefoil can be used for undersowing, although you may need to take action to prevent it from becoming too vigorous. You could also try clover. If you've got perennial plantings (such as fruit bushes) then they can benefit from being undersown with a winter hardy nitrogen fixer in the autumn – with the green growth cut down and left on the soil surface in spring, to feed the bush.

U is for...

Unusual

I can't tell you exactly why I love growing unusual edibles, because I don't know. I suspect it's a combination of a lot of factors. When I started gardening I was very much an armchair gardener, with more room in my head for ideas than there was room in the garden for plants. That's always going to be the case, I fear. And my lifestyle at the time was one of pretty conspicuous consumption and I was driven to collect gardening books and seeds and plants in the hope that they would make up for the deficit in other areas of my life.

Things have changed now, but I still love unusual edibles. If you think of a well-balanced life as a series of small moments, then gardening (of any kind) has the potential to fill it with the kind of "oh, wow!" moments that memories are made of. Ornamental gardeners will see a perfect bloom, or remember the scent of a old-fashioned rose. Kitchen gardeners enjoy the sight of a plate of steaming vegetables being tucked into by their loved ones, or the simple joy of digging up your potato plants and finding... potatoes!

I'm not immune to any of those things, but I choose my plants the same way I choose the people in my life – for their individuality. I'm not one to anthropomorphise, but plants have what amounts to a personality, a collection of traits that sets them apart from the others.

Achocha is vigorous, fearless in its explorations and very private – its flowers are tiny and pale, and it hides its green fruits among plentiful foliage. But it's also very hospitable, providing a friendly welcome for all the hoverflies in the garden.

Peppers are some of my favourite plants. To begin with, they're attractive but restrained. Glossy green leaves, grown at regular intervals, are followed by small white flowers. Only when they're ready do they display their true colours and put on a spectacular display.

Oriental brassicas are speed freaks. They shoot up out of the ground, linger just long enough to bulk up a bit, and then flower in a shower of yellow fireworks.

Jerusalem artichokes are practical jokers. They spring up from the ground and then sway in the wind like a jack-in-the-box. If you're lucky then they'll show you sunny yellow faces, but it's later in the year that you discover their true passion – fart jokes!

The kiwi seems to be a real cutey – all furry leaves and cuddly. I don't know the kiwanos well yet, but they're already out-growing their support, and very hearty plants. There's no comparison between them and the tiny, straggly mouse melons.

Growing a new plant is like meeting a new person. It takes time to find out what they're really like, and whether they're going to be a permanent resident, a frequent visitor, an occasional guest or simply a passing acquaintance.

U is for...

Urine

One of the most popular episodes of the Alternative Kitchen Garden show was one I did on Pee (episode 29). It sticks in people's minds, for some reason! Dealing with human waste is a topic that a lot of people are squeamish about, but it's one that we have to keep on top of if we want to stay healthy and keep the planet healthy.

Leaving aside the more thorny issue of solid human waste (which is admirably covered by books such as The Toilet Papers and the Humanure Handbook), there's no real reason why we can't all make more use of our urine. At the moment we use it to contaminate our drinking water, leading either to energy-intensive denitrification processes down at the water treatment plant, or pollution of our rivers and streams.

Instead we could use it as a sustainable source of nitrogen fertiliser (and other minerals) for our gardens, and avoid all that wasted water and energy. And although it might sound like a step back in time, it's actually a space age solution – NASA has used urine in their hydroponics systems.

Pathogen levels in fresh urine are low, and you can't give yourself a disease you don't already have by coming into contact with your urine. There are, however, some things to bear in mind before you start splashing it around the garden.

The first is that urine is acidic and can be salty. As with so much of life, too much of a good thing can be a problem, and urine should be used in moderation. Spread it around, don't concentrate it on one or two plants – especially if they're in containers. For the same reason, don't add it to your worm composters.

Use it fresh – once urine starts to smell then the nitrogen it contains is turning into ammonia gas and escaping. Not only is fresh urine far more pleasant to handle, it's also more nutritious for your plants.

Neat urine is incredibly strong. So strong, in fact, that it can be used as a weedkiller. If you're trying to feed plants rather than blast them, you need to dilute it with at least five parts water. 10:1 is probably better for most plants, and definitely for young ones.

And when you're feeding your garden with urine, don't forget that you should only use nitrogen fertilisers on plants that will appreciate the boost. Leafy vegetables in spring will love it; later in the year too much nitrogen will encourage leafy growth in place of fruit production, and soft growth that won't last long in harsh weather.

If you don't fancy wandering around the garden with a watering can full of wee, then there is another option with the same benefits. You can compost urine, adding all of the nutrients to your home-made compost. Urine adds a lot of nitrogen to a compost heap and if you've got lots of woody stuff or 'browns' to compost then it makes an ideal compost activator. How the urine gets onto the compost heap is up to you – but if you have an urban garden then don't forget you have neighbours!

The *Alternative* Kitchen Garden

V is for...

V is for...

Vacciniums

The *Vaccinium* plant family includes lots of fruit bushes – most notably blueberries and cranberries, but there are plenty more and some (including the cowberry and the bilberry) are native to Britain.

All of the *Vacciniums* need acidic (ericaceous) soil, which I don't have – and so I have to grow them in containers of ericaceous compost. And make sure that the pH of the compost doesn't rise, by adding sulphur chips each season and trying to water them only with rain water (which hasn't been a problem this year!).

Blueberries are said to be easy to grow in containers, and to a certain extent this is true. They are naturally bushy plants that don't mind being contained. However, they do need a lot of water, and for someone as shy of the watering can as myself, that can be a problem. In my experience, a blueberry that is short of water doesn't look any different to a blueberry that's perfectly happy. What happens is that it loses its foliage as normal in the winter, and then dies. It doesn't look any different to a dormant blueberry, but it won't be making any kind of comeback in the spring. In a dry summer you'll need a big water butt and a regular watering routine to keep your blueberries happy.

Blueberries tend to crop better if you have two different varieties for pollination. They are also an absolute magnet for birds, so you will need to net them if you want to eat any of the fruit yourself. The birds will eat them long before you think they're ready – which is when they're a deep blue colour with a whitish bloom.

They seem to be unfazed by everything other than birds and drought, and rarely bothered by disease. Although they need quite large containers, they don't grow a dense canopy of leaves, and so you can make more productive use of the space by growing them with a low-growing relative like the cranberry. The cowberry (also known as the lingonberry) can be put to the same use. They both also make good ground cover plants – if you have the right sort of soil.

I've killed off two or three blueberries over the years, but I currently have three healthy ones (living in the fruit cage), so I think I've cracked it. I'm still waiting for a harvest large enough to be worth bringing back to the kitchen (Pete loves blueberries and will happily eat them straight from the bush), but the signs are hopeful. As with any soft fruit, it takes a while for the bushes to settle in and mature before they're ready to produce large crops.

V is for...

Vegan

Animal products (and by-products) abound in organic gardening. There's bulky manure, poultry manure pellets, packets of 'blood, fish and bone' and 'hoof and horn', all designed to return nutrients to the soil that have been taken out in crops. Using animals to replace fertility has been the standard, pretty much, for as long as people have been growing things.

But there are plenty of people who, for a wide variety of reasons, don't want to use animal products in their lives, and that includes in their gardens. And there's no need for them to turn to synthetic products instead – there's a whole area of vegetable gardening known as 'vegan organics' that aims to keep vegetable gardens in good heart without using animal products.

Most of the techniques used for vegan gardening have been mentioned already, because they're good gardening practise for any organic gardener. Vegan gardeners need a good supply of home-made compost, and a comfrey patch and a supply of nettles can be turned into hearty liquid feeds. Green manures can be worked into the crop rotations to rest the soil and add fertility, as well as bringing all the other benefits of weed suppression and soil improvement. And every gardener brings with them an almost inexhaustible supply of nitrogen fertiliser – their urine.

Even if you need, or want, to buy in additional fertilisers, vegan options are available. It's now possible to buy comfrey liquids, or comfrey pellets, and seaweed feeds and meals. The Organic Gardening Catalogue also carries fertiliser pellets made from alfalfa, comfrey and seaweed and have an animal-free fertiliser based on soy.

And as most vegetarians will want to grow a plentiful supply of beans (and peas and other legumes), they'll have plenty of help from nitrogen-fixing bacteria. When you clear away your pea and bean plants at the end of the season, remember to leave the roots in the soil, so any excess nitrogen that has been collected will feed the next crop, and the soil bacteria will be ready and waiting to help with the next bean crop. If you're starting a new garden, it might be worth spending a few pounds on packets of suitable bacteria (often called bean boosters) to kick start the process – it's something you should only need to do once.

V is for...

Vegetative Propagation

Plants don't necessarily have to flower and set seed to reproduce themselves. They can also do so vegetatively, which is what we're encouraging them to do when we take cuttings, divide established perennials or try and get them to layer.

Vegetative propagation is often used for perennials, but is also used to reproduce plants that are slow growing (and take a long time to mature from seed) and those that are difficult to grow from seed. There are also named varieties of plants that don't come true from seed, and hence have to be propagated vegetatively. It's often the case for variegated plants, seedlings of which tend to revert to being plain green. And there are some plants that don't normally set seed at all – I've mentioned at least two already, saffron and garlic.

Division is pretty straight forward. You dig up a mature perennial plant, and chop the root ball into chunks. I've done it with small plants, like mint, but it's still quite a tough job. The traditional way to do it is to insert two garden forks, back to back, into the rootball and then lever them apart. You can also chop through with a spade. Each root chunk can be replanted to make a new plant.

Taking cuttings involves cutting of a piece of a plant and then encouraging it to root and grow into a whole new plant. There are lots of different types of cutting, taken at different times of the year, from soft cuttings in the spring through to root cuttings (used for comfrey). There is a preferred method for propagating every plant, and a good book on propagation is a must if you want to get seriously involved.

Layering is when a branch of the plant forms roots where it touches the ground. Blackberries are famous for it, but there are plenty more plants that can be encouraged to root this way. You can even air-layer some plants (usually house plants) by wounding a branch and then encasing the wound in a plastic bag of compost. Once it has started to root you can sever it from the parent to become a new plant.

Grafting is almost always done for fruit trees. Wood from a named variety of fruit tree is attached to a root stock with known qualities – often vigour, or disease resistance. The grafted wood governs the fruit that is produced, but the rootstock decides how large the mature tree will be.

Some plants (again, mainly houseplants) reproduce themselves vegetatively without much help from us. The classic example is the spider plant, which grows plantlets at the end of long stems. If they touch the soil they will root, or they can be removed and potted up to make separate plants. Plenty of succulents are almost as easy, and will grow new plants from leaves that fall off, or root from stems that break off. Plant a leaf from an African violet, and eventually it will grow tiny plantlets – each one of which can be potted up to make a new plant.

In the vegetable garden, vegetative propagation is most obvious in the plants that grow from tubers – like potatoes and Jerusalem artichokes. Planting one tuber leads to a plant that grows many more tubers. Clumping onions do something very similar with their bulbs.

V is for...

Vermiculture

Vermiculture is worm composting. My first worm composter was a Can-O-Worms. They're a bit of an investment, but mine has lasted over six years, so they are worth it. The Can-O-Worms is round and comes with three stacking trays that sit on top of a base unit with a tap, and legs to keep it all off the ground. It also has a lid with air holes.

    I inherited a second wormery (a Waste Juggler, it's like a small wheelie bin) from a family member who stopped using it after two tragic accidents – a freezing and a drowning. Worms need similar conditions to ourselves. They don't like getting too hot, or too cold. Although they live in wet conditions, they breathe air and can drown. Kitchen waste is largely water, which is why the wormery has a tap. Most wormery owners learn to leave the tap open, with a bucket underneath to catch the run off. It makes a superb liquid plant feed, diluted with water to the colour of weak tea.

Composting worms aren't earthworms, they're a different species of worm that doesn't make burrows in the soil, and eats decomposing organic matter – which makes them perfect for life in a composter. They're often known as red wigglers, because they're a darker shade of red than earthworms, and they wriggle a lot.

Red wigglers love vegetable kitchen waste – tea bags, coffee grounds, vegetable peelings and rotten fruit. They also like cardboard and newspaper. Crushed eggshells help to keep the pH in the wormery high – worms don't like acidic conditions. You can also use garden lime to balance out the pH, as you might in a normal compost bin.

Worms don't like spicy food, or greasy food. And you shouldn't add meat, dairy or fish products to the wormery. They can poison the worms, and make for a very nasty wormery environment.

When you set up a wormery, the worms explore their new habitat for a few days, after which they call it home. If your worms are happy then they stay in the bin. It's warm, dark and moist – it's a five star worm hotel. If they're climbing up the insides of the bin then they may be unhappy with the service you're providing. If the contents of the wormery are very wet, make sure the tap is working properly and drain off any excess liquid. Add shredded paper or cardboard to even things out. If the waste is very dry, add some water. If it looks just right, then you might have a problem with the pH. If you've got a pH meter, you can check it. Otherwise try adding some lime or crushed eggshells to the mix and cut down on adding acidic foods like onion waste and citrus peel.

If the food waste is going putrid before the worms compost it, then you're adding it too fast. If you have a problem with flies wrap kitchen waste in newspaper before you add it, or add a layer of newspaper or shredded paper to the top of the bin.

I empty out my wormeries about every six months. I have stopped trying to remove every worm from the finished compost; escapees will do some good in the garden and the wormery population recovers in time. Worm compost is very nutritious, and can be dug into the soil or used as a mulch, as part of a potting mix, or as a top dressing for containers.

V is for...

Vines

In January 2007 I went on a little bit of a shopping spree to a certain high street store that sells cheap fruit trees and bushes (it seems they're branching out!). For around £20 I bought a redcurrant, three tayberries, a kiwi, a gooseberry and a couple of vines. Oh, and a pair of asparagus crowns. Not all of the plants survived a year in containers, but the remaining ones were planted out this spring. One of the tayberries fruited, the other is still catching up. The redcurrant grew one string of fruits, which the birds took because it was left outside the fruit cage. The kiwi, the gooseberry and the asparagus all died.

I planted the two vines out last autumn, in the chicken run orchard, up against the fence. They weren't impressive specimens, being little more than twigs. This spring, I thought they had died. I didn't dig them up, though, and eventually they did start to leaf out – it turns out that it takes a long time for the spring sunshine to reach the back of the chicken run.

It's now August and we've just noticed that one of the vines has sent up a tall shoot on the wrong side of the fence – in our neighbour's garden. On my side of the fence they're still much shorter, and the other one is having trouble latching onto the fence. For some reason the chickens don't seem to eat vine leaves, though, so they have a chance at surviving.

I have one white grape and one red (a Sauvignon blanc and a Cabernet sauvignon). I'm told that they're not the best varieties I could have chosen, may be prone to disease and may not produce any grapes worth eating. The instructions say they like well-drained soil, which is something in very short supply in my clay-rich garden. But they survived one wet winter, so they may do just fine. And if they don't grow any grapes then we'll just have to develop a taste for dolmades!

V is for...

Vine Weevils

There are very few creatures for which I don't have a good word to say. Slugs and snails do important work in the garden, helping to decompose organic matter. Aphids and similar small insects provide food for ladybirds and birds. Caterpillars grow up to be beautiful moths and butterflies. But there's nothing nice about vine weevils.

Vine weevils are black beetles. They have big feet that point out to the side, which makes them look rather comical, but they feed on the foliage of plants.

They particularly like plants that are in containers, for some reason. They take distinctive notches out of the edges of leaves, but it's their offspring that do the real damage. Vine weevil larvae live underground, and they eat plant roots. A bad infestation could easily kill a container-grown plant, especially a young one.

There's an easy rule of thumb to remember with beetles – if it's fast moving then it's likely to be predatory and one you should encourage in the garden. If it's slow moving then it's almost certainly there to munch on the plants, which don't give it much of a reason to run.

If you see adult vine weevils, step on them (or feed them to your chickens!). But then you'll know that you have vine weevils, and need to take steps to prevent the larvae from devastating your patio pots. I try to remember to put a layer of newspaper over the drainage holes in the bottom of my pots as I fill them. Not only does it prevent the soil from falling out, but I think it helps prevent ants and vine weevils from climbing in and making themselves at home. For a long term container planting, you could use something that will last longer, like an old cotton t-shirt.

There is a biological control for vine weevils, and this is where organic gardeners score points because the chemical controls for vine weevils can't be used on edible plants or on open soil. The biological control is simply watered into the pots, and takes care of the larvae for you – it's a parasitic nematode (a microscopic worm). It doesn't kill the adults, though, so you'll have to do that.

If you encourage wildlife into your garden, then you'll have an army of little helpers to control vine weevils for you. Birds, frogs & toads, shrews and hedgehogs will all eat vine weevils, given the chance. As will some of those speedier, predatory beetles.

There is another creature in the garden that deserves no mercy. Red spider mites are horrible things. They suck the life out of plants, leaving behind nothing but dead leaves and tiny webs. They like dry conditions, but even so are most likely to be seen in the greenhouse, attacking prized specimens like my nectarine tree and the pepper plants. Keeping humidity high by damping down the floors and regular watering helps to deter them.

Red spider mites can be killed with a fatty acid based spray (but so can some beneficial insects, so you have to be careful when and where you spray). They attack stressed plants more rapidly, so if you have some then either help them to perk up or compost them before they infest everything else. There is a biological control for red spider mite, too, but it can only be used when the temperature conditions are right, so read the instructions before you buy a packet (biological controls have a short shelf life). Oh, and there are two different sorts of red spider mite – one which lives outdoors and the one which infests greenhouses. And they're not red all the time, either. But they are always mites.

The *Alternative* Kitchen Garden

W is for...

W is for...

Water

During dry weather the hosepipes come out and garden water consumption soars. If there's a hosepipe ban in place then lawns parch, plants wilt and tempers flare, but there are lots of things you can do to make your garden more water-wise.

   The first step is to collect rainwater, which is best for plants anyway. The next is to look at your soil. Adding organic matter helps to store water in the soil and, paradoxically, allows soil to drain properly. Mulches help slow evaporation from the soil surface and prevent heavy rainfall from damaging the soil structure.

Grey water is water that has been used for washing up, bathing or laundry. It contains dirt and detergents and can't be stored without being filtered. It can be used to save ornamental plants and trees during droughts, but shouldn't be used on vegetable plants because of the bacteria it contains. Grey water makes a great addition to dry compost heaps.

Water that has only been used for washing vegetables can be used anywhere in the garden. And there are also places that we waste clean water that could be collected. Some people place a bucket in the shower while they're waiting for the water to warm up; I do the same at the kitchen sink. It's an eye-opening thing to do, as you'll be amazed how much water comes out of the tap in the few seconds it takes to run hot.

Small changes to your watering habits can make a big difference to your water requirements. Water early in the morning or during the evening to avoid evaporation during the heat of the day. Water onto the soil, not plants. For large plants it can be helpful to sink a flower pot (or a cut-off plastic bottle) into the soil to direct water to the roots where it is needed.

The fine spray produced by sprinklers encourages evaporation and they indiscriminately water the area around them, even if it's a hard surface. Get yourself a hose with a trigger gun instead, so that water only goes where it's needed.

In most cases it is better to water plants well once or twice a week than a little bit every day. Plants will send out deep roots, looking for water, and be more drought tolerant. Watering every day encourages the growth of roots near the soil surface, where they are more affected by dry weather.

Check the water level in the soil before you water. The soil surface will look dry, but if you push your finger into the soil you may find that it's still damp lower down.

Water should be rationed out to the plants that need it most. First on the list should be seedlings and any plants that have just been planted out. Once they're established they can survive longer without water, but if you want good crops then they need more water when they're flowering or fruiting or otherwise cropping.

Some crops are more drought tolerant than others. Perennial plants such as asparagus and rhubarb survive for longer without water. Fruit trees and bushes normally survive too, although a dry summer affects yields. Underground crops are also water-wise: Jerusalem artichokes, beetroot, carrots, parsnips, swedes and turnips, onions, garlic and shallots can all be placed lower down on the watering hierarchy. Leaf beet and chard are tougher plants than many other leafy veg and survive weather that causes lettuce and spinach to wilt or bolt.

W is for...

Watercress

A couple of months ago Pete and I took a short trip out to the edge of the Chilterns to see what was once a commercial watercress farm. Streams running off chalky hills are the natural home of watercress, and watercress farms were once common in suitable locations all across the country.

Ewelme (pronounced Ewe-elm) watercress beds went out of business in the 1980s, a victim of the modern food supply system that can easily provide fresh vegetables from all over the world, every day of the year. Prior to that, watercress was a staple vegetable and prized for its nutritional value.

After a decade or so of neglect, the Ewelme watercress beds are being restored as a heritage site and a wildlife sanctuary. The beds themselves have been cleared, although the watercress is not now sold. The simple dams that regulate the water flow have been repaired, and a new bridge gives access to the wildlife areas on the other side of the stream. On the days that the site is open, it's also a great place to get a cup of tea and a big slice of home made cake.

Work continues to enhance the wildlife value of the site, but it is already home to a population of water voles, more than 20 species of butterfly, and 65 species of birds.

Watercress grows wild in parts of the UK, but it's not always safe to forage – watercress can be contaminated by liver flukes, a parasite that lives part of its life in sheep and then passes into the water and the watercress via their droppings. If the affected watercress is eaten, the liver flukes can be passed on to humans.

On a brighter note, there are now varieties of watercress that can be grown in the garden – without a supply of running water. They can be grown in containers, given a plentiful supply of water. The usual recommendation is to sit the pot in a saucer and keep topping up the saucer with fresh water. You may also be able to root stems of watercress from bunches bought in the supermarket, simply by putting them in a glass of water for a few days.

I grew watercress for the first time this summer, in a small trough with a built-in water reservoir at the bottom. It grew very well, and we used it to make a very green and tasty soup with some frozen peas and mint from the garden. You can also eat it as a salad vegetable. Later in the season it's quite ornamental as it's covered in tiny white flowers.

An alternative to watercress, more suitable for those in dry conditions, or as a winter crop, is land cress (sometimes known as American land cress). It has a very similar growing habit and flavour and can be sown in late summer for autumn and winter crops.

W is for...

Weeds

Weediness is in the eye of the beholder – one person's weed is another's ornamental or useful plant. I considered the brambles at the bottom of my garden weeds. They made picking blackberries a doddle, and secured the bottom of my property, but were taking up space I wanted to use for something else.

Many people would consider nettles weeds. I consider them a wildlife habitat and a source of compost goodness. Until recently, nettles were used for food and herbal medicine and as a source of fibre for clothing and rope.

The daisies in my driveway could be considered weeds. When we moved in there were one or two, but I have selectively pulled up the dandelions and left the daisies and they have spread into pillowy drift and look lovely.

One of the big questions people have about organic gardening is how you deal with weeds. And while it's true that there are no instant weed solutions that doesn't mean that organic gardeners spend countless hours on their knees weeding. Nor does it mean that all weeds are tolerated – weeds are unwelcome where they are in competition with your plants for light, nutrients and water, are unsightly or are providing a host for pests and diseases.

The first stage in organic weed control is understanding what you're dealing with. Perennial weeds are some of the hardest to remove, but knowing how the plant reproduces is the key to stopping it doing just that.

Brambles, in one sense, are easy. If you dig out the root ball then they don't come back. Established brambles layer themselves – branches that touch the ground root and form a new plant. Bramble thorns make clearing them a chore; thick gloves and persistence win the day.

Japanese knotweed was introduced as an ornamental plant, but has become an 'alien invader' to the point that disposing of it incorrectly is an offence. Killing it involves digging out the crowns, but you'll have to contact your local authority to find out how to dispose of the plant material – it can't go on the compost heap because it just keeps growing.

Bindweed, couch grass and dandelions are some of the plants that spread from sections of root or underground stem. Digging them out is a painstaking business, but you can also try and starve them by cutting off their supply of sunlight. Plastic sheeting or weed control fabric is the best mulch to use, because there are few gaps that the plants can grow through – but you'll need to leave it down for a couple of years.

Annuals and biennials are easier to remove, but harder to prevent. The trick is to prevent them from flowering and setting seed. A thick mulch over the soil surface prevents weeds seeds from germinating, and No Dig gardening avoids bringing buried seeds to the surface.

Hand weeding, or hoeing, keeps weeds under control in areas where you don't have a mulch. You can put annual weeds (as long as they're not flowering, setting seed, or diseased) in the compost, but perennial weeds are more problematic. Send them for commercial composting (which guarantees to kill weeds and diseases) or incarcerate them in a plastic bag until they die, or drown them in a bucket, and then add the resulting mess to the compost heap.

W is for...

Welsh Onions

In late spring or early summer, my garden lights up as fluffy white flower heads the size of golf balls appear all over the place. The bees go mad and some of the raised beds become virtual no-go areas until the flowers have faded and the bees move on. At that point I have to dead head the flowers and remove them from the garden if I don't want seeds sowing themselves all over the place and a hundred more plants springing up next year. If I want to save seeds to pass on to other gardeners, then I simply hang a few flower heads upside down in a paper bag, and the seeds drop out as the flowers dry out.

The source of this bounty – flowers, bees and seeds – is an edible plant, the Welsh onion. It's a perennial onion, growing in neat clumps. It sends up pointy, hollow leaves, about a foot tall, almost all year round. You can chop them up as green onions, or pull up some of the small bulbs as salad onions. However you choose to eat them, you can have onion flavour from the garden all year round with very little effort. The only time you can't harvest them is when the flowers are out and the bees get their turn.

Welsh onion seeds are usually in the herbs section of seed catalogues. They're very easy to grow, being unfussy about soil and location. You don't even need to bother watering them. I keep meaning to sow the seeds I collect in a bed or a container, and then harvest the plants young instead of spring onions, which I find quite difficult to grow (ask every gardener, no matter how experienced, and there are always plants they struggle with).

The only problem I have with Welsh onions in my garden is that they're a magnet for slugs and snails. If I go on a slug and snail hunt then they're the first place I look. They don't do much damage to the Welsh onions, but they seem to use them as a base of operations for attacks on other plants. The chickens know this too, and regularly patrol the Welsh onions when they're free ranging in the garden.

Welsh onions will happily grow in containers, and are very ornamental when they flower. And, like spring onions, you can get two different bulb colours – the normal 'white' Welsh onions, and the more unusual 'red'.

W is for...

Wildlife

When asked to think about wildlife, a lot of people come up with tigers, pandas, orang-utans, or something equally exotic and endangered. If pressed for something closer to home, they might think of foxes, badgers, kestrels and sparrows. But the truth of the matter is that most wildlife is invisible – it's either too tiny, too shy or too rare to be seen, or it simply lives underground.

This hidden wildlife plays a vital role in the garden ecosystem. Soil animals, microbes and fungi do so many things that we have yet to figure them all out. They certainly move nutrients around the place, improve the soil structure, and break down organic matter and even poisons and toxins. Plants don't live in isolation, they form relationships with other organisms and are much healthier when allowed to do so.

There's a whole range of garden creatures that are slightly easier to see. Slugs, snails and woodlice might not be the most welcome garden visitors, but they also have an important part to play in breaking down organic matter and feeding nutrients into the bottom of the garden food web. Then there's beetles, millipedes, centipedes, moths, butterflies, flies, spiders and other arachnids, tiny mites and a lot of other things that you don't get to hear about unless you're friends with an entomologist.

The point is that the easiest way to encourage wildlife – birds, reptiles, mammals and amphibians – is to make sure you're a good host to all of the unseen creatures in your garden. They're the ones driving the ecosystem, making sure there's plenty of food available. Make them happy, and everyone else will turn up to the party.

Since chemical fertilisers and pesticides damage the soil ecosystem, it's best to stop using them and garden organically. Soil organisms will flourish, your plants will be healthier (although not instantly, there will be a time lag as the ecosystem restarts itself) and you'll find yourself with more of the critters that larger animals like to eat.

You can also make homes for wildlife. You don't need to invest in purpose-built condos; try leaving that corner at the bottom of the garden to run wild, don't be too hasty when you're clearing up the garden at the end of the season, and make sure you have a compost heap (basically an all-you-can-eat buffet for the things that eat decomposing organic matter). If you have the space then plant a hedge or build a pond – but make sure it has sloping sides so that animals that fall in have a chance of getting out.

Dot some rocks and the occasional log pile around the place – both are good for nooks and crannies, and rotting wood is one wildlife habitat that's generally missing from gardens.

Birds will appreciate natural sources of food in the autumn – seed heads that haven't been removed, shrubs that grow tasty berries. Butterflies and bees are grateful for a succession of flowers from early spring right through to the first frosts.

Although it's good to garden with wildlife in mind, you don't need to worry too much or try and cram every possible habitat into your garden. Have a look at the neighbouring gardens and see what's available there – there could be plenty of trees and ponds without you adding one to your garden. Your local wildlife is likely to either live out its entire life without ever wondering what lies beyond your fence, or to roam around the neighbourhood with no respect for property boundaries.

W is for...

Window Boxes

One of the earliest garden books I read was *Window-box Allotment* by Penelope Bennett. It encourages people with tiny spaces to grow some of their own food, and manages to encompass the magic and wonder of plants – from the moment they unfurl their first tiny leaves to the contribution they make when they slowly rot down on the compost heap.

I persuaded Pete to put up some window boxes for me. There are four long ones at the front of the house, where for the last couple of years I have grown cherry tomatoes and marigolds during the summer. Last autumn I replanted them with violas and curly leaved parsley.

At the back of the house Pete put up eight smaller window boxes, in what I now call the window box wall. This year I used two to raise my leek seedlings, out of the reach of slugs (but not snails!). I also filled two pots with sorrel seedlings, which have done very well, but one morning when I went outside I saw that one of the pots was looking very sad – it had definitely been munched by something.

We have a flock of house sparrows who nest in the eaves of our house. We're very glad to have them – they're cheeky chaps and their antics are fun to watch. You can see them on insect patrol whenever they're flitting around the garden, helping to control the aphid population. But this particular week they were doing something different. They were swooping down, perching on the edge of the window boxes and taking great chunks out of the sorrel. I swapped the two pots around, to give the beleaguered sorrel a rest, and left them to it.

When you're choosing plants for window boxes, there are a few things to bear in mind. Firstly, there is very limited root depth. Some plants don't mind, but you're never going to be able to grow long, straight carrots. Try the mini varieties instead. Secondly, you'll need to be very regular with feeding and watering to get a good crop from most plants. Herbs are the obvious exception, some of which flourish in dry conditions.

Some plants grow happily together in a confined space, but some are too vigorous and some are simply too tall or too big. Mint is too much of a thug to share a container with anything, even another variety of mint. Leafy vegetables give you a good and continuous harvest from a small space for weeks and it's always worth having a few suitable plants waiting in the wings to fill gaps if your window boxes are going to be on display.

Most of the crops that do well in window boxes are vegetables, or used as such. Cherry tomatoes and even dwarf peppers do well in a sunny spot. Anything leafy is fine on the shady side of the house. One fruit you can try is strawberries, especially the tiny and very attractive alpine strawberry. Flowers, edible or otherwise, add a touch of colour and anything that trails over the edge makes good use of the space.

On a practical note, if you're fitting your window boxes above the ground floor then make sure that they're secure – they weigh a considerable amount and could cause a nasty accident. Plastic containers are lightest and compost is far lighter than a soil-based potting medium, but it does need more regular feeding.

The *Alternative* Kitchen Garden

X is for...

X is for...

Xanthopyll

Most people know that plants are green because their leaves contain chlorophyll, and that chlorophyll is used in photosynthesis to produce food (sugars) using only sunshine and carbon dioxide.

Some people also know that plant leaves contain other coloured chemicals, and that when deciduous tree leaves turn gorgeous colours in the autumn it's because the tree is taking back the chlorophyll to save it for next year, but leaving the other coloured chemicals behind.

These coloured chemicals are also used for photosynthesis – including several xanthophylls, many of which are yellow. Carotene, the chemical that makes carrots orange, does the same for some leaves. Anthocyanins may also be present, causing purple or red colouration, but they're not involved with photosynthesis. In variegated leaves the distribution of these pigments is what causes the colour variations.

Leaf discolouration is often one of the first, and most obvious signs, that something is wrong with a plant. Pests, diseases and physiological problems can all change the colour of leaves. To be certain of the cause you need to check which leaves are being affected (Where are they on the plant? Are they new leaves or mature leaves?) and what colour they are turning.

Fungal diseases usually cause coloured patches or spots, or a coating on the leaf surface. Viruses create interesting patterns on the leaves (the first time I saw it, I thought the natural silver patterning on courgette leaves was caused by a virus). Pests usually cause holes or transparent patches, but they can also cause leaf distortion and affected leaves often turn brown prematurely.

Nutrient deficiencies also affect the leaves. A magnesium deficiency causes leaves to go yellow or brown around the edge and between the leaf veins. The older leaves will be most affected. Iron and manganese deficiencies cause a similar yellowing, but the youngest leaves will be most badly hit. A potassium deficiency shows as scorched edges to the leaves, and a nitrogen deficiency will cause small, yellow leaves. The older leaves are affected first, but symptoms will spread throughout the plant and cause stunting.

Nutrient deficiencies are usually seen in container grown plants that need a good feed. Out in the garden they can be quite rare if your soil is in good heart and you add plenty of compost, but they are sometimes seen in hungry plants like tomatoes and squash. A good first step if you suspect one is to give the plant a light seaweed feed, which supplies a lot of different nutrients without giving an overdose of any one. The nice thing about seaweed feeds is that you can apply them (properly diluted) directly onto the leaves, which allows them to be absorbed almost immediately and is a very quick way of giving a plant a pick-me-up. You may find that there is no improvement in leaves that have been discoloured, but the new growth should be a much better colour.

A good book on pests and diseases will give you clear photos to refer to when you suspect you have a problem. They don't make comfortable reading though, and it is better to focus on improving plant healthy generally, so it's a book to have on the shelf rather than the coffee table!

X is for...

Xeriscaping

Xeriscaping is a much more common term in drier parts of the world, because it is the process of designing a garden that thrives without being watered. The benefits of xeriscaping are obvious – it means less water is used, conserving water for other uses. If your water supply is metered then you save money by not watering the garden. If the water supply is interrupted (perhaps by a hosepipe ban) then your garden will happily survive, and in hot weather you don't need to be out there sweating to give your plants a much needed drink.

Xeriscaping goes beyond water-wise gardening because it involves a significant element of design. Plants are chosen that are native to the habitat and therefore have evolved to live in the local, dry conditions. Plants commonly used are cactus and agave, or herbs like lavender and thyme – depending on where in the world the garden is located. Plants are primarily chosen for their habitat requirements rather than their ornamental or useful features.

Dry gardens are also landscaped to prevent unnecessary run-off, with retaining walls and sunken planting holes that allow water to sink in around the plants. Mulching also features heavily, helping to slow evaporation. They are often used to replace a water-hungry lawn.

Like forest gardens, dry gardens need to be properly designed before planting. They are therefore more work to set up than more standard garden designs, but give benefits later with reduced maintenance. However, dry gardens are not normally productive gardens.

Even so, it is worth taking a look at your garden and thinking about how well it would survive if you could not water, and what long-term steps you can take to improve its self-sufficiency, rather than always taking the 'quick fix' option and reaching for the watering can or hose pipe on hot days. And if you're designing a new garden then water use should be one of your primary concerns.

I've already talked about water-wise gardening at some length, so I will just reiterate the importance of adding as much organic matter to the soil as possible and investing in some nice, deep mulches. You may also want to consider creating some shade in your garden, even if it's just temporary shades that you can move around. Shading seedlings and new transplants will drastically reduce their water consumption while they get established. If you can cut down on their wind exposure then that will help as well. If you have fleece to protect plants in cold weather, or mesh tunnels to keep the insects off, then consider making more use of them in the summer as sun shades. Or bash together a wooden frame and cover it in shade cloth so that you can use it wherever it's needed most.

X is for...

Xylem

There are lots of nearly unpronounceable words used in botany, and you can be a perfectly good gardener without being able to remember any of them – but a vague idea of how plants work is always helpful.

Like us, plants have a vascular system to transport things around. The xylem tissues allow water (and dissolved plant nutrients) to be brought up from the roots right to the tops of the plants. It's one of the engineering miracles of the plant world that water can be taken from ground level up to the tops of the highest trees; water pressure at the bottom pushes water upwards, and loss of water from leaves sucks it upwards.

Another sort of plant tissue, the phloem, transports the plant food made in leaves through photosynthesis downwards to areas of the plant that don't produce food – most notably the roots.

Plants can control, to a certain extent, the amount of water they lose through their leaves. But the signs of an insufficient water supply are obvious – droopy leaves followed by wilting stems followed by very unhealthy crispy bits.

What's not so obvious is that even before dehydration does permanent damage to the plant, it will stop these vascular systems from functioning properly. If there's not enough water coming up from the roots then there won't be enough nutrients being brought up either. And there won't be any food being transported down the plant. Photosynthesis in the leaves is likely to be shut down until the water supply is reconnected – the plant won't grow until conditions improve. This is what is referred to a 'check to growth' (there are other causes, including cold snaps) and should be avoided if possible. A happy plant is a more productive plant.

One of the most common problems with tomatoes is blossom end rot. The bottom of the fruits turn black, and are often then also attacked by mould. Blossom end rot is not caused by a pest, or a disease, but rather by a physio-logical problem – the plant has been unable to supply sufficient calcium to the forming fruits. Although this can be down to a calcium deficiency, it's more often due to fluctuations in water levels.

Water supply problems are also implicated in issues with pollination and fruit set (flowers falling from runner beans being a common problem in dry weather), cause leafy plants to grow tough and unappetizing leaves, and can encourage plants to bolt and run to seed early.

The *Alternative* Kitchen Garden

Y is for...

Y is for...

Years

Years take on a new significance when you have a garden. You become attuned to the turning of the seasons, seeing autumn and winter as a necessary part of the year, rather than the sad end of summer and the cold months we just have to endure. You also come to appreciate, in ways that many people perhaps don't, just how different each year is.

I remember 2006 as a horribly hot summer, in which I had to do a lot of watering in sweltering heat to prevent all my plants from dehydrating in front of my eyes. It was the year of the unending onion crop (they lasted well into 2007!), the first time I grew achocha and the last time I managed to get the wall of window boxes outside the kitchen to look anything other than straggly.

2007 will be remembered (throughout England at least) as the year of the floods. I was wandering through the streets in my wellies during the worst of the weather, and the garden was thoroughly soggy for most of the summer. I had huge trouble germinating any seeds, and even the courgette plants didn't thrive. Somehow, though, I managed a decent sweetcorn crop and the garden was full of flowers.

And 2008? Well I'm writing this in September and we've just about given up hope of any summery weather this year. It has been damp and humid and many gardeners have been plagued with slugs and blackfly. My onion harvest was good again, we enjoyed the early potatoes and anything leafy is having a whale of a time. The chickens are looking sleek and healthy. The most memorable thing this year has been the effect of the weather on the gardener – the miserable days and enervating effect of the humidity combined to keep me indoors much of the time, and the garden suffered.

The point I'm trying to make is two-fold. Firstly, if you are a new gardener and have a disappointing first (or even second and third) season, you should not blame yourself. Yes, you will be learning as you go along, but every year has its challenges and even experienced gardeners can't grow everything all the time. And although it's useful to have a guide to what should be growing when, you have to go with the flow of the season rather than slavishly following instructions.

And secondly, next year will be different. Over the winter, when the garden is all but dormant, a magical change occurs in gardeners. In autumn they are battle-weary, dispirited troops who have succumbed to the combined armies of Pests, Disease and Bad Weather and hung up their trowels for good. They are surrounded by a supporting cast of friends and relatives who refuse to eat another courgette, or to accept another jar of green tomato chutney. But at some point during the cold months they become people who are champing at the bit to get outdoors. They rake through the seed catalogues with hope, and order far more seeds than they have room for, and then impatiently calculate the earliest possible sowing date that gives their plants a chance of survival. Jars of sprouting seeds appear on the kitchen counter, just to give the appearance that some gardening is taking place.

And, early in the year, on the first day with acceptable weather, gardeners charge outside to see which of the perennials are starting into life and which may have died overwinter. They prepare the soil, making sure to do everything properly – because this year… this year will be DIFFERENT!

Y is for...

Yellow Plants

Every so often, ornamental garden design goes through phases where it's fashionable to plant up a bed in just one colour. Some of these gardens are very famous – including the White Garden at Sissinghurst Castle.

If you wanted to do something similar with edible plants then your options would, at first glance, seem limited. But in actual fact there are plenty of edible or otherwise useful plants that are white (or green and white, since colour gardens always have green as a backdrop). Most fruit blossom is white, and highly ornamental in the spring. Welsh onions and garlic chives both have impressive white flowerheads. It's possible to find nasturtiums that are almost white, and there's also white clover as a green manure. Plenty of herbs, including parsley and coriander have white flowers when they bolt, and broad beans have black and white flowers (unless you have the crimson flowered heritage variety). White vegetables include Swiss chard, turnips, kohl rabi, white sprouting broccoli and cauliflower.

Red would be easy, with raspberries and strawberries in the summer, ruby chard and rhubarb and red lettuces and cabbage. There's also red peppers and tomatoes, the red flowers on runner beans, the flaming red pods of borlotti beans and cranberries.

Yellow is even easier, although sweetcorn counts as green because you don't see the colour of the cobs until you harvest them. Instead you'd want nasturtiums, marigolds and pot marigolds, sunflowers and yellow chard. Courgettes and squash have very impressive yellow flowers, and you can even find varieties with yellow fruit. There are some beans with yellow pods, and Crystal Lemon cucumber grows round, yellow fruits. Yellow peppers and tomatoes are also reasonably easy to track down. It seems as though yellow is quite a common colour in the kitchen garden.

Surprisingly, purple is too. You can get purple cauliflowers (in fact, these days you can get orange cauliflowers, too!) and purple sprouting broccoli. Peas and beans both come with purple pods and aubergines frequently ripen to purple. Plums and globe artichokes can also come in purple. Flowers are possible too – try chives and phacelia, along with some varieties of lavender.

Blue is one of the most problematic colours. Only blueberries spring to mind, but there are plenty of blue flowers – including borage, lavender and rosemary.

A coloured garden may not appeal to you, but a theme garden can be a lot of fun. You could try a pizza garden – a favourite with children – where you grow onions, tomatoes and peppers, perhaps with sweetcorn and oregano. Or you could have a chocolate garden, although in the UK it's sadly not feasible to grow your own cocoa. But chocolate cosmos are the right colour and smell like hot chocolate, there's a chocolate scented daisy and chocolate mint will allow you to have an edible chocolate flavoured harvest!

Y is for...

Yellow Sticky Traps

The yellow sticky trap is a useful weapon in the organic gardener's armoury. It's literally a piece of yellow card or paper, covered in something sticky. If you're being very frugal then you can make your own by painting something yellow and then covering it with petroleum jelly.

For some reason, a lot of insect pests are attracted towards the colour yellow. Once they land on the trap, they stick fast and can't move – and so they die. Yellow sticky traps can be used to control populations of some pests, and monitor the populations of others.

They are designed for use under cover. I use them inside the house to control the population of fungus gnats (the ones that the carnivorous plants in the bathroom don't get). They're pretty icky things – the flies get stuck and then they stay there – but it's also quite fascinating to see what happens. You can watch their progress over a few days as they become less and less fly-like and more flat and squished. You can certainly tell which are the fresh ones and which have been there for a while. Once they get covered in bugs you have to replace them, and you have to watch out that they don't get too close to your plants – leaves get stuck to.

Whether you're using sticky traps to control pest populations, or simply monitor what's happening pest-wise, you need to make sure they're in the right place. Fungus gnats are terrible fliers. In fact the females don't fly much at all, preferring to crawl around on the surface of the compost. The males are the ones that go out and about, and they fly rather feebly and quite low – so there's no point hanging your sticky traps a foot above the plants to catch fungus gnats. Prop them up lower down and they'll do much more good.

To monitor potential pest problems, it makes more sense to have sticky traps in a range of places, with some higher above the plants, to catch a wider range of bugs. You may also need to replace them more frequently so that they give you an 'up to the minute' reading about what's flying around in your greenhouse.

The main problem with sticky traps is that they collect creatures that aren't pests. Ladybirds and spiders get stuck, as will anything which isn't strong enough to break free of the goo. To a certain extent it's inevitable, but careful siting of your sticky traps will help to reduce the problem.

Sticky traps don't have to be yellow. Bright blue is used for monitoring thrips... and bright white traps are useful against flea beetles.

Y is for...

Yields

Modern agriculture is obsessed with yields. Counted in tonnes per acre or per hectare, the figures are used for everything from determining the market price to comparing different forms of agriculture and their ability to feed the world.

Kitchen gardeners can also become obsessed with their yield – competing to grow the largest crops of tomatoes and courgettes, aiming to increase production year on year and feeling it very keenly when the weather, or some other phenomenon, prevents them from achieving their target.

Permaculture has a slightly different view of yields. The underlying philosophy of achieving the maximum output from the minimum input looks as though it's a fairly standard model of efficiency – but the truth is very different. Permaculture 'calculations' of yield go far beyond mere tonnes per acre, to include everything of value.

So while our permaculture garden may have an obvious yield of food crops (vegetables, fruit and herbs) it also gives us other things of value. Some may still be obvious – material for the compost heap, or for mulching, twiggy sticks for supporting peas, or willow for making supports or basket weaving.

Then there are the less obvious benefits to gardening this way – including the ability of gardens to soak up excess water and help prevent flooding, provide shade or wind breaks, wildlife value and a contribution to clean air. And there is the contribution gardens make to providing the environmental services we depend on – oxygen production, nutrient cycling, water cycling and soil management.

There are even less tangible benefits to growing a sustainable garden. We could include in the yield the contribution we aren't making to climate change when we grow our own food rather than having it flown in, and the indirect savings we make when we don't send our biodegradable rubbish off to landfill (with its ever increasing costs). Our home-made comfrey (or nettle) fertiliser is a yield, as is the run-off from the worm bin that we use as a liquid feed. How much would it cost (the true figure, including the environmental cost) to buy these things in?

And on top of all this there are the personal yields. The time spent working outside in the fresh air, and the health benefits that brings. The impact on physical and mental health, and the reduced cost of medical care that brings. The value to communities of beautiful, productive, shared spaces that help to reduce poverty and crime. The opportunity to share your garden, and its produce, with family and friends and neighbours – adding immeasurably to your quality of life and theirs.

When you think about it this way, there really is no comparison between an enormous wheat field, with its one yield of tonnes of wheat, and a thriving garden with its productive mixed cropping, and wildlife and aesthetic values. Not only that, but a garden can turn any space into an oasis – it doesn't rely on having a prime agricultural location. Windowsills, roof tops, driveways and wasteland can all be turned into sustainable, productive spaces – and that's what permaculture is all about.

The *Alternative* Kitchen Garden

Z is for...

Z is for...

Zero Waste

One of the ideas that's gaining popularity at the moment is Zero Waste – the idea that we can live our lives without producing any waste that cannot somehow be reused or recycled. An increasing number of people are trying to do just that, having a surprising amount of success (given the fact that we don't design many products with recycling in mind) and also some interesting failures.

An easier concept to achieve is something I first saw at the Eden Project

– being waste neutral. The idea is to try and balance any waste you produce, so that you would try and buy recycled products to balance out the waste you send for recycling (or to landfill), which helps to build the market for recycled products and hence make it easier for people to recycle. The Eden Project has well-thought out purchasing strategies, and plenty of recycling bins, which let them do just that.

Both Zero Waste and Waste Neutral strategies rely on the three Rs – Reducing the amount we consume and the amount of things we buy that will ultimately become waste, Reusing things rather than buying new ones, and Recycling as much waste as possible by turning it into something else. Composters add a fourth R – Rot – but composting can also be seen as recycling as you take a waste product and process it into something different with a value of its own.

Having a garden can make a big difference to a Zero Waste effort. For a start you can have a compost bin (or several) and compost all of your biodegradable waste at home. It's possible to keep a small worm bin indoors, if you don't have a garden, to compost your kitchen waste and produce liquid feeds and small amount of compost for container plants. Making your own compost avoids having to buy in soil amendments, which usually come in a plastic sack or a bulk bag that cannot be recycled.

Growing your own, even if it's just a few herbs on the windowsill, means that you don't have to buy as much fresh produce. Not only does it save you money, but it saves on packaging to. If you shop at the supermarket then it can be surprisingly difficult to come back with fresh produce that doesn't have any plastic packaging. Plastic bags and films are notoriously difficult to recycle at the present time, and hence have to be avoided for a Zero Waste lifestyle.

Gluts can be preserved for future use or given away (cutting back on shopping and packaging again).

And the garden is a great place for reuse and recycle as well. I've already talked about recycling in the garden, and about using Freecycle to find items for your garden rather than buying new ones.

As the price of landfilling waste increases, the public and companies alike will become better at recycling, designing products with reuse in mind and avoiding waste. In the meantime, it's time to go outside and plant an apple tree or sow a pot of mixed salad so that you can think global, eat local and end up with nothing in the bin.

Z is for...

Zea Mays

Sweetcorn (Zea Mays) is one of the biggest kitchen garden treats. It's not the easiest thing to grow, but you haven't really tasted sweetcorn until you've eaten it fresh from the garden – ideally you should put the water on to boil before you go out and harvest the cobs.

Sweetcorn is a tall plant, and you don't get much of a harvest in return for the space – even in a good year, two cobs from each plant would be a push.

Baby sweetcorn is even worse. The plants are the same size and you only get a few cobs per plant, and they're tiny. It really brings home why baby sweetcorn is very expensive to buy.

For the best chance of a good harvest in the UK you need to choose your variety carefully, so it matures early. Then you need to make sure that you sow your seeds and have your plants in the ground as soon as the weather makes it feasible, so they have plenty of time to grow.

Sweetcorn is an unusual kitchen garden plant in that it's wind pollinated. It is planted in a block, rather than a straight row, because that gives the pollen the best chance of falling down from the male tassels at the top of the plant onto the female silks at the end of the developing cobs. Patchy pollination leads to cobs that don't fill out properly. The usual cause is the pollen not transferring properly – try tapping the plants when you walk past when they're flowering. In my case, this year, it was caused by the slugs eating the silks before the cobs had developed, something I had never even heard of before it happened to me!

Some people have problems with birds or squirrels attacking the cobs as they ripen. If that happens then you can give them armour plating by cutting a large plastic bottle down the middle so that it hinges at the bottom. Pop the bottle over the cob, with the neck over the stem and close it up, and your sweetcorn should be safe from everything but badgers – who tend to trample the plants down to eat the fruit. You'll have to make sure the cobs are properly pollinated before you add the bottle, though, or your cobs won't be full.

Sweetcorn is one of the native American 'three sisters' – three crops grown together for their mutual benefit. Traditionally the corn is used to support climbing French beans, and a trailing squash is planted at the bottom. The beans fix nitrogen to feed the squash and the corn, and the squash acts as a living mulch and keeps things nice and cool and damp at the roots. The idea is that you get three crops from the same space. I haven't tried it yet, but it's becoming more popular. You have to get the timing right so that the corn is growing away before you plant the beans and the squash, and I have heard that harvesting the beans can be problematic (although it might be good for a crop of dried beans), but there are still plenty of people who give it a go each year to see how it works.

Z is for...

Zucchini

On the other side of the Atlantic, courgettes are called zucchini. Over here they tend to be thought of as under-developed marrows, and indeed if you let them get out of hand they soon grow into something you could use as an offensive weapon.

Although they're tender plants and can't go outside until the weather has warmed up, courgettes are ridiculously easy to grow. They have large seeds that are easily shoved into the soil. They spring up quickly into vigorous plants that are only vulnerable to slugs and snails when they're young. Once they get established, they're too tough to be bothered by much, and their hollow stems are a bit hairy and unattractive to most pests.

You can grow courgettes in a container, if you choose the right variety. There are bush plants, which are quite well-behaved, and trailing plants that are utter thugs. You can get them under control to a certain extent by giving them a support to clamber up. Or you can wind them round themselves and peg their stems to the ground to stop them becoming a trip hazard.

You can even try growing a courgette plant in the top of your compost heap, as it will love the damp and the heat and the unending supply of plant nutrients, and grow like a triffid.

And courgettes provide a good return on your investment – they're hungry and thirsty plants, but each one can provide more courgettes than a person can happily eat in one summer. Plant more than two and you'll spend the season ever more frantically searching for people to offload your surplus onto, or hunting for chutney recipes.

You can get a surprising number of different courgette varieties. There are the long ones that look like baby marrows, but come in different shades of green and even in bright yellow. You can get round ones, too, that are great for stuffing. Again, they come in different shades of green and also in yellow. The one I'm growing (Tromba d'Albenga) has long, curving fruits with bulbous ends. It can be grown as a winter squash, but young fruits are lovely and firm eaten as courgettes, with no hint of bitterness. The knobbly variety I grew last year (Friulana) is described as being the ugliest and tastiest courgette available. And if you wander into summer squash territory then you can grow things that taste like courgette but look like flying saucers.

As autumn comes round your courgette plants will be affected by powdery mildew. You can take off the affected leaves if you want to, but this is just nature's way of telling you that the courgette harvest is finally coming to an end. More problematic are the rots that set in where the fruits touch the ground. It's not normally a problem with courgettes unless the weather is damp, but you might need to raise them off the ground (using a tile or a rock or something like that) to give them some air flow. That also keeps them out of the way of slugs, who have the occasional nibble when the fruits are young and their skin is soft.

And early on in the season you might find that you don't get any fruit because you only have male flowers. But you just need to be patient – they will fruit, and fruit, and fruit, just as soon as they are ready.

The *Alternative* Kitchen Garden

Directory

Blogs

The internet is, by nature, a very dynamic place. Blogs are especially so — springing up like weeds and then dying away. The blogs listed here are some of my favourite perennials and seem well established, but there is no way to encompass the wealth of gardening knowledge out there on the internet on paper.

Fluffius Muppetus   http://coopette.com/blog
My blog details what I'm doing in the garden, what the chickens are up to and a few bits and pieces here and there about more general environmental topics. There are links to many more gardening blogs and websites in my 'blogroll'.

Bifurcated Carrots   www.patnsteph.net/weblog
Patrick is an ex-pat American in Amsterdam. He blogs about his kitchen garden and in particular about heirloom and heritage vegetable varieties. He also delves more deeply into the politics of gardening and agriculture than I do. Patrick was a guest on the AKG podcast for three episodes in 2007 (22, 23 & 24), talking about heirloom seeds.

Daughter of the Soil   http://daughterofthesoil.blogspot.com/
Rebsie is a folk musician and keen gardener. Her blog is awash with interesting information about her latest pea breeding experiments, complete with beautiful photos. Rebsie was kind enough to talk about one of her favourite vegetables, beetroot, in episode 23 of the AKG podcast.

Soilman   www.soilman.uk.com/
Soilman talks about the trials and tribulations of having an allotment. He even records occasional videos, so you can really see what he gets up to. He's an expert on brassicas, and in episode 16 of the AKG podcast he shared some tips on how to grow good cauliflowers.

Mad About Herbs http://madaboutherbs.org
Madeleine is a herb expert, and has shared her knowledge in quite a few episodes of the AKG podcast. She blogs about seasonal herb topics and crafty herb projects.

Horticultural http://perrone.blogs.com/horticultural
Jane used to blog about everything she got up to on her allotment. A baby, a new job and a house move later and she's still going strong – but now she talks about her garden, and gardening in general.

My Tiny Plot www.mytinyplot.co.uk
Gillian at My Tiny Plot reminds us that you don't have to have a huge garden to grow your own vegetables and cook with the seasons. Careful planning is all you need, and Gillian talked about that in episode 53 of the AKG podcast.

The Garden Monkey http://thegardenmonkey.blogspot.com
The mysterious garden monkey blogs about the world of gardening and is a self-confessed gardening book addict. He's a very naughty simian who likes to poke fun, and can therefore be hugely entertaining.

Compost Lover http://allanshepherd.com
There are more blogs than you would think that are dedicated to compost. Allan Shepherd has written a book on the subject (among others) and is very involved with the Centre for Alternative Technology (CAT) in Wales. As well as being keen on compost, he's obsessed by slugs.

Transition Culture http://transitionculture.org
Rob Hopkins, author of The Transition Handbook, blogs about the progress of the Transition Town movement, building resilience back into communities and maintaining the skills we are in danger of losing – including growing our own food and darning socks.

The Rubbish Diet http://therubbishdiet.blogspot.com
The Rubbish Diet started as a blog of one family's attempt to produce absolutely no waste during their local Zero Waste week. It has become a national phenomenon, with regular posts about what's being thrown away in Almost Mrs. Average's wheelie bin as well as waste issues in general.

Podcasts

A podcast is like a radio show that you listen to via the internet. You can choose when you listen, and where. Some podcasts allow you to listen to the show directly from the website. For others you need to download the files. If you want to listen to a show regularly you can normally subscribe via iTunes or a feed reader so that you're automatically notified when there's a new episode available. iTunes will also download the files for you, so it's really easy to use.

The Alternative Kitchen Garden   http://coopette.com/akg
I try and produce a new show for the Alternative Kitchen Garden each week, on a particular topic (ranging from techniques like composting to particular plants or pests). I have guests on the show to talk about their favourite gardening subjects, and some shows are recorded in the Grow Dome or outside with the chickens.

The Wiggly Podcast   www.wigglywigglers.co.uk/podcasts
Heather and the team at Wiggly Wigglers produce a weekly show about farming, composting, wildlife and environmentally friendly gardening. They also have regular guests on the programme, or take a trip and do outside broadcasts.

Recommended Reading

There are far more good books on gardening than I could possibly mention here. These are the ones that have most inspired me, or those that I constantly refer to.

Asian Vegetables   Sally Cunningham, Eco-Logic Books.*
A guide to growing edible plants from the Asian subcontinent.

Back Garden Seed Saving   Sue Strickland, Eco-logic Books.*
A very helpful guide to saving your own vegetable seeds.

The Book of Rubbish Ideas   Tracey Smith, Alastair Sawday.
A witty and quirky book to set you on the path to a more sustainable home and garden.

The Edible Container Garden   Michael Guerra, Gaia Books Ltd.*
A good guide to growing fruit and vegetables in containers and small gardens.

Encyclopedia of Organic Gardening   Garden Organic, Dorling Kindersley.*
An indispensable reference book on all aspects of organic gardening.

Growing Unusual Vegetables   Simon Hickmott.*
A very accessible manual on growing some 90 unusual plants – organised into greens, roots, fruits, seeds, grains and flavourings.

Liquid Gold   Carol Steinfeld, Green Books.
Urine: it's uses in the garden, the problems it causes and the uses to which it has been put through history. If this book doesn't get you weeing on your compost heap then nothing will!

No Nettles Required   Ken Thompson, Eden Project Books.*
A book that shows, with reference to research done in Sheffield, just how easy it is to have a wildlife friendly garden.

Oriental Vegetables   Joy Larkcom, Frances Lincoln Publishers.*
Essentially an encyclopaedia of oriental vegetables, complete with growing and cooking instructions and a general gardening techniques section.

Permaculture, a Beginner's Guide   Graham Burnett, Spiralseed.*
A friendly and engaging book about what permaculture is and why we need it. The illustrations are quirky and perfect.

Permaculture In A Nutshell   Patrick Whitefield, Permanent Publications.*
A concise and accessible introduction to the principles and practice of permaculture. Covers how permaculture works in the city, the country and on the farm.

The Pip Book   Keith Mossman, Penguin.
Currently out of print but available second hand. A helpful guide to germinating pips and seeds from bought produce.

Plants for a Future   Ken Fern, Permanent Publications.*
An indispensable book for people interested in unusual edible and useful plants. Takes gardening, conservation and ecology into a new dimension.

Urban Eden   Adam and James Caplin, Kyle Cathie.
An inspiring book on growing your own food in tiny urban spaces.

Window-box Allotment   Penelope Bennett, Ebury Press.
As mentioned in the section on Window Boxes on page 336.

Worms Eat My Garbage   Mary Appelhof, Flower Press.
The recognised authority on worm composting.

Books marked with an * are available from: ***The Green Shopping Catalogue***:
www.green-shopping.co.uk or tel: 01730 823 311.

Suppliers

A few places where you can find unusual plants and seeds, and shop without guilt.

Agroforestry Research Trust   www.agroforestry.co.uk
A registered charity that carries out research on temperate agroforestry (tree crops), the Agroforestry Research Trust also produces publications and sells plants and seeds.

Kore Wild Fruit Nursery   www.korewildfruitnursery.co.uk
A small-scale nursery in Wales that specialises in unusual edible plants from all over the world.

The Organic Gardening Catalogue   www.organiccatalog.com/catalog
A one-stop-shop for organic gardeners, which also helps to fund the work of Garden Organic. You can order online, over the phone or by mail order.

The Real Seed Catalogue   www.realseeds.co.uk
As mentioned in the text, a supplier of open-pollinated vegetable seeds guaranteed to grow well in the British climate and chosen with gardeners in mind.

Seeds of Italy   http://seedsofitaly.co.uk
Suppliers of genuine Italian seeds, including a mind-boggling array of courgettes, plus a few unusual edibles and truffle trees.

Wiggly Wigglers   www.wigglywiggers.co.uk
Mail-order and online suppliers of environmentally friendly products for the home and garden, and worm composting specialists.

Gardens and Organisations

Common Ground www.commonground.org.uk
The organization linking nature with culture and championing local distinctiveness through publications and projects such as Field Days, Parish Maps, Flora Britannica, Apple Days, Community Orchards and the campaign for local distinctiveness.

Eden Project www.edenproject.com
A beautiful garden, and an educational masterpiece, in Cornwall. It has the most amazing rainforest and mediterranean biomes as well as extensive external planting ranging from kitchen garden vegetables to tea.

Garden Organic www.gardenorganic.org.uk
The UK's organic gardening charity, and home of the Heritage Seed Library. They have a special website: www.homecomposting.org.uk to promote home composting and the Master Composter programmes.

The Harlequin Ladybird Survey www.harlequin-survey.org/
The website for reporting sightings of the Harlequin ladybird. There's also plenty of information about identifying the Harlequin, and about ladybirds in general.

Permaculture Magazine www.permaculture.co.uk
The online home of *Permaculture Magazine – Solutions for Sustainable Living*, Permanent Publications, Permaculture Information and the *Green Shopping Catalogue* – everything you need to get started in permaculture.

RecycleNow www.recyclenow.com
WRAP's website aimed at households is a mine of information about recycling and has plenty of helpful information about composting.

RISC's Edible Roof Garden www.risc.org.uk/garden
An edible haven among the roof tops of Reading. It has a forest garden complete with over 120 species of edible and medicinal trees, shrubs, vines and plants.

Thrive www.thrive.org.uk
A UK charity which uses horticulture to change lives. Their website about easier gardening is www.carryongardening.org.uk

Photo Credits

All pictures copyright Emma Cooper except:

Author, P Cooper. **Annual**, S Fedarenka/Shutterstock; **Apples**, Margo Harrison/Shutterstock; **Beans**, T Harland; **Bees**, Gorilla/Shutterstock; **Birds**, Avalon Imaging/Shutterstock; **Cats**, D Rajszczak/Shutterstock; **Climate Change**, Asharkyu/Shutterstock; **Coffee**, Bigelow Illustrations/Shutterstock; **Compost**, Latentlight/Shutterstock; **Dandelions**, Vaclav/Shutterstock; **Digging**, N Cornes/Shutterstock; **Earwigs**, Z R Swadzba/Shutterstock; **Eden Project**, L Kelly/Shutterstock; **Environment**, D Gustavsson/Shutterstock; **Footprints**, D Milinkovic/Shutterstock; **Forest Gardens**, T Harland; **Freecycle**, L Howard/Shutterstock; **Garlic**, Slavcic/Shutterstock; **Goji Berries**, Stephen Shirley/Victoriana Nursery Gardens; **Happiness**, D Dohnal/Shutterstock; **Hardening Off**, Ason/Shutterstock; **I is for..**, J Calev/Shutterstock; **Impoverished Soil**, E Chan/Shutterstock; **Inter Cropping**, T Harland; **Inspiration**, J Adams; **J is for...**, Picamaniac/Shutterstock; **Jam and Juice**, Yxowert/Shutterstock; **Jerusalem Artichokes**, Stephen Shirley/Victoriana Nursery Gardens; **Jostaberries**, T Harland; **K is for**, T Davis/Shutterstock; **K (Pottasium)**, Mitzy/Shutterstock; **Kiwi**, Ljupco Smokoyski/Shutterstock; **Kohl Rabi**, M Barbone/Shutterstock; **Lemons**, C Frost/Shutterstock; **Mint**, R Mackenzie/Shutterstock; **Mushroom**, E Phillips/Shutterstock; **N is for...**, Kirschner/Shutterstock; **Native**, Naturaldigital/Shutterstock; **Nectarine**, Stephen Shirley/Victoriana Nursery Gardens; **Nitrogen**, I Marx/Shutterstock; **Onions**, Colour/Shutterstock; **Oranges**, P Cowan/Shutterstock; **Organic**, J Hatch/Shutterstock; **R Paz**, S Fedarenka/Shutterstock; **P is for...**, Basil101658/Shutterstock; **Peas**, Mifid/Shutterstock; **Phosphorus**, K Degreef/Shutterstock; **Potatoes**, E Eginton/Shutterstock; **Q is for...**, T Boland/Shutterstock; **Quamash**, L Guo/Shutterstock; **Quick Return**, D Barger/Shutterstock; **R is for...**, E Shweitzer/Shutterstock; **Rotation**, Garasia/Shutterstock; **S is for...**, Vaklav/Shutterstock; **Saffron**, Turtleman/Shutterstock; **Shallots**, D Kay/Shutterstock; **Strawberries**, Joy Wang/Shutterstock; **Thrive**, J Gynane/Shutterstock; **Tubers**, M Makela/Shutterstock; **Umbellifers**, A Haase/Shutterstock; **Undersowing**, J Adams; **Unusual**, M Bukovski/Shutterstock; **Urine**, P Rose; **V is for...**, SSS Photos Inc./Shutterstock; **Vacciniums**, Stephen Shirley/Victoriana Nursery Gardens; **Vegan**, I Montero Verdu/Shutterstock; **Vegetative Propagation**, A Kitzman/Shutterstock; **Vermiculture**, ENOXH/Shutterstock; **Vines**, J Kershner/Shutterstock; **Vine Weevils**, Plastique/Shutterstock; **Water**, R Hackett/Shutterstock; **X is for...**, D Pannala/Shutterstock; **Xylem**, Pakhnyushcha/Shutterstock; **Y is for...**, E Ray/Shutterstock; **Yields**, Erkanupan/Shutterstock; **Z is for...**, N Cousland/Shutterstock; **Zero Waste**, S Mann/Shutterstock; **Zucchini**, Stephen Shirley/Victoriana Nursery Gardens.

Inspiration
for Self Reliance

SOME OTHER BOOKS
from
PERMANENT
PUBLICATIONS

ALL THESE & MORE AVAILABLE FROM:
The Green Shopping Catalogue,
www.green-shopping.co.uk
or any good bookshop

If You Enjoyed This Book You Won't Want to Miss This Magazine!

Permaculture Magazine helps you live a more natural, healthy and environmentally friendly life.

Permaculture Magazine offers tried and tested ways of creating flexible, low cost approaches to sustainable living. It can help you to:

- Make informed ethical choices
- Grow and source organic food
- Put more into your local community
- Build energy efficiency into your home
- Find courses, contacts and opportunities
- Live in harmony with people and the planet

Permaculture Magazine is published quarterly for enquiring minds and original thinkers everywhere. Each issue gives you practical, thought provoking articles written by leading experts as well as fantastic eco-friendly tips from readers!

permaculture, ecovillages, organic gardening, sustainable agriculture, agroforestry, appropriate technology, eco-building, downshifting, community development, human-scale economy... and much more!

Permaculture Magazine gives you access to a unique network of people and introduces you to pioneering projects in Britain and around the world. Subscribe today and start enriching your life without overburdening the planet!

Every issue of *Permaculture Magazine* brings you the best ideas, advice and inspiration from people who are working towards a more sustainable world.

Permanent Publications

The Sustainability Centre, East Meon, Hampshire GU32 1HR, UK
Tel: 0845 458 4150 or 01730 823 311 Fax: +44 (0)1730 823 322
Email: orders@permaculture.co.uk Web: www.permaculture.co.uk